BRIDGING THE GAP

Bridging *the* Gap

Connecting What You Learned
in Seminary with What You Find
in the Congregation

CHARLES J. SCALISE

Abingdon Press
Nashville

BRIDGING THE GAP:
CONNECTING WHAT YOU LEARNED IN SEMINARY WITH WHAT
YOU FIND IN THE CONGREGATION

Copyright © 2003 by Abingdon Press

This book is printed on recycled, acid-free, elemental-chlorine–free paper.

Library of Congress Cataloging-in-Publication Data

Scalise, Charles J.
  Bridging the gap : connecting what you learned in seminary with what you
find in the congregation / Charles J. Scalise.
     p. cm.
Includes bibliographical references.
  ISBN 0-687-04564-9 (alk. paper)
    1. Pastoral theology—United States. 2. Protestant churches—United
States. I. Title.

BV4011.3.S332003
253—dc21

                                                              2003004961

All scripture quotations are taken from the *New Revised Standard Version of the
Bible*, copyright © 1989 by the Division of Christian Education of the National
Council of the Churches of Christ in the United States of America. Used by
permission. All rights reserved.

Excerpts taken from *Feminist and Womanist Pastoral Theology*, edited by Bonnie
Miller-McLemore and Brita L. Gill-Austern. Copyright © 1999 by Abingdon
Press. Used by permission.

Excerpts taken from *Family Ministry: A Comprehensive Guide* by Diana R.
Garland. Copyright © 1999 by Diana R. Garland. Used by permission of
InterVarsity Press, P.O. Box 1400, Downers Grove, IL 60515. www.ivpress.com.

Excerpts taken from *Pastoral Care and Liberation Theology* by Stephen Pattison.
Copyright © 1994 by Cambridge University Press. Reprinted with the permission of Cambridge University Press.

03 04 05 06 07 08 09 10 11 12—10 9 8 7 6 5 4 3 2 1

MANUFACTURED IN THE UNITED STATES OF AMERICA

To the students
at Fuller Seminary Northwest
who have also been my teachers

Contents

Acknowledgments

Although scholarly writing is a solitary task, it cannot be accomplished effectively without the assistance of a host of helpers. It is my pleasant task here to thank many of those who have enabled this book to move from idea to reality. Given the diversity of persons upon whom I have personally relied in the writing process, it should be obvious that the limitations of, and any errors remaining in, this work are solely my responsibility. In writing this book, I have been blessed with a host of students, colleagues, and friends to whom I am grateful.

I would like to express my appreciation to the faculty and trustees of Fuller Theological Seminary. The sabbatical I received during academic year 2000–2001, which included some special financial support of this project from former Provost Russell Spittler, provided the time to complete a draft of the chapters of this work. Special thanks are due to my colleagues in the Department of Church History of Fuller's School of Theology: James Bradley, Cecil M. Robeck, Jr., John L. Thompson, and Nathan P. Feldmeth. They not only encouraged this project, but also refrained from too much wondering aloud why a colleague who teaches history and theology courses should be working in the interface between theology and ministry. I trust that historical case studies in this project will provide some rationale for my theological wanderings. Also, I would like to express gratitude to my Seattle colleagues, Richard Erickson and Charles Kim Anderson, who effectively kept the ship of Fuller Northwest afloat during the sabbatical year.

Thanks are also due to the Fuller staff, including especially Gayle McFarland and Alyssa Younger, who appreciated the need for some uninterrupted time for writing, even when I was working on this project in Seattle. In addition, special gratitude is due to the staff of Fuller's McAlister Library, especially Gail Frederick of the Interlibrary Loan Department. Along with my graduate assistant, Jeff Phillips, the McAlister Library staff graciously navigated through the flood of my many requests. Anna Lindvall assisted with the preparation of the bibliography, and Jeff Phillips provided help with the index preparation.

I want to record my appreciation to the editors of *Cross Currents* ("Teresa of Avila: Teacher of Evangelical Women?" 1996) and *The Journal of Pastoral Theology* ("Agreeing on Where We Disagree," 1998; and "Revelation and Pastoral Theology," 1999) for permission for the use and revision of these articles; and to Edwin Mellen Press for similar permission for my article "*Lex Cantandi, Lex Credendi:* Theology and Hymnody" in *Learning from Beauty*, the 1997 Festschrift for William L. Hendricks. Also, early versions of chapters 1 and 4 were presented as workshops at the 1999 and 2001 annual meetings of the Society for Pastoral Theology. In addition, the Lilly Foundation made it possible to present "Connecting Christian Doctrine and Pastoral Practice" in a revised version to the School of Theology faculty at Fuller Seminary.

I would like to express my gratitude to the many persons who served as readers for this project at various stages of its development. Besides anonymous referees, the following persons read and offered feedback on chapters of this project: Herbert Anderson (now of Seattle University), Kerry Dearborn (Seattle Pacific University), Carrie Doehring (Boston University School of Theology), Sumarme Goble (Fuller Northwest alumna), Roslyn Karaban (St. Bernard's School of Theology and Ministry), Joyce Lawlor (pastor, Good Shepherd Baptist Church), Lisa McCullough

(Fuller Northwest alumna), Bonnie Miller-McLemore (Vanderbilt University Divinity School), Jane Plantinga Pauw (pastor, Woodland Park Presbyterian Church), Richard Steele (Seattle Pacific University), Dan Stiver (Logsdon School of Theology, Hardin-Simmons University), Miriam Glover Wetherington (pastoral counselor, Durham, North Carolina), and Laurie Wheeler (pastor, Church at the Center). Special thanks are offered to Herbert Anderson, Roslyn Karaban, Lisa McCullough, Jane Plantinga Pauw, and Dan Stiver who read drafts of the entire book. Carrie Doehring, Roslyn Karaban, and Bonnie Miller-McLemore were particularly helpful in correcting and sharpening my understanding of the arguments of feminist pastoral theology. Herbert Anderson's expertise in pastoral theology and family issues helped me avoid some major detours in the development of this project; his editorial eye also rendered my rhetoric more understandable. I am particularly grateful for his gracious hospitality and collegiality, now that he resides in Seattle.

My editor at Abingdon Press, Kathy Armistead, graciously granted me the freedom and encouragement to develop this cross-disciplinary project in a way that would best serve seminarians and others seeking to deepen their understanding and practice of ministry.

My sons, David and Daniel, continue to challenge and encourage me to communicate my faith in enthusiastic dialogue with Christians who have only known postmodernity. They even patiently endure their father's middle-aged tennis playing! My partner in life and learning, Pamela Scalise, Old Testament professor for Fuller Seminary, has supported this project in ways that are beyond telling.

Finally, the Fuller Seminary students I have taught, particularly those among whom we live and work at Fuller Northwest, have raised the questions that have animated this research. So, it is appropriate that this work should be dedicated to them, in hope of their faithfulness in the ministry of the gospel of Jesus Christ.

Charles J. Scalise
Seattle, Washington
Pentecost 2002

Preface

Pursuing the question of how Christians who minister make connections among Scripture, theology, and practice has led to the writing of this work. As a teacher of theological students preparing for ministry, I encounter in every class the demand to make reliable connections between theology and practical ministry. The vignette of "Cheryl" in the first chapter reveals the continuing challenge to integrate the classical disciplines of theological education with the needs of persons and groups in ministry. How do the history and theology courses I teach connect with Cheryl's role as a minister to youth and their families?

My two previous books, Hermeneutics As Theological Prolegomena[1] and From Scripture to Theology,[2] explored the interface between Bible and theology through a canonical hermeneutic—a theory of interpretation that treats the Bible as theologically authoritative Scripture for communities of Jews and Christians. This study seeks to complete the circle of Scripture, Christian teachings, and ministry by exploring models for integrating theology and practice. Unlike my earlier work, which sought to develop one recommended route for Protestants who begin with Scripture and move to theology, this study seeks to describe and evaluate a variety of models. The interface between theology and ministry—like the interaction between theory and experience—is a more diverse and messy affair than the relationship between Bible and doctrine. So, this study seeks to examine critically five different models used by contemporary Western Christians to connect theology and ministry. A series of historical and contemporary case studies—in addition to a master case study running through the chapters—tests the models described against the practical realities of ministry.

The book has been designed to accommodate diverse reading strategies. The various ways in which readers may use this study include the following three possibilities:

(1) The work may be read from start to finish as a critical survey of contemporary types of models connecting theology and the practice of ministry, which are tested both by case studies in the individual chapters and by the master case study.

(2) The master case study, initially developed in chapter 1, may be read "horizontally" across the chapters of the book, independently from the presentation and evaluation of the individual models. To facilitate this approach to reading, the analysis of the master case study will always be found at the ends of chapters 2 through 6.

(3) Likewise, the chapters may be read independently from the master case study as description and critical analysis of each type of model. Readers who choose to focus upon only one or more models will be able to select

the chapters related to their interests and read them apart from the continuing case study.

In this study, I intentionally do not advocate the superiority of one theological model to the others. Rather, I maintain that each of the five types of models is legitimate and offers assistance in making connections between theology and ministry. I seek to demonstrate through the case studies both the value of each model and some significant limitations. The final chapter proposes a way to supplement a primary model with others (a planned hybrid), rather than succumbing to a random or indiscriminate "potpourri" of approaches to ministry.

I have labored diligently to be fair to all of the approaches I describe. Whether I have succeeded is, of course, for my readers to judge. Since I am a white male, I have been especially attentive to perspectives offered by writers who are women and people of color. These perspectives often sharply reveal the limitations of dominant cultural perceptions and values. Since I am an evangelical, I have worked especially hard to treat fairly the views of Catholic and other Protestant writers whose theological presuppositions differ markedly from my own. In short, I hope I have been fair to all the writers whose work I have examined.

Given the controversial nature of the nontraditional family issues discussed in the master case study, I want to emphasize my intention to avoid any appearance of advocacy. The issues are developed as part of scholarly research that seeks to evaluate through case studies the usefulness of various theological models for ministry. I am not intending through this research to propose or defend any position in the debates over heterosexuality or homosexuality that continue to divide Protestant and Catholic communities and denominations in North America. Instead, I trust that my analysis of theological models may be of assistance to readers across the boundaries formed by controversy concerning issues of sexuality and nontraditional families.

As I prepared this book, my own intensive study of these conflicted issues has resulted in greater clarity regarding the nature of the complex choices confronting Christian communities today. I hope that a similar benefit may be experienced by my readers. I strongly believe that Christians learn best by grasping the hard cases—such as our contemporary struggles with the difficult subjects of sexuality and nontraditional families—and by examining these issues through different types of theological reflection. I invite my readers to approach this book as a journey of exploration of paths through which our faith can lead to greater understanding.

In this era of postmodernity, many readers desire that authors acknowledge their own social location and presuppositions. Beyond the descriptors provided above, I am an ordained American Baptist minister and a faculty member of Fuller Theological Seminary, who happily endorses the seminary's Confession of Faith and Formal Statements of Community Standards (in other words, I am "a card-carrying evangelical").

This work was written as a result of the demand of seminary students who desired practical assistance in the task of integrating theology and ministry. Although the models examined are certainly not exhaustive, they do provide a range of responsible alternatives for making connections between what Christians believe and how they minister. I pray that this work may offer some useful assistance to Christians who seek to hold their heads and hearts together with the needs of those they serve in the calling of ministry.

CHAPTER 1

Models for Making Connections[1]

Thoughtful examination of the ways Christians connect their theological beliefs and practices of ministry is an urgent task for contemporary theological studies. In Euro-American theological education, the challenge of assisting students in integrating their personal spirituality, knowledge about the faith, and ministry practice in concrete situations is at the heart of the educational mission. How can teachers assist students and other persons in ministry in developing and articulating a working theology for pastoral practice? How can leaders in ministry integrate their beliefs and actions with teachings or doctrines of the Christian faith?[2]

In Western culture, the dominance of instrumental reason has eclipsed the vision of God.[3] Too many Christian leaders have been seduced by programs claiming to show "five simple ways" to build a great church, "six easy steps" to sanctification, or "seven perfect practices" to know God. The shelves of Christian bookstores are lined with volumes on ministry or "pastoral theology," which, instead of offering critical reflection upon Christian action, consist of marketable "helps and hints" on succeeding in ministry or exploit the latest fad or social issue. Christian ministers—whether vocational or volunteer—need a more reliable guide than this dumbed-down commercialism to connect what the Christian faith teaches with what they do.

We will begin our study by listening to the questions—and suspicions—of those who are struggling to integrate their faith and action into a coherent theology that guides, supports, and evaluates their ministries. Case studies and other reports of pastoral practice offer useful ways to illumine empirically the problem the study addresses.[4] The "thick description" of a case study opens a "window" onto some of the cross-disciplinary complexity of theological reflection upon Christian ministry.[5] The following composite case study[6] seeks to introduce the problem of connecting Christian theology and pastoral practice from the particular perspective of "the living human web" of a beginning seminarian.[7]

Cheryl's Suspicions About Seminary: An Introduction to the Problem

I first met the thirty-year-old student we will call "Cheryl" at the annual M.Div. Retreat of Fuller Seminary Northwest, held on the Olympic Peninsula of Washington State. Cheryl's exploration of vocational Christian ministry represented a major (and ongoing) shift in both her professional and personal self-understanding. Probing these issues of identity and call, particularly as they related to a possible career in ordained ministry in the Presbyterian Church, was the principal lure that drew Cheryl toward seminary. Naturally, she was especially interested in the roles and struggles of women in Protestant ministry in North America. She hoped that seminary study, particularly in the community afforded by a continuing cohort of students, might help her clarify her own calling both to serve and to transform the church.

After some preliminary introductions and conversation regarding the retreat, Cheryl suddenly looked directly at me and emphatically asked: "Well, now that I'm finally here and committed to taking all of these different classes, what I want to know is how they are all supposed to fit together. I mean, how will all of these classes come together to make me a 'professional minister'?"

I muttered something about "integrating the classical and practical disciplines." Then Cheryl continued, "I've already done a good bit of volunteer work in the church, working with children, youth, and senior adults. So, I don't want *all* of seminary just to be training in skills to do more of that. I guess I could use *some* skills, especially in preaching. I want to know more about the Bible. Fuller certainly requires lots of that. Those Greek and Hebrew courses worry me some, especially since I will need to know the languages for ordination exams (unless I change denominations again). But I don't want to become a biblical scholar. I want to be somebody who works in the church to change the church, especially for women."

Then Cheryl politely inquired, "Did you say you teach history and theology?" "Yes," I admitted with a nervous smile. "Well," Cheryl interrogated, "how will the abstract stuff we learn in those classes help me be a minister? How will it *connect* with the needs of the students in my youth group at Community Presbyterian Church on the East Side? Perhaps I shouldn't be telling you this, but I would rather *handle snakes* than study all those old facts and dates of history! One of the reasons that I left my old job in accounting was that I was *bored* with all those endless facts and figures, which didn't seem relevant to life. I wanted to work with *people*, and I felt the Lord was leading me to work in (and sometimes against!) the church. So, tell me, how does what you teach connect with the woman minister I think I want to become?"

The subsequent exploration of theological models for connecting Christian theology and pastoral practice represents an attempt to respond to Cheryl's tenacious questions. We will seek to alleviate Cheryl's suspicions regarding the value to her ministry of studying the doctrines and historical traditions of Christianity. Research connecting theology and practice assumes that "people skills" alone are insufficient for the authentic performance of Christian ministry. Rather, *Christian* ministry requires knowledge of the truth claims and traditions of the faith, wise practical reflection upon them in the context of specific ministry situations, and concrete actions of implementation. In order to avoid the reduction of the truth of Christian faith to the "whatever works" of pragmatic instrumentalism, we will seek to hold Christian theology and ministry in a dynamic tension, which points metaphorically beyond the limitations of each dialogue partner toward the mystery of God.

We will examine case studies to assist us in visualizing and evaluating critically various theological models connecting theology and ministry. Later in this chapter, a master case study will be developed. This case study will serve as a continuing comparative reference for our subsequent presentation and evaluation of each of the models.

Connecting Theology and Ministry: The Value of Models

Christian communities, throughout their history, have commonly sought to enable their members to make connections between the teachings of the faith and their experiences in the world.[8] This task of forging meaningful and reliable connections between Christian theology and Christian practice has held special significance for those charged with the leadership of the communities. Not only have the leaders of Christian communities been entrusted with the development of Christian doctrine or theology—through the interpretation of Scripture and the shaping of tradition—but also they have been responsible for guiding the practice of Christian life and ministry. This guidance includes both spiritual and moral formation of those within the community and direction of the community's mission throughout the world.[9]

In the twentieth century, such guidance among Protestant Christians has frequently sought to achieve the practical integration of psychology and theology through pastoral care and counseling.[10] The rise of the Clinical Pastoral Education (CPE) movement and other educational movements in supervision and training for professional leadership in ministry point out the perceived need for connecting psychologically interpreted human experience with Christian theology and spirituality.[11] These movements have also raised the issue of the balance between psychology and theology in various forms of proposed integration. One might describe this historical tension in a shorthand way as the question "*pastoral* counseling or pastoral *counseling?*" Also, some recent North American theological discussion has begun to focus upon the examination of a rather wide range of Christian practices that connect faith and Christian living.[12]

Beyond expectations of calling and giftedness, effective service in Christian ministry presumes the capacity of church leaders to articulate the connections between theology and practice. For example, Christian leaders may proclaim the teaching that Christ sets us free from the bondage of sin, from both individual and corporate sin. Yet, if these leaders fail to model how Christians can live as free people, and if they fail to lead their communities in following Christ's mission of seeking to free those in bondage, their proclamation is empty.

Furthermore, precisely at this point, one observes an absence of thoughtful reflection and reasoned discussion in the rhetoric of contemporary church leaders. Far too often it is simply assumed—and frequently loudly proclaimed—that if one merely knows the Scripture and adheres to a particular doctrinal teaching, then specific practices of Christian life and ministry are easily and obviously warranted.

Critics of the Christian faith are quick to point out the spectacle

—particularly common in North American Protestantism—of opposing Christian groups, each loudly proclaiming that Scripture and theology clearly and unambiguously support their specific position in a controversial political or social conflict. Christian polemics over abortion and gun control are dramatic recent examples of this pattern in American culture. After repeatedly observing such conflicting Christian rhetoric regarding issue after issue, one comes to suspect that the determinants of each side's "Christian view" are substantially economic, social, and cultural factors, rather than simply exegetical or theological matters. Faced with these recurring conflicts, a number of scholars have attempted to use "worldview analysis" to describe and offer steps toward reconciliation between opposing groups.[13]

Similarly, Christians—in both postmodern Europe and North America—are confronted with a bewildering array of religious and moral practices that appeal to Scripture and Christian teaching for justification. Such appeals imply that Scripture and theology possess some sort of authority, but often this authority is left unspecified and commonly reduced to "prooftexts."[14] How does one sort through the competing claims in search of trustworthy connections? How can Christian leaders form durable connections between the doctrines they teach and the practices they support or advocate?

This research, of course, is not able to offer any simple method to resolve these questions. Rather, the intention is to seek greater clarity through careful, critical examination of a variety of models that Christian theologians have proposed can be used to connect theology and practice. Ian Barbour offers a useful general definition of models and their function:

> A model is a symbolic representation of selected aspects of the behavior of a complex system for particular purposes. It is an imaginative tool for ordering experience, rather than a description of the world. There are, of course, some objects of which actual physical replicas can be built—such as a "scale model" of a ship or a "working model" of a locomotive. We will be concerned, however, with mental models of systems which for var-

ious reasons cannot be represented by replicas, such as the economy of a nation, the electrons in an atom or the biblical God.[15]

Similarly, the models examined in this study are not attempts to replicate or simulate the features of a fixed system of Christian teachings or practices.[16] They are neither historical nor empirical descriptions of Christian life and thought, but "imaginative tools" or extended metaphors used to order some of the complexities of Christian experience and reflection.[17]

Avery Dulles in *Models of Revelation* offers the following broad description of a model: "a relatively simple, artificially constructed case which is found to be useful and illuminating for dealing with realities that are more complex and differentiated."[18] Dulles's models differ from those in our study, since his models are more image-based and lack an operational base or action orientation.[19] Stephen Bevans points to this difference: "Instead of symbolic images like 'Mother' for God or 'sacrament' for the church, we will be speaking about models of operation, models of theological method."[20] Yet Dulles's work clearly shows how metaphorical models may be useful in theological discussion.[21]

The models in this study are interpretive or hermeneutical constructs, which describe various types of theological methods used in both systematic and pastoral theology. The models are symbolic ways of analyzing selected aspects of the teachings of the Christian faith and selected practices of its adherents, so that they may be coherently connected. Through deeper understanding of various ways of linking the teaching of the faith with the practice of Christian life and ministry, we will be able to gain valuable perspective on the confusions and conflicts that beset Christian communities today.

The final third of the twentieth century saw a renewed awareness by many thinkers of the significance of "paradigms" in the philosophical process of understanding changing perceptions of "reality."[22] As Dulles observes, "A model rises to the status of a paradigm when it has proved successful in solving a great variety of problems and is expected to be an appropriate tool for unraveling anomalies as yet unsolved."[23] None of the theological models described in this study will reach a status historically comparable to Newtonian physics or quantum mechanics in elegantly solving problems and powerfully unraveling anomalies. Yet comparative study, which not only describes but also critically analyzes the strengths and limitations of various theological models, enables Christian theologians to do more than merely advocate—with the passionate single-mindedness of tunnel vision—one limited approach to the complex interface between Christian theology and practice. Furthermore, such critical study makes available to Christian ministers and other practitioners the resources of a diversity of perspectives, which in turn may encourage the development of "blended" approaches. Wisdom in the daily practice of effective pastoral ministry commonly entails the sort of intentional, thoughtful eclecticism that insightfully matches different resources to different needs.[24]

This study will argue for the value of planned hybrid, or blended, theological approaches to Christian ministry, which begin by choosing one primary model and then thoughtfully supplementing it with others.[25] Students like Cheryl should be empowered to discover some of the wisdom of the Christian tradition, which both identifies a primary theological tradition and allows the blending of diverse approaches to ministry. Making effective connections between the traditions of Christian theology and the needs of the adolescents in her youth group, as well as with her own developing professional identity, involves encountering the strengths and limitations of diverse approaches. Rather than swallowing whole the claims and implementing by rote the strategies of any one approach, or creating an indiscriminate potpourri or seeking to invent a new approach from scratch, Cheryl could benefit from a blended approach.

Before offering a brief overview of the various theological models that later chapters will consider in detail, we need to deepen the questions this study seeks to address. We will examine a rather complex case study, which complicates Cheryl's questions about the connections between theology and practice, through the thick description of a specific ministry setting. Although the case study is set in the Pacific Northwest region of the United States, the questions it raises about the redefinition of "traditional" understandings of family are common to many post-industrial Western societies.

Redefining "Families" at Valleywood Presbyterian Church

Jackie and Dale are a clergy couple who copastor Valleywood Presbyterian Church.[26] They have served together at Valleywood for five years—long enough to know fairly well the people and community of this suburban congregation. They are also now well aware of some of the major problems and challenges that face the church and shape its ministry.

After much prayer and reflection—and numerous committee meetings—Jackie and Dale have decided to focus their attention on what has been inadequately labeled the issue of "nontraditional families." Jackie declares, "The North American church—despite all of its family-values rhetoric—has done a poor job of responding to the diversity and difficulties of the family life of people like those at Valleywood. Dale and I have come to the conclusion that we aren't even completely clear about what we mean by the word "families," when we use it so freely in our ministry."

"Yes," Dale adds, "when we started looking at the life situations of specific people at Valleywood with whom we are trying to minister, the boundaries of "family" really started to blur. We wanted to give you a picture of some of the people with whom we have ministered and the questions about family that they raise for the church. But before we start, I guess you need some background about the church and about us."

The Church: Valleywood Presbyterian

Founded in 1959, Valleywood Church is located in what used to be a semirural community north of Seattle, Washington, in the

Pacific Northwest region of the United States. At the church's fortieth anniversary celebration in 1999, many of the long-term members of the congregation commented how dramatically the community of Valleywood had changed over the years. Not only has Valleywood become more urbanized—it incorporated as a separate city in 1998 under the county growth management act—but also the environment has changed. Instead of single-family homes—surrounded by conifers and apple trees—apartments, condos, and commercial properties are more prominent.

The people who live in Valleywood have changed, too. Although the population still barely shows a Euro-American plurality (40 percent), the fastest-growing group is Pacific Rim Asian American (30 percent). Only 5 percent of the population is African American. The churches growing numerically in the community are Korean and Filipino. In fact, Valleywood Church now shares its facilities with the First Korean United Presbyterian Church of Valleywood—a congregation started by Valleywood—which is now more than twice the size of its mother congregation. The Korean congregation meets on Saturday evenings and Sunday afternoons in the church facilities.

During the 1960s, Valleywood Church viewed itself as a "family-centered but socially progressive" congregation in a fairly conservative new community. For example, the first African Americans to live in Valleywood (Henry and Rosa Parker and their three children) were welcomed by and affiliated with the church. Unfortunately, due to local harassment (by persons unrelated to the church), the Parker family soon moved away. The charter members of Valleywood—a few of whom are still living and active in the congregation today—continue to recall with pride both the church's large Sunday school program and its active involvement in the community. Besides their continuing commitment to fighting racism, they frequently mention their successful opposition in the early 1960s to a dance club and bar, which originally opened across the street from the church. The site is now the location of one campus of the large, well-funded Valleywood Community College.

During the late 1960s and 1970s Valleywood Church was led

by a succession of young married male pastors (known familiarly to the congregation as Pastor Bob, Pastor Ron, and Pastor Todd), who graduated from state universities in Washington and then were trained at San Francisco Theological Seminary—a Presbyterian school in San Anselmo, California. Mainline Protestant seminary education during that period was shaped by an emphasis on pastoral counseling, with a growing emphasis upon civil rights issues.[27] Pastors Bob, Ron, and Todd focused upon counseling ministries in the church, which had begun to recognize an unprecedented number of divorces and other family counseling issues. Also, they involved Valleywood in a variety of small-group ministries and alternative church experiments. The experiment most remembered from this era was the "house church" model, which resulted in the congregation being led by a team of pastors who served a consortium of local churches.

During the 1970s, the size of the congregation first stabilized at a plateau of about 150 members and then began to decline.[28] Despite a variety of attempts to revitalize the congregation, as the cost of living in the region increased dramatically during the 1980s, the church struggled to afford a full-time pastor. All paid office assistance was eliminated; and the church choir director and organist, Jean, continued to volunteer her services, receiving only some reimbursement for expenses and a thank-you present at Christmas. Part-time pastors Jon and Louisa, though not a clergy couple, served together in a team ministry, which tried a variety of experimental worship experiences to renew the congregation. Some in the congregation began to fear that the church might not survive.

The congregation saw an opportunity for a new beginning when Jackie and Dale—supported in part by a grant from the denomination's congregational ministries program—were called five years ago as copastors. Valleywood Church had significant experience with copastors, but the church had never been pastored by a clergy couple. Jackie and Dale's combined gifts were "a good match" for the needs of the congregation, which has shown some slow growth both numerically and financially under their leadership.

The Copastors: Jackie and Dale

Jackie grew up in Southern California and attended high school in Claremont. Her father was an ordained denominational administrator in the Presbyterian Church USA. Jackie's mother was a homemaker who supported her father's church career. Jackie's family were long-term members of a very large urban Presbyterian church, where she was actively—if sometimes reluctantly—involved in a wide range of children's and youth ministry activities. When she graduated from high school, Jackie rejected her parents' suggestion to attend the "nice Presbyterian liberal arts college" where they had met. Instead, Jackie attended UCLA, where she majored in psychology because she "wanted to understand and help all kinds of people." Then, despite family expectations and advice, she attended Fuller Theological Seminary in Pasadena, where she enrolled in the M.Div. program with a concentration in family pastoral counseling. In addition to her classical and practical theological studies and a local church internship, Jackie completed two units of clinical pastoral education at a major Los Angeles hospital. She worked with an "awesome" woman supervisor who played a formative role in the development of Jackie's identity as a pastor.

Dale grew up in the Pacific Northwest. His father was the pastor of a number of small Presbyterian congregations in both Oregon and Washington. Meanwhile, Dale's mother worked at a variety of social service positions in the communities that Dale's father pastored. Dale was actively involved in Young Life during his high school and college years. He attended a small liberal arts college in Oregon, where he majored in both religious studies and music. During the summers, he worked with underprivileged youth in a variety of church and Young Life camps. After graduation, Dale spent a year working for Church World Service in India, an experience that played a large role in his call to pastoral ministry. Then he attended San Francisco Theological Seminary.

Jackie and Dale met at a denominational conference for seminarians. After a long-distance romance, they each graduated from seminary and were married. The next year, they both were serving as ministry interns for a large Presbyterian church in the

San Francisco Bay area, which strongly emphasized worship and its connections with pastoral care. The following year, with assistance from a special denominational program for revitalizing struggling churches (which Jackie's father helped develop), they received a call to serve as copastors of Valleywood Church.

After a warm reception by the church and the initial "honeymoon" period, Jackie and Dale found themselves confronting the difficult realities of the church's decline. Their joint pastoral ministry has been well accepted by most members of the congregation. Now after five years, they find themselves struggling to understand how to help the people at the church and others in the community move beyond the places where they are spiritually and relationally "stuck." Jackie and Dale believe that, empowered by the grace of Jesus Christ, the lives of individuals and families can be transformed at Valleywood. Yet they find themselves with nagging questions, particularly about the nature of the families that make up the people of God. As Jackie and Dale reflected upon their ministry with the people of Valleywood, three examples of the challenge of "nontraditional families" emerged. Each of these examples raises in a different way the question of the nature and boundaries of their use of the term "family" in the church.

The Lesbian Couple: Darlene and Sue

Darlene and Sue have become regular attenders at Valleywood Church during the last year. They are both "thirtysomething" women who have been living together for the past three years in a small home, which they jointly own. When they moved into the neighborhood, they were seeking a congregation that would seriously care about the religious needs of their children, Tom (age 10) and Harrison (age 8). Valleywood's small but creatively led Christian education program for children, staffed largely by teachers who work in several local public school districts, was the church's primary attraction to Darlene and Sue. During their first two years in the neighborhood, they occasionally attended Valleywood, as well as some other local congregations, to check out the possibilities. Then Darlene and Sue finally risked a heart-to-heart conversation with Jackie and Dale regarding whether the church would truly welcome a "blended family" of their sexual orientation. During "the talk," Darlene and Sue shared their stories.

Darlene grew up in Minneapolis. All of her grandparents were Swedish immigrants who arrived in the U.S. and settled in the Upper Midwest during the early 1920s. Darlene's parents met and married in high school. After they graduated, Darlene's father started an independent plumbing business, with some office assistance from Darlene's mother. When the business failed after five years, he began a long-term career working for a large plumbing supply company, while she worked at various domestic jobs until Darlene was born.

Unlike her parents, but with their encouragement, Darlene excelled in school. She graduated first in her high school class and was a National Merit Scholarship finalist. She was also active in children's and youth activities in her family's Lutheran church, even serving as Luther League president during her senior year. After graduation, Darlene attended Yale University on scholarship, where she was a Saybrook College pre-medical student majoring in biochemistry. She also developed a strong interest in the writings of C. S. Lewis and other members of the Inklings. So, rather than become involved in the Lutheran campus ministry program at Yale, Darlene chose to become active in the Yale Christian Fellowship—the local chapter of InterVarsity Christian Fellowship, where Lewis was widely read and virtually accorded the status of "patron saint." During her junior year, she met Gordon, a Silliman College pre-medical student, who attended an InterVarsity dorm fellowship group, hosted by one of his suite mates. Gordon was the son of British parents from the Midlands, who migrated to the U.S. in the 1970s to work in the nascent computer industry in California's Silicon Valley. He and Darlene began dating and soon became a committed couple. They applied to similar lists of medical schools; they were surprised and delighted when they both were accepted to the University of Minnesota. Darlene and Gordon were married at Darlene's home church during spring break of their first year of medical school.

Darlene and Gordon's son, Harrison, was born during the summer before their third year of medical school. With both Darlene and Gordon in medical school, life was highly stressful. With the added responsibilities of taking care of "little Harry," the marriage began to show the strain. By the end of their fourth year of medical school, Gordon had become embroiled in a long-term affair with another woman medical student and wanted a divorce, to which Darlene reluctantly agreed.

Following the divorce, Darlene decided to leave the Midwest. She moved to Washington State for her internship and subsequent residency in psychiatry. Also, after much struggle with religious guilt—over both her divorce and some post-divorce sexual experimentation—Darlene publicly affirmed what she described as "a long-repressed lesbian orientation." She enjoyed her work at the University of Washington (UW) not only because of its excellent medical resources, but also because of its hospitable cultural attitude toward gays and lesbians, as compared to her experience in the Midwest. Following her training, Darlene decided to remain in the area and pursue a career in research in academic medicine. She is currently working on studies of psychiatric disorders among patients with AIDS.

Darlene first met Sue during a psychiatry rotation during her internship, and their relationship slowly developed during the years of Darlene's residency. After many intimate conversations and much personal sharing, they came to realize that they loved and were committed to each other. When Darlene decided to stay in the area, she and Sue agreed to pool their resources and buy a home in Valleywood, where they could raise their children.

Sue grew up in Louisville, Kentucky, and was raised by a single mother. Sue's father was a soldier assigned to Fort Knox, who abandoned Sue's mother when she became pregnant. Sue's mother then worked at a variety of unskilled domestic and retail jobs, while trying to raise her daughter alone. She eventually managed to find some acceptance and help in a single-parents group sponsored by a large "moderate Baptist" congregation in suburban Louisville. The church sponsored some children's and youth ministries, in which Sue occasionally participated. Sue fondly remembers a special church youth mission trip to Oregon during her junior year in high school. She worked on a puppet ministry team, enjoying the anonymity, as she visited the Pacific Northwest for the first time.

Sue graduated from a large suburban high school, which was a magnet school for health-care industry careers. After four years of working in entry-level jobs in a large Humana hospital, Sue attended Jefferson Community College part time. After receiving her associate's degree, she transferred to a small local Catholic college to study nursing. There, she met a student named Frank. After dating Frank for two months, Sue moved into his apartment, with plans to marry him soon. After she became pregnant, Frank began to abuse her. When Tom was born, the pattern of abuse intensified. With the help of some Catholic sisters who taught at the school, Sue managed to find an apartment of her own and child-care assistance. She was also helped by some personal and vocational counseling from a church-related organization that supports young women in crisis and transition.

After graduation, Sue wanted to make a fresh start in life both for herself and for Tom. So, she accepted an opportunity to move to Seattle and begin a position in psychiatric nursing at a major urban teaching hospital. Several of her friends on the hospital staff were openly gay or lesbian. Sue was attracted to the openness and nonviolence of their sexual expression, in contrast to her experiences in Louisville. After several years working at the hospital, she met Darlene. Following many talks with Darlene and other friends in a support group for gay, lesbian, bisexual, and transgendered employees at the hospital, Sue decided that she should "come out" in Seattle. In a few months, encouraged especially by her intensifying relationship with Darlene, Sue worked up the courage to make the announcement to her mother in Louisville. Then she and Darlene decided to move in together and, with their sons, become a blended family.

Beyond their discussion with Jackie and Dale regarding the congregational dynamics involved in Valleywood Church's accepting their lesbian blended family, Darlene and Sue raised several other issues that the copastors need to consider carefully. First, since Darlene and Sue are involved in church primarily out of concern for the religious and personal development of their children, Tom and Harry, they have some critical questions about what the church will teach both publicly and by example about sexuality, marriage, and families. "I grew up with years of guilt-producing talk about 'God's design for marriage,' and we don't want that stuff inflicted on Harry and Tom," Sue exclaimed. "Yes," Darlene added, "we want our children to know about the reality of abuse and how it can be prevented in both heterosexual and homosexual relationships. We want our children to be taught about the sins of homophobia and heterosexism, which pervade our culture and many churches today. Above all, we want our children and their peers at Valleywood to learn that God loves all kinds of families, not just the 'traditional' ones!"

Darlene and Sue shared that they plan to add another child—perhaps a girl this time—to their family. "We were thinking about adoption," Darlene commented, "but now we're exploring the possibility of artificial insemination by a donor." "I feel as if I was robbed of the joy of carrying Tom by Frank's abuse," Sue confided. "So, I would like the chance to experience the blessing of carrying a child supported by Darlene's love and care."

A final issue with which Jackie and Dale are struggling is Darlene and Sue's strong desire to have their union blessed by the church. "We are both Christians who regularly attend church. We own a home together and parent each other's child," Darlene observed. "We are entitled to domestic partners insurance and health-care benefits at the hospital. Why can't our family be blessed by the church? Since the church has an interest in the success of our relationship—at least for the sake of our kids—doesn't that mean that the church has an obligation to pray for and bless our long-term commitment to each other?"

The POSSLQ: Jim and Jenny

Jim and Jenny think it is humorous that the United States Census classifies them as POSSLQ—persons of opposite sex sharing living quarters. "We are not just shacking up temporarily," Jim declares, "but Jenny and I have a long-term commitment to each other."

Jim grew up in Valleywood. His maternal grandparents were

charter members at Valleywood Church, and his parents—Loren and Judy—are still "pillars" of the church. Loren directs a large, nonprofit social service organization, while Judy is a middle-school social studies teacher in Valleywood.

Jim was brought to Valleywood Church as an infant and enrolled in the Cradle Roll department. He spent his preschool, elementary, and middle-school years in the Sunday school and children's ministries programs of the church. Long-term members of the congregation still laugh about the year Jim was the "confused angel" in the church children's Christmas pageant, who enthusiastically proclaimed: "Behold, I bring you good tidings of great joy. Santa Claus is coming to Valleywood!"

Jim's parents—shaped by American cultural values of the 1960s and 1970s—adopted a rather laissez-faire style of parenting, especially as their three children became teenagers. Jim fell in with a group of friends in his high school who were indifferent to religion. During his sophomore year, he stopped attending church and announced he was an atheist. His parents took this declaration in stride as a developmental phase. After Jim graduated from Valleydale High School, he attended Valleywood Community College as a pre-engineering student. He then transferred to Western Washington University in Bellingham, a city on Puget Sound, north of Seattle. During the first semester of his junior year, Jim began dating Jenny, whom he remembered first meeting at the annual Christmas dinner that Valleywood Church held with First Korean Church.

Jenny is a third-generation Korean American, who also grew up in Valleywood. Her maternal grandparents owned and operated a local dry cleaning business, while her paternal grandparents founded a very successful Korean specialty grocery store, which was bought out by a larger chain. Jenny's father, Sam, attended Valleywood Community College for two years and then went to work for Boeing. He worked his way up to a middle management position. Sung Hee, Jenny's mother, continued to work long hours in her parents' dry cleaning business, while taking care of Jenny, their only child.

Jenny's grandparents and her parents were pillars in First

Korean Church. Like Jim, Jenny was brought to church each week. She also attended a Korean language and culture school, held in the church fellowship hall on Saturday mornings. When Jenny turned thirteen and began middle school, however, she rejected what she now describes as the "conservative, patriarchal" church and refused to attend. This break became the focus of a continuing conflict between Jenny and her "authoritarian" father that continues today.

When she finished Valleyview High School—on the other side of the town and the tracks from Valleydale—Jenny eagerly left home to attend Western Washington University. She "connected" with Jim during her first semester. In a few months, much to her family's chagrin, she and Jim were living together. Jenny finished her degree in elementary education in four years, while Jim worked almost full time and spread out his program in plastics engineering to graduate at the same time as Jenny. During their last year of college, Jenny became pregnant with Mary, who was born during the summer following graduation. Jim then accepted a position at a start-up plastics manufacturing company in Seattle, founded by some friends from college.

When Jenny and Jim moved to Seattle, Loren, Judy, Sam, and Sung Hee were united in their hope that since their children now had a baby, they would "do the right thing—settle down and get married." As parental pressure increased, so did Jim and Jenny's resistance. They flatly continue to refuse to be married. Mary is now two years old. She is brought to Valleywood Church almost every Sunday by Jim's parents. Jenny refuses to allow Mary to be brought to First Korean Church.

Occasionally Jim and Jenny show up at Valleywood Church for social functions, especially the annual joint Christmas dinner with First Korean, but they do not attend services. Jim now describes himself as an agnostic, and Jenny sees herself as a feminist who is alienated from the institutional church. Other than the Christmas dinner, both Jim and Jenny avoid any contact with First Korean. Jenny and her father do not speak directly to each other. On rare occasions they communicate through Jenny's heartbroken mother.

Loren and Judy have repeatedly asked for Jackie and Dale's

advice regarding the cohabiting couple. Recently, Loren suggested that since Jim and Jenny soon will have lived together for seven years, they should consider applying for common-law recognition of their relationship, if they do not want to get married. All of Mary's grandparents and great-grandparents—except Jenny's father—are fervently praying for a wedding. Also, the baptism of Mary, which has been pointedly not requested by her parents, despite the desire of Mary's grandparents, great-grandparents, and others in the congregation, raises difficult issues. Jackie and Dale are in a genuine quandary about how to approach this situation pastorally. Should they consider this twenty-something cohabiting heterosexual couple with a toddler on the church's Cradle Roll a "family," a "church family," or even a "Christian family"?

The Single-in-Church Woman: Jill

Jill is a "forty-something" woman who grew up in Ballard, a Seattle neighborhood south of Valleywood. Her father is a commercial fisherman who rarely attends church; her mother, Jane, who died last year, was a faithful member of Valleywood. Jill has one brother who followed his dad into a fishing career and likewise has little interest in organized religion.

Jill's mother taught her that God had a soul mate for her. Following her mother's leadership, Jill began to pray in elementary school that "God would show me the one prepared to be my life partner." In the summer of her junior year in high school, Jill went with the Valleywood Church youth group to Tall Timbers—the Presbyterian camp near Mount Rainier. At camp, Jill met Michael and was sure that God had answered her prayers. Michael came from University Presbyterian Church, a very large urban congregation in Seattle. He was beginning study at the University of Washington (UW) and wanted to major in business.

Although Jill was intelligent and did well in school, she had no interest in pursuing further education after high school. She found a job waitressing at a local restaurant and continued to see Michael regularly. Her friends used to tease that she was pursuing an "M.R.S." degree. Jill and Michael were married in a well-attended ceremony at University Presbyterian (rather than at

Valleywood) the summer following his college graduation. They both gave their personal testimonies of faith as part of the service.

Michael began a career working for a major bank, while Jill worked for a large grocery store chain. They soon bought a home in Valleywood. Since they decided to postpone having children, it seemed like a good idea for this recently married, devout young couple to work with the church's college group. So, when Pastor Jon invited them to assume this ministry, which involved many evenings and weekends, they accepted. On nights when Jill had to work at the grocery store, Michael would attend the college group meetings by himself.

Jill still doesn't know—and perhaps doesn't want to know—all the details of how it happened. During the second year of their volunteer ministry, Michael had an affair with Kathy, a college sophomore in the group. Although the affair was hushed up in the church, it was widely rumored that Michael and Kathy became romantically involved during church-sponsored events at which Jill was unable to attend. Despite Pastor Jon's efforts at marriage counseling, Michael soon left both the church and Jill. He divorced Jill as soon as possible.

Kathy graduated from the UW and married Michael during her senior year. They now live in Redmond, Washington, and have three children. Since Kathy's parents, Terry and Karen, are long-term members of Valleywood, Michael occasionally comes back to Valleywood with Kathy's family, particularly for special events such as the Christmas dinner.

Following the divorce, Jill remained at Valleywood with her mother. She sought help from a professional pastoral counselor at Presbyterian Counseling Service and participated in a divorce recovery group at University Presbyterian. Ten years ago, after much soul-searching, Jill married Ed, a successful bank manager (previously married but with grown children) who is not interested in the church. "Ed is not a Christian," Jill reports, "but he is the kindest man I have ever known." With Ed's encouragement, Jill enrolled in a computer technology training program at Valleywood Community College. This experience led to her current job in the medical records office of a major health insurance company. Jill reports sadly that she and Ed have decided that it would be unwise for them to have children.

During the two decades following her divorce, Jill regularly participated with her mother at Valleywood Church. Now, since her mother's death, Jill feels truly alone at church. She sits by herself in church and feels alone in her faith. She wearily observes, "There are some Sundays when I feel like a fallen nun." Both Jackie and Dale have talked with and prayed for Jill, especially during the time of her mother's death. They, however, are at a loss as to where Jill—like a number of other "single-in-church" women at Valleywood—fits into the "church family."

"So," Jackie concludes, "after much prayer and reflection, Dale and I think that somehow we must redefine what we mean by 'family' at Valleywood Presbyterian Church. Although our own families were pretty "traditional," many of the families of the people whom God has called us to serve are not." "That's an understatement," Dale added. "We really need to find better ways to connect what the Christian faith teaches about love relationships and families with examples like these from our ministry."

Outlining Theological Models of Ministry: An Overview

In the subsequent chapters of this book, we will return to the context of Valleywood Church and the complex web of issues this context raises for the problem of defining families in contemporary Christian ministry. Along with a wide variety of model-specific case studies and illustrations accompanying our discussion of the models, we will test each approach against the thickly described Valleywood context. What are the strengths and weaknesses each model offers to Jackie and Dale's struggles with the nature of families at Valleywood?

One way to image our task is to envision the models as various proposals for "building a bridge" between Christian theology and pastoral practice. We are describing and critically evaluating the "design, materials, and durability" of each proposal to connect the teachings of the faith to the empirical situations of Valleywood and to other test cases. The strongest bridges may combine features from more than one proposal.

Our next step is to offer a brief overview of the theological models for connecting theology and pastoral practice with which this study is concerned. Detailed analysis and critique is offered in subsequent chapters. We are examining five distinct, but somewhat overlapping, approaches to connecting Christian theology and the practice of ministry. Taken together, these models encompass much, but not all, of the significant work being done in developing approaches to connect theology and ministry in Europe and North America. In other words, these categories offer a representative overview of the subject but make no claim of offering an exhaustive survey.

Correlational Models

The first category in our overview is correlational models, which will be explored in detail in chapter 2. During the 1950s and 1960s, Paul Tillich popularized the "method of correlation" in both systematic and pastoral theology.[29] In Tillich's view, human existence gave rise to ultimate questions that were then correlated with the symbols of the Christian faith. This method provided a way to connect individual human needs with the traditions of the Christian community.

Later systematic theologians—particularly David Tracy—have revised and further developed Tillich's approach. Following advances in philosophical hermeneutics,[30] Tracy argues that what is needed to connect culture or society with theology is a "mutually critical correlation."[31] Chapter 2 examines correlational approaches, as they have been embodied in *both* the "pastoral care and counseling" and the "Christian counseling" movements. The development of these two competing movements to connect theology and psychology in pastoral practice parallels the major twentieth-century division between mainline and evangelical Protestants.

Particular attention is given to Don Browning's use of the revised correlational model in his effort to revision the task of Christian theology from the perspective of practical theology[32] and to Diana Garland's recent comprehensive approach to family ministry.[33]

Contextual Models

Chapter 3 examines the use of contextual models to connect Christian theology and ministry. These models focus upon human experience analyzed through the lens of a specific context. This context may be geographic, as in indigenous local mission theologies.[34] It may be racial or ethnic, as in the development of African American,[35] Hispanic,[36] or Asian[37] theologies. Alternatively, the context may be politically and economically based, as in many liberation theologies.[38] In addition, gender may be studied as its own context[39] or in relationship with a wide variety of models (for example, eco-feminist theology).[40]

Contextual models generally proceed through the empirical examination of the "lived experience" of whatever group is being examined (for example, according to race, gender, or class). It is the human experience of this particular group that supplies the norms that govern theological language connecting practice (or, more accurately, "praxis") with Christian teaching. A modified version of Aristotle's idea of *praxis* is commonly used in these approaches to overcome the separation between theory and practice.[41]

Amidst the wide diversity of these approaches, we seek to locate common theological assumptions and methodological approaches that identify them as members of the contextual family of models. We particularly use the context of Valleywood to portray and evaluate the strengths and weaknesses of contextual models.

Narrative Models

The rise of "narrative theology" among Protestant and some Catholic theologians in the 1970s and 1980s[42] was in part a hermeneutical response to the continuing crisis over the doctrine of revelation.[43] "Story theology" provided a way around some of the unresolved historical dilemmas of propositional theology.[44] With a practice-centered focus upon ethics, narrative theology, in James McClendon's words, viewed the "narrative community" of the church as "the home of doctrine."[45]

Narrative models seek to recover the loss of ethics, particularly following the failure of what is labeled "the Enlightenment project."[46] By returning to the storytelling traditions of the ancient world—whether Aesop's fables, Homer's epics, Hebrew narratives, or Jesus' parables in the Gospels—narrative theologians seek to recover ways to create character and virtue. The goal is to connect the stories of our lives and communities with the formational master stories of the traditions of the past. The concern for historical critical adequacy in making these connections between traditional stories and contemporary stories of faith communities presents an important challenge to narrative models.[47]

In addition to examining in chapter 4 a narrative approach to the Valleywood case, my case study of Teresa of Avila and evangelical women represents another example of the use of a narrative model. In that investigation, I argue that the historical themes of status inconsistency and ecclesiastical authoritarianism and also Teresa's model of Christian community as "friends of God" help account for her remarkable appeal to Protestant women today.[48]

Performance Models

Beginning with the New Testament, models of performance—particularly singing—have been used to connect Christian teaching and pastoral practice. As Ralph Martin exclaims, "The Christian Church was born in song."[49] The British theologian Frances Young has developed a performance model that examines the Bible and its use in the early church as a guide to the dilemmas of biblical interpretation today. Her *Virtuoso Theology* was originally published in Britain under the title *The Art of Performance.*[50] As Young maintains, the problems of "authentic performance" of classics on stage, film or in concert hall are somewhat parallel to discussions about valid interpretation of the Bible. The thesis of this book is that such tensions can be contained within the context of Christian Doctrine as a whole, so as to become coherent with the theological landscape of Christianity.[51]

In addition to examining how a performance model might work in the Valleywood case, chapter 5 examines how one might use a performance model to illumine the connection between theology and hymnody for Christians in the Free Church and evangelical traditions.[52] Developing a historical contrast between Prosper of Aquitaine and Augustine of Hippo, I argue that, instead of learning their theology from liturgy, Baptists and other Christians in the Free Church and evangelical traditions principally learn their theology from song. Thus, the standard liturgical slogan *lex orandi, lex credendi* ("the law of praying is the law of believing") should be modified for these nonliturgical traditions to *lex cantandi, lex credendi* ("the law of singing is the law of believing").

Regulative Models

Chapter 6 examines a fifth type of model for connecting Christian theology and the practice of ministry: a regulative approach.[53] In this area, the pioneering work of George Lindbeck's cultural-linguistic model has shaped a new alternative.[54] Like performance models, with which it is often linked,[55] Lindbeck's model constructs a cross-disciplinary analogy. In Lindbeck's case, however, the root analogy is not between theology and a cultural practice (such as musical performance), but rather between Christian doctrine and language. Out of concern to understand the process of doctrinal change in the context of candid ecumenical dialogue, Lindbeck develops an analogy between understanding Christian doctrine and learning a new language.[56] Following Wittgenstein, Lindbeck argues that learning doctrine works something like learning grammar when one speaks a new language.[57]

The chapter invites Christian ministers to consider seriously the value of a practice-centered approach to Christian theology that reflects Lindbeck's cultural-linguistic approach. By utilizing a cultural-linguistic approach to Christian theology, Christians would at least have enough common language to agree on *where* they disagree![58] Without lapsing into relativism or "lowest-common denominator" theology, such an approach would both allow for doctrinal change through historical development and foster a candid view of ecumenical dialogue. Furthermore, I think that Lindbeck's functional, community-based view of Christian doctrine may provide a way of reconnecting pastoral and systematic (constructive) theology. A functional theological analysis of narratives of pastoral care may do much to clarify the pluralistic perplexity that characterizes much contemporary constructive theology.[59]

The final chapter briefly summarizes the results of the book's critical comparisons of the five types of models, with particular attention to their value in illuminating the Valleywood Church case. The book concludes with some exploration of blended models and strategies for assisting persons in developing their own approaches to connecting Christian theology and pastoral practice.

Crafting Theological Models: The Search for Wise Approaches to Pastoral Practice

To return briefly to the opening composite case study, how does this careful examination of theological models enable a helpful, honest response to Cheryl's questions about her studies in seminary? How will learning about the connections between Christian theology and pastoral practice empower Cheryl to be a more effective Christian minister with her youth group at Community Presbyterian Church?

I would respond to Cheryl that one of the primary tasks of seminary is to develop a working theology of ministry, which is globally aware yet culturally specific to the concrete needs of the persons and communities she is serving.[60] Through both *what* we teach and the *way* we teach in seminary, we seek to model the integration of the second-order discourse of theological reflection and the concrete lived experience of ministry. As part of the process of shaping her identity as a Christian minister, Cheryl needs to develop a way to connect Christian theology and pastoral practice. Exploring theological models that integrate the teachings of the faith with pastoral practice could alleviate some of her suspicions about the value of studying Christian doctrines and traditions. What Cheryl learns about the traditions of Christian faith in her courses on Bible, history, and theology is integrated with her personal appropriation of the Christian faith. This working theology must be linked with her pastoral assessment of the individual, corporate, and even global needs—both personal and structural—found in her ministry setting. In short, Cheryl must learn to develop a wise approach to connect her theology and ministry. Critical study of a wide range of models that attempt to connect Christian theology and pastoral practice will assist her in developing a personally crafted, culturally sensitive practical theology of Christian ministry. If Cheryl's seminary experience can aid her in moving toward this goal, then the outcome of theological education will truly justify the effort and expense. To adapt the famous maxim of Irenaeus, "The splendor of God is a [Christian minister named Cheryl] fully realized."[61]

CHAPTER 2

Correlational Models

When Christians engaged in ministry seek to connect their beliefs and actions, they become "reflective practitioners."[1] For example, in our master case study in the previous chapter, Pastors Jackie and Dale seek to reflect upon the ministry of Valleywood Church with nontraditional families. Jackie and Dale are reflective practitioners who seek to relate their theology and their pastoral practice.

Each of the models for connecting theology and ministry that we will examine in the following chapters assumes some kind of mutual relation between the Christian tradition and the practices of ministry. One common pattern is the formulation of some sort of *correlation* between authoritative pieces of the Christian tradition and action in ministry. This correlation may be as simple as citing a biblical text that states the theme of a ministry, or as complex as a hermeneutical theory that connects a social scientific analysis of action and philosophical theology.

Approaches linking theology and ministry commonly describe the correlation between the Christian tradition and ministry as *communally shaped* and frequently, though not always, as *reciprocal*. The ministry is portrayed as the outgrowth of a community's obedience, or insight into the demands of the faith. The Christian tradition is appealed to for authorization of the ministry, but the community's appropriation of the tradition should also be reciprocally shaped by the ministry. At times, a Christian community's experiences in ministry will challenge the adequacy of its previous formulations or interpretations of the Christian tradition. Then, depending upon the particular Christian community's processes for change, the correlation may become the vehicle for revision or reinterpretation of the tradition.

Correlational models may connect Christian doctrine and pastoral practice in two different ways. First, a correlation may be used to provide doctrinal warrant or authorization for a particular ministry. For example, the Gospel narratives of Jesus' feeding the hungry may be used to warrant the involvement of a church community in both direct service and political action ministry to persons experiencing hunger. Second, a correlation may be used to challenge the inadequacy of the church's past teaching. For example, the experience of the church's complicity with unjust power structures that create and maintain situations of continuing hunger may be used to confront previous limited interpretations of Jesus' ministry to the hungry. So, correlational models for connecting doctrine and practice may be warranting and transformative.

This chapter analyzes both the formal and the informal uses of correlational models to connect Christian doctrine and pastoral practice. The discussion first traces the development of the model of critical correlation in pastoral theology, with particular attention to the revised correlational model formally proposed by Don Browning. Then several informal models of correlation, found in evangelical "Christian counseling" and Protestant family ministry movements, are examined. The obvious differences and some surprising similarities between Browning's and these approaches point the way to a general critical evaluation of the strengths and weaknesses of correlational models. The chapter concludes by returning to the case of Valleywood Church and offering some direct application and evaluation of correlational models.

Models of Critical Correlation

Since the high middle ages, Christian theologians, particularly those in the Thomistic tradition, have sought to correlate aspects of nature and grace. The assumption of an "analogy of being" (*analogia entis*) between God and creation, which seeks to justify human speech about God, also underlies attempts to correlate theology and human experience.

The middle of the twentieth century saw the emergence of a formal concern with correlation as a theological method. Paul Tillich (1886–1965) proposed that the task of theology was to analyze the changing existential questions that arise in each period of history and to correlate these questions with the answers found in the symbols of the Christian faith.[2] As Tillich described the process, "In using the method of correlation, systematic theology proceeds in the following way: it makes an analysis of the human situation out of which the existential questions arise, and it demonstrates that the symbols used in the Christian message are the answers to these questions."[3] For example, questions that arise from humanity's self-estrangement are correlated with the New Being in Jesus as the Christ, which conquers estrangement.[4]

An important limitation to Tillich's approach is that the interaction between the Christian tradition and the human situation only goes in one direction: Basic existential questions defined by the human situation find their answers in selected symbols of the Christian message. The possibilities for two-directional mutual interaction—for example, the Christian message raising questions for the human situation or culture responding to questions raised by the Christian message—are ignored. Although the experiences of pastoral practice are correlated with the themes of Christian theology, Christian doctrine is not informed by the concrete experiences of ministry.

Awareness of this limitation led theologians to revise Tillich's method of correlation in the direction of greater interaction between theology and the cultures in which ministry takes place. For example, the pastoral theologian Seward Hiltner (1909–84) strongly advocated moving the model of correlation toward a genuine two-way dialogue.[5]

David Tracy proposed a significant revision of Tillich's method of correlation to include a "mutually critical correlation" between theology and contemporary cultural experiences and practices.[6] Tracy's approach seeks to establish a critical dialogue between interpretations of the Christian "classics" and interpretations of the lived experience of contemporary communities.[7] Under the banner of the "revised correlational method," Tracy's approach provided the framework for a range of projects in practical and pastoral theology.[8]

In *A Fundamental Practical Theology*, Don Browning utilizes Tracy's revised correlational method to ground his constructive proposals for reorganizing the disciplines and practices of theology.[9] Browning develops correlations between detailed case studies of three diverse congregations—Wiltshire Methodist, the Church of the Covenant, and the Apostolic Church of God—and his own model of practical moral reason. Browning argues that his five dimensions of moral thinking—the *visional*, the *obligational*, the *tendency-need*, the *environmental-social*, and the *rule-role*—are rooted in the theological ethics of Reinhold Niebuhr and can be used to describe and analyze the actions that occur in the congregations.[10]

Browning's correlations reflect his liberal Protestant background and its reduction of theology to ethics. His method works effectively with the two white mainline churches he analyzes, which each possess a history and social location related to his own. For example, Browning uses his five dimensions of moral thinking to analyze two complex conflicts in Wiltshire Methodist Church: (1) the pastor's desire to purchase the parsonage and (2) plans to expand the Christian education facilities. Reinhold Niebuhr's view of sin as "inordinate self-concern" offers a critical theological dimension to the analysis.[11] Similarly, Browning's revised correlational model critically analyzes the process of religious education around the Church of the Covenant's decision to become a sanctuary church for Salvadoran refugees.[12]

The African American Apostolic Church of God, however, provides the real test of the strengths and weaknesses inherent in Browning's correlational method. We now focus on Browning's analysis of families in this highly visible Pentecostal congregation.

Revised Correlation and the Apostolic Church of God

The Apostolic Church of God, a large congregation affiliated with the Pentecostal Assemblies of the World, is located in the midst of Chicago's deteriorated Woodlawn neighborhood. Although the Apostolic Church of God is geographically near the University of Chicago, where Browning works, the social and cultural differences between the two institutions are great. Browning comments that "within a few blocks, vastly different ways of life unfold."[13] Browning attempts to bridge this gap through "a hermeneutical dialogue" with the church. The dialogue seeks to be "mutually critical." Browning declares, "The Apostolic Church affirmed and judged my world in a variety of ways. In turn, my world both affirmed and judged the Apostolic Church."[14] The tension in this dialogue becomes very acute as Browning examines the issue of congregational care of families.

Browning candidly admits the need that motivates his interest in this dialogue: "I wanted to know what a pressured, inner-city church did for its families because of my fear that mainline, white congregations were losing their capacity to cope with the growing pressures on their families."[15] He delineates the obvious conflict between the Apostolic Church's understanding of families and both liberal and feminist views of family held by his constituencies in the university.

The Apostolic Church of God developed extensive, well-organized programs of ministry to families, particularly through its Christian Action Lay Ministry program (CALM). Browning confesses,

> As a professor who had written rather widely in pastoral care for over two decades, I was astounded by the range and depth of CALM and by the philosophy behind it.... The crystal-clear value framework that surrounded the CALM ministries...was far different from the value assumptions behind much of mainline Protestant care and counseling.[16]

The theology that guides the Apostolic Church's ministries to families reflects the church's pentecostal-holiness understanding of "the biblical model of the family."[17] Ministry leaders not only could quote the key passages that supported their programs, but also "could advance nuanced interpretations" of them.[18] The key text for comprehending the church's understanding of the "sanctified family" is Ephesians 5:21–6:4. The leadership of the church accepted the theme of male headship of the family, but interpreted this to mean that the husband was to be the "chief servant" of the family. Browning reports that

> If husbands and fathers used their authority to mistreat their families, the church instructed wives and children not to obey or submit. Wives were thoughtfully capable of knowing how a sanctified husband should act. If husbands did not act correctly, that was to be brought to the attention of the pastor.[19]

At this point, Browning's method of revised correlation presses him to make a rather surprising hermeneutical leap. Instead of acknowledging and analyzing the clear—even if sometimes benevolent—patriarchalism of the power structure of the church, particularly as embodied in its authoritative pastor, he correlates the church's teachings and practices with Reinhold Niebuhr's ethic of equal regard.[20] It seems doubtful that the congregation's pastor would accept Browning's interpretation that the pastor, in his preaching on families, "inserted an *implicit* ethic of equal regard."[21] Browning claims, "What appeared at first glance to be a rhetoric and ethic of male authority worked out in the end to be an ethic of male responsibility *guided by an ethic of equal regard.*"[22]

Browning's correlational model leads him to assimilate genuine cultural and theological differences under a broad ethical umbrella. He uses life cycle theory[23] to support his claim that "the Apostolic Church recognizes that the ethic of mutuality means different things for men, women, and children at different moments in the life cycle."[24] At best, this effort yields an awkward fit, due to the gap between Browning's culture and that of the Apostolic Church of God. Browning's claim seems particularly questionable when one recalls that Browning earlier reported that the pastor of the Apostolic Church "explicitly denounced the 'liberal tendency to derive the entirety of the Christian ethic from the principle of neighbor love.' "[25] It seems that the presuppositions of Browning's method, rather than the theology and practice of the Apostolic Church, are displayed in his insistence on finding an ethic of equal regard in the congregation.[26] Elaine Graham has offered a similar criticism of Browning's approach: "Browning is, I believe, still firmly rooted in a modernist, Weberian rationalist tradition. His understanding of the human subject and pastoral agency illustrates this, in the primacy he affords to moral reasoning."[27]

The revised correlational approach, so articulately embodied in Browning's research, reveals its limitations when it struggles to interpret broad differences of theology and culture. Understandings of, and ministries to, families in the Apostolic Church of God resist assimilation into the five broad dimensions of Browning's moral reasoning. Yet the tendency to use correlation as a vehicle to "reinterpret" the challenging views of others so that they fit within one's preestablished categories and interpretive scheme may be irresistible. The distance between

Browning's theological worldview and that of the leadership of the Apostolic Church of God creates a hermeneutical gap, which the revised correlational method seeks, but fails, to bridge.

Our examination of Browning's hermeneutically sophisticated model of revised correlation may foster the inaccurate perception that correlational models for integrating theology and practice must necessarily be complex. In fact, much contemporary Christian ministry relies upon simpler models of correlation to connect social scientific claims with those of Christian teaching. Sometimes these models are explicit, as in attempts to foster integration between psychology and theology; but often the correlation is implicit, as in the Apostolic Church's biblical model of "the sanctified family." We now examine several examples of these less formal correlational models, found in evangelical Protestant circles, that attempt to establish a more direct connection between the Bible and ministry.

Informal Models of Correlation

Christian Counseling and Correlation

The divisions in twentieth-century Protestantism between liberal and conservative factions not only expressed differences in theology and culture, but also shaped ministry practice.[28] Among conservative Protestants, the rise of "Christian counseling" included diverse attempts to integrate a biblically centered theology with the increasing cultural acceptance of psychological understandings.[29]

Lee Eliason surveyed and critically examined the counseling literature used in the 1980s in a range of evangelical seminaries in the United States and Canada.[30] Amidst the variety of materials cited, Eliason discerned three basic approaches to the relationship between psychology and theology: (1) an "exclusively biblical" type, (2) a "unity of truth" type, and (3) a "pastoral theology" type, based most commonly upon the mutual correlational approach of Seward Hiltner.

Eliason's exclusively biblical type used deductive approaches that sought to develop counseling practice by directly applying selected "biblical teachings." Proponents stressed the inadequacy—or even falsity—of psychological knowledge.[31] This separationist view rejected the possibility of meaningful correlation. Its reactionary approach to ministry now represents a conservative minority of contemporary North American evangelicalism.

Eliason's remaining two approaches to integrating psychology and theology in evangelical seminaries both may be characterized as correlational models. Both types seek to bridge the gap between psychology and theology by reciprocally relating themes from each discipline. The primary differences lie in assumptions about the normative role of Scripture in Christian theology and the need for a unified understanding of truth. According to Eliason, respondents who advocated the unity of truth approach affirmed in various ways "the normative authority of the Scriptures as *the foundation* for pastoral counseling theory and practice."[32] Although integration is done in various ways, the assumption is that there is no *inherent* conflict between the truths of Scripture and the truths of psychology.[33] From this perspective, all truth is God's truth. Therefore, although misinterpretations and misunderstandings of the truths of both disciplines abound, the unity of truth type assumes there are no final contradictions.

In contrast, evangelical respondents in Eliason's third type (pastoral theology) tended to allow more scope for the authority of truth from the behavioral sciences. An approach centered upon the practices of ministry (such as Hiltner's "shepherding" perspective),[34] rather than upon the unity of truth, characterized this type of correlation.[35]

Thus, despite diverse approaches to the integration of psychology and theology, the Christian counseling movement has frequently used correlational models to describe and analyze much of its ministry. Although Christian counseling has sought to distinguish itself from "more liberal" Protestant versions of pastoral counseling and spiritual care, the movement has ironically found

~~itself subject to similar methodological limitations.~~ For example, the dynamics of assimilation to the correlator's own culture (and consequent struggles with clients who embody significant cultural differences) limit correlational models, regardless of the theological differences of their proponents.

Beyond the psychological focus of Christian counseling, our discussion of correlational models now returns to encompass the broader concerns of congregational care of families.

Family Ministries and Correlation

As Browning's work exemplifies, in recent years, correlational models have been broadened to include systemic approaches to congregational care. The dialogue between theology and psychology has been extended to include the whole range of the human sciences. This wider dialogue has been especially apparent in the rapid development of "family ministries" among congregations. Driven by anxiety-producing challenges to traditional family patterns in Euro-American societies, as well as by explosive conflicts over the nature and boundaries of families, congregations are focusing significant energy and ministry resources in developing ministries to families. Furthermore, in the United States, "family ministry" is developing as a specialty field, with programs in seminaries and in Christian colleges and universities. These programs are often separate from pastoral care and sometimes maintain close ties to graduate social work.

Our analysis of correlational models in family ministry focuses upon Diana Garland's extensive survey of the field.[36] Garland adopts an ecosystemic framework for understanding families.[37] This perspective "uses ecology as a metaphor for the relationships human systems (families) have with their physical and social environments."[38] Although she concedes that some structural aspects (for example, biological and legal) are part of the definition of family, Garland argues for "a functional family definition as the ideal to which we strive."[39] She contends:

The functional definition seems to better fit Jesus' teachings about family. For followers of Christ are not to be bound by the structures of legally recognized or biologically based relationships. Rather, family relationships are defined by relationship processes—loving one another, being faithful to the same Lord, and adopting one another as brothers and sisters in the household of faith.[40]

Whether one agrees with Garland's definition of the family, the question with which we are concerned is the *method* she uses to connect her understanding of "biblical foundations" of the family with the findings of recent social scientific research on families.

In addition to some careful exegesis of the power relationship between husbands and wives in key biblical texts and a brief historical survey of the church's influence upon family life, Garland's work spends three chapters examining "biblical foundations for family ministry today."[41] Numerous biblical texts are examined, with an eye to their implications for issues facing contemporary American families. Garland is aware of the role of hermeneutical preunderstandings in biblical interpretation and gives some attention to critical historical studies.

Yet Garland offers no explicit discussion of her theological method. The reader is left to discover by observation how this wealth of biblical material is used to illumine current social scientific research on the family. The method that emerges is one of *implicit correlation.* Carefully selected biblical texts and themes are correlated with social scientific research findings. For example, Garland *interweaves* Scripture and social scientific research in a way that moves beyond mere parallelism, as she deals with the problem of venting anger:

> Vented anger is discussed often by biblical authors, since it is the expression of anger that most often develops into physical assault or verbal hostility (Gen. 34:18-31; Exod. 2:11-15; 2 Sam. 13; Prov. 14:17). Obviously, anger expressed in physical or emotional attack on another is intent on doing harm, not on problem-solving. Anger expressed in venting becomes the first step toward murder, not toward reconciliation (Matt.

5:22). Social science research indicates that expressing negative emotions actually tends to keep families from being able
to resolve difficulties (Forgatch 1989).[42]

Although this example cites a number of biblical references, it is
the language of modern social science—"venting anger" and
"problem-solving"—that supplies the categories within which
the biblical texts are cited. The horizon of interpretation is the
social psychological situation of the contemporary middle-class
American family, and differences from families in ancient Israel
are downplayed. Selected scripture and selected research findings
are carefully correlated to give a unified result.

Garland's discussion of intimacy offers another example of this
theological correlation of biblical material and the findings of
social science:

> One of the major themes of the Bible is intimacy. God wants
> to be known by us; God knows our innermost being. Jesus
> instructs us to stay connected, to be intimate with him by abid-
> ing in his love (John 15:4-7). Before the Fall, Adam and Eve
> were "naked" and "not ashamed" before each other and before
> God (Gen. 2:25). At the culmination of Jesus' life, he was
> stripped naked and held up for all to see, God with us (John
> 1:14-18), allowing us to know and see who God is.
>
> Intimacy is not a feeling or an act of romantic endearment.
> Intimacy is "a fundamental bonding between persons' inner-
> most senses of identity" (Heyward 1982:44). It is the outcome
> of attachment, communication, and problem-solving.
> Intimacy is a sense of knowing and being known by the inti-
> mate other, which grows out of a generalized sense of closeness
> between persons. It is often characterized by self-disclosure,
> feelings of cohesion, physical acts exchanged...or communi-
> cation of thoughts and feelings (Moss and Schwebel 1993).[43]

Theological interpretation of the Bible plays a more predomi-
nant role in this example than in the previous one. The theme of
"intimacy" provides a category for correlating relationally interpreted biblical material and contemporary psychological descrip-

tion. Garland weaves together a harmonizing interpretation of diverse, carefully chosen biblical texts, with a compatible empirical definition of intimacy.[44] The resulting correlation offers a ministry-focused understanding of the processes of family development.

Garland's method of implicit correlation is most effective in illumining the situation of families whose history and social location are similar to her own. In a fashion strikingly reminiscent of our earlier analysis of Browning's critical correlation, limitations of Garland's approach are clearly revealed when she attempts to reach beyond her own culture and social location to analyze family life in cultures quite different from her own.

For example, Garland offers a brief overview of African American family life, culminating in some "suggestions for culturally relevant family ministry."[45] Although she discusses a selection of significant social scientific studies of African American family and church life, the section fails to make the theological connections that would guide family ministry with African American congregations. Given the powerful place of biblical stories in the worship of African American congregations, and considering Garland's own extensive discussion of "biblical foundations," one is surprised to find a complete absence of biblical references in this section of Garland's work. The only discussion of worship consists of a story of a teenage girl preparing to read the announcements for a service.[46]

Whether we are examining Browning's methodologically sophisticated revised critical correlation or Garland's biblically harmonized implicit correlation, the limitations seem strikingly similar. Likewise, correlational models in Christian counseling exhibit difficulties in moving beyond their own culture to embrace significant cultural differences. Correlational models work best when the social location and culture are closely connected to the correlator's background and social location. Even in the hands of thoughtful and skilled practitioners, correlational models struggle when they encounter significant theological and cultural differences. A deeper analysis of these and other strengths and weaknesses of correlational models is the task to which we next turn.

Assessing Correlational Models

When persons engaged in ministry seek to provide a theological justification—or at least a theological rationale—for the actions of their ministries, correlational models offer a natural response. The ministry situation, frequently perceived through the language of the human sciences, is connected with authoritative pieces of the Christian tradition in reciprocal fashion. As we have already begun to see, the method of correlation has some significant limitations and weaknesses for the task of relating theology and ministry. We will begin our critical assessment of correlational models with some general evaluation. Then we will specifically analyze the use of a correlational model in the case of Valleywood Church.

Critical Evaluation

Correlational models exert a broad appeal that is not restricted to one part of the theological spectrum. They enable insights from theology and insights from the human sciences to engage one another, ideally in an open forum. For example, both the mutually critical correlations of Browning and the unity-of-truth correlations of Christian counseling claim to support such open engagement. Yet Christian traditions that view ministry through a "theology and culture" paradigm—for example, Christians whose traditions see God and creation connected through an analogy of being—find themselves more comfortable with correlational models than those traditions that understand their ministry through a paradigm that sharply separates theology from culture.

The great difficulty with the ideal of mutual engagement found in correlational models is that the presuppositions and analysis of one discipline often *compete* rather than cooperate with one another. Instead of mutual enhancement, over time, each discipline seeks to subordinate the other. It is this tension between the correlated disciplines of biblical exegesis and family sociology that shapes the skillful harmonizing efforts of Garland's family ministry correlations. Similarly, tension between theological ethics and the human sciences may partially account for Browning's reliance upon an abstract schema of moral reason to describe the congregational care of families in the Apostolic Church of God.

Over a period of time, carefully crafted correlations between theology and the human sciences tend to unravel. Since there is no common language that can mediate the tension, typically one discipline or another eventually dominates the correlation, with the other(s) assuming an adjunctive role. For example, as Brooks Holifield has shown, much of the history of pastoral care and counseling in twentieth-century America can be understood through the lens of a continuing tension between the disciplines of psychology and theology. In Holifield's view, the theological goal of "salvation" was subordinated to the psychological goal of "self-realization."[47] A negative reaction to this transition of emphasis from theology to psychology may partially help account for the rise of a separate Christian counseling movement among conservative Protestants.

Correlational models exhibit the strength of promoting openness to dialogue with current cultural themes and trends. Both Browning's and Garland's approaches, for instance, draw heavily upon recent understandings of families and congregations advocated in a spectrum of literature from a variety of disciplines in the human sciences. This cultural openness is particularly useful for ministries that begin with a focus upon "lived experience." Contemporary training for ministry commonly utilizes methods such as verbatims, case studies, and oral histories to enable practitioners to describe the experience of a ministry situation phenomenologically. By first describing a ministry situation as it unfolds, pastoral theology maintains a concrete point of departure in human experience for its subsequent analysis and theological reflection. For example, the *Journal of Pastoral Theology* privileges such description of contemporary personal experience as it describes its mission: "To maintain a view of pastoral theology as a constructive theology growing out of the exercise of caring relationships, with attention both to *present lived experience* and to knowledge derived from the past."[48]

Yet this openness to dialogue is limited by the preunderstandings of the correlator's culture. As we saw both in Browning's efforts to apply his method to the Apostolic Church of God and in Garland's struggle to describe family ministry that is culturally relevant to African American families, extensive theological and cultural differences prove difficult for correlational models. This difficulty becomes most acute when the encounter involves culturally critical themes, such as those raised in the struggle for peace and justice.

Correlational models risk the subordination of the culturally critical aspects of the Christian gospel. The gospel call for repentance becomes buried beneath the dominant values of the correlator's culture. Ministers using correlational models then easily become labeled as "bourgeois" defenders of the status quo. For example, Rebecca Chopp has criticized liberal-revisionist practitioners of correlation for "compliancy" with "bourgeois existence," which participates in oppression of the poor.[49] The proponents of correlational models need to be self-critical, lest their openness to dialogue leads them to be caricatured as "modern Sadducees"—those who have traded the particularity of the gospel for a mess of changing cultural pottage.[50]

Comparative Case Evaluation: Correlational Models and Valleywood Church

Our critical evaluation of the strengths and limitations of correlational models now leads to the question of the practical evaluation of a correlational approach in the master case study we developed in the previous chapter. Using a correlational model for connecting theology and practice involves reciprocally relating themes from the experience of persons and groups (often interpreted through the human sciences) to authoritative themes in the Christian tradition. Jackie and Dale, the copastors of Valleywood Church, seek to identify and connect themes from the life of the congregation and from each of the examples of nontraditional families in the case to their interpretation of the Christian faith.

The Congregation

The ministry of Valleywood Church can be characterized by a tension between "socially progressive" and traditional "family-centered" aspects of the church's heritage. The socially progressive ministry is grounded in the biblical prophetic tradition, with its concern for peace and justice, particularly among the socially marginalized. The family-centered ministry is grounded in priestly pastoral traditions of Scripture, with concern for both Christian nurture and healing, particularly in the context of sanctification through daily Christian living. The challenge for Jackie and Dale's pastoral leadership is guiding the congregation to find a balance between these traditions, especially when the dynamics of a particular ministry situation would push the congregation to affirm only one aspect of its heritage.

On the one hand, dating back to its welcome of Henry and Rosa Parker, the congregation has expressed strong opposition to the injustice of racial discrimination. This commitment was further strengthened under the church's pastoral leadership during the civil rights era of the 1960s and 1970s. The congregation's opposition to racism is not merely a reflection of American egalitarian national ideals ("liberty and justice for all"). Rather, opposition to racial discrimination expresses Christian beliefs about creation (that each person is created in the image of God) and redemption (that God's saving love in Christ is freely offered to all, as both persons and social structures stand in need of redemption). The congregation's socially progressive stance is rooted in its Christian identity and may be extended to include opposition to other forms of discrimination.

On the other hand, the members of Valleywood Church also maintain a deep commitment to the Christian nurture of families, particularly the Christian education of children. This is reflected in both a desire to welcome new and returning families into the life of the congregation and a deep suspicion of alternative lifestyles. Dating back to the church's successful opposition to a dance club and bar that opened across the street in the 1960s, the congregation has voiced strong concern about sexually permissive lifestyles.

A central feature of the congregation's traditional family-centered ministry has been its long-term involvement in counseling and supporting marriages and families in crisis. In this ministry, biblical understandings of the church as a community of forgiveness and healing have been correlated with a variety of psychological approaches emphasizing both nonjudgmental acceptance and a transformative understanding of the dynamics of family systems.

The Lesbian Couple: Darlene and Sue

The situation of Darlene and Sue challenges the congregation to confront the tension between the socially progressive and traditional family-centered aspects of its heritage. Given the continuing bitter debates about sexuality, which are dividing churches and denominations, Jackie and Dale are painfully aware that confronting this challenge could result in explosive conflict and permanent division in the congregation.[51]

The strong opposition of the congregation to unjust discrimination would encourage a significant number of members to take a proactive stance in supporting the *civil rights* of Darlene and Sue and their children. Although some members might urge the congregation to extend this support further to include church recognition of Darlene and Sue's lesbian lifestyle, many in the congregation probably would not want to include any endorsement of this lifestyle. The congregation's history of deep suspicion of alternative lifestyles, which tends to see all noncelibate lesbian lifestyles as sexually permissive, would likely lead to strongly voiced opposition to any such move. Furthermore, as Jackie and Dale seek to serve as pastors to Darlene and Sue, they continue to look with considerable confusion to their denomination for direction regarding any official blessing of homosexual unions.

The teachers in Valleywood's Christian education program, most of whom work as professional educators in the public schools, have been delighted to welcome Harry and Tom (Darlene and Sue's children) into their classes. Although these teachers strongly believe that discrimination against gay persons is sinful, they would probably resist Darlene's desire to revamp the congregation's Christian education program to focus on the evils of homophobia and heterosexism.

In addition, Darlene and Sue's attitudes regarding the legitimacy and healthfulness of their present relationship would challenge the long-term emphasis upon forgiveness and healing in the church's marriage and family counseling ministries. Darlene and Sue do not experience any need to repent of their present family situation and to receive forgiveness and healing. They do not see their family as one in crisis, but rather as one seeking to grow through the possible addition of another child.

In this example, the model of correlation sharply reveals the significant religious and cultural differences between Darlene and Sue's worldview and the worldview of Valleywood Church. Unfortunately, in the face of such extensive differences, correlational models lose much of their effectiveness in guiding toward specific pastoral action. Hermeneutical preunderstandings tend to control the outcome of conflicted situations. For example, Jackie and Dale struggle over what direction to take in their ministry with Darlene and Sue. Should they emphasize God's unconditional love and grace in Christ to assure Darlene and Sue that their lesbian blended family will be welcomed and truly accepted at Valleywood? Alternatively, should they emphasize the biblical theme of God's costly grace and transformation to encourage Darlene and Sue to accept God's forgiveness and healing in Christ? If Jackie and Dale hold a preunderstanding of themselves (and the congregation) as either affirming or not affirming the Christian acceptability of a lesbian lifestyle, it will predetermine the result.

The POSSLQ: Jim and Jenny

The situation of Jim and Jenny vividly raises the question of the status of personal Christian commitment in Valleywood's family-centered church life. Clearly, Valleywood Church is more flexible—or some might say lax—in this area than Jenny's home congregation, First Korean Church. The boundaries separating the church and "the world" are clearer, but also more excluding, at First Korean than at Valleywood. Yet, even if occasional attendance is the minimal standard at Valleywood, Jim and Jenny are emphatic about placing themselves outside of the *religious* fellowship of the church. They are explicit in stating their alienation from the faith professed by the church. As a result, despite the pressures of two-year-old Mary's grandparents and great-grandparents, she cannot yet be baptized at Valleywood. Jackie and Dale believe they should follow their denomination's requirements of parental consent (including parental profession of faith) for the baptism of a child. These requirements are based on a covenantal theology of Christian baptism.

Jim and Jenny's long-term relationship raises the matter of the place of legal or other structural aspects in the church's theological understanding of family. If a couple *functions* as a family, should the church simply recognize it as one? In contrast, Jackie and Dale have ministered to families at Valleywood, assuming that the role of the pastors is to hold up a Christian ideal or vision of family life, while showing the greatest possible pastoral discretion to all those who fail to realize it. Are the legal, social, and theological reasons that support Valleywood's deep suspicion of alternative lifestyles *necessary* assumptions for its ministry to persons who define themselves outside the boundaries? Jackie and Dale wonder if the church's understanding of, and ministry to, families should follow the patterns and trends shaping family life in contemporary culture or resist them or perhaps find some middle way.

Correlational models strive to connect the perspectives of theology and the human sciences. When the definitions of the family are debated and various disciplinary perspectives do not fit together, correlational models experience difficulty in guiding pastoral practice. In confronting contemporary North American conflicts over sexuality, correlational models often prove powerless either to warrant ministry or to transform it.

The Single-in-Church Woman: Jill

Jill has both suffered from the church's inadequate teaching about marriage and benefited from its provision of counseling ministries. Although she has experienced some healing in the nonjudgmental acceptance of pastoral counseling, Jill continues to experience an intensifying isolation in her congregational life.

The community of faith that Jackie and Dale proclaim and facilitate in their ministry needs to function as community in Jill's daily life. One approach might be the involvement of Jill in small group ministries, in which she can find nurture and support for her changing Christian identity. In addition, Jackie and Dale can lead in the creation of contexts in which Jill's marriage to her non-Christian husband, Ed, can be recognized in the life of the congregational community. Such ministry might not only help address Jill's isolation but also offer opportunities for ministry to Ed (cf. 1 Cor. 7:14).

Correlational models can provide ministry connections between Christian ideals of community and the sociocultural dynamics of group process and community formation. Effective ministries using correlational models must adapt both to changing interpretations of Christian beliefs and to changing social contexts in the lived experience of those the church seeks to serve.

CHAPTER 3

Contextual Models

Christian theology and ministry have never existed in a timeless cultural vacuum. Christians, despite their frequent focus upon eternal matters, have always expressed and practiced their faith in specific cultural contexts. These contexts are inextricably involved in the shaping and the distortion of Christianity. Christianity is always embodied in the midst of culture.

Yet, throughout much of the history of Christianity, cultural contexts were understood to be *incidental* to Christianity's message and practices. Christians might *apply* the Christian message and practices within a particular context. Perhaps they might *adapt* Christianity to changing or different cultures, but the cultural contexts themselves were not understood as a major emphasis or starting point for Christian practice and reflection.

Contextual models for integrating Christian theology and ministry reflect a shift of theological perspective. Cultural contexts, which were once in the background, are moved to the front and center of Christian thinking about faith and practice. Contextual models offer an analysis of lived human experience in specific cultural contexts, which interactively shape theological reflection.[1]

Christianity, in both its historical and contemporary expressions, is found in an amazing diversity of cultural contexts. Moreover, a given situation may be viewed from a wide variety of contextual perspectives. For example, one may analyze a group of individuals through the lenses of gender, race, ethnicity, geography, social class, and so on. Therefore, contextual models for connecting theology and ministry are correspondingly diverse.

Rather than merely chronicling some of the diversity, this chapter analyzes some theological assumptions and methodological similarities that characterize contextual models. This "family resemblance" among carefully selected contextual models will enable us to examine strengths and weaknesses inherent in the *method* of this approach. First, we briefly examine some of the factors that have shaped the development of approaches to theology through the lens of cultural context. Second, we critically examine efforts to adapt the Latin American theology of liberation to pastoral theology in a Euro-American context. Next, we consider some recent feminist and womanist contextual models of pastoral theology. Our analysis of these diverse examples of significant contextual models leads us to a critical assessment of the strengths and limitations of contextual methods. The chapter closes with an application of a contextual approach to the master case study.

Theology Through the Lens of Cultural Context

Christian theology, dating back to the writings of the apologists of the second and third centuries, has struggled with the relationship between the gospel and the surrounding culture. Early Christian writers such as Justin Martyr (c. 100–c. 165)[2] and

Clement of Alexandria (c. 150–c. 215)[3] favored development of a dialogue between Christianity and truths found in Greek culture, although other writers such as Tatian (c. 160)[4] and Tertullian (c. 160–c. 225) bitterly opposed such openness.[5] Early Christian doctrines of God and Jesus Christ adapted the terminology of Greek philosophy, particularly Neoplatonism, to describe the central mysteries of the faith. As Christianity became the dominant religion of the West, the dynamic between the gospel and culture was often lost from view, buried beneath the ideological demands of "official theology" and political needs for social control.

The modern period in the West witnessed the development of critical philosophy and critical historical study of the Christian past, including the complex relationship between the church and culture. Friedrich Schleiermacher (1768–1834) sought to respond to the modern "cultured despisers" of Christianity, developing a liberal Protestantism focused upon personal religious experience.[6] Schleiermacher's theology, along with the emphasis upon religious subjectivity in pietism and revivalism, prepared the way for the rising importance of psychology in twentieth-century pastoral theology.

Beginning in the nineteenth century, the "masters of suspicion"—Karl Marx (1818–1883), Friedrich Nietzsche (1844–1900), and Sigmund Freud (1856–1939)—played major roles in the development of serious cultural challenges to the values of Christianity and Western culture.[7] Despite their antireligious rhetoric, these thinkers' insights into the underlying dynamics of both culture and personality confronted theologians with new approaches to understanding human life and society. For example, Marx's analysis of culture through the conflict of social classes still plays a major and controversial role in shaping the approach of contemporary liberation theology.

Although Christianity may be in a period of decline in the West, the expansion of Christianity in non-Western cultures represents a major force in the development of contextual models. As Stephen Bevans maintains, "the growing identity of local churches," particularly in postcolonial Africa and Asia, is leading to the necessity of contextualization in both theology and mission.[8] This concern for contextualization is found not only among Catholic leaders, who often use the term "inculturation," but also among Protestant missiologists concerned for "indigenization."[9]

The geographic spread of Christianity has given rise to a variety of ethnographic approaches that seek to connect Christian theology and local cultures. As Robert Schreiter observes, these approaches focus upon the changing "cultural identity" of a group.[10] Although Western missionary movements originally played a role in intensifying the development of these non-Western Christian cultures, the rise of indigenous theologies and the global mission movement have challenged Western hegemony. Theological categories based upon a universalizing, modernist perspective are contested by third world Christian communities whose traditions are not shaped by these assumptions. Vincent Donovan's account of his mission experience among the Masai people of East Africa dramatically portrays such a situation.[11]

Yet, the increasing mobility of people and cultural commodities in an age of globalization complicates theological approaches that rely upon *geographical* boundaries for cultural identity. A complex mosaic of cultural identities characterizes many local communities. A wide range of diverse groups may struggle to live together peacefully in a single geographically defined community. Therefore, contextual models are also organized around a particular aspect of human identity or social location, rather than merely around geographical boundaries. For example, race or gender often serves as the principal organizational focus for a contextual approach to theology and ministry. Also, writers may combine aspects of identity—as may be seen in recent "womanist" approaches to pastoral theology— which explicitly combine race and gender.[12] In addition, liberationist approaches commonly use social class theory to call for freedom from oppression and for social change. These basic themes of race, gender, and social class are especially in evidence among the diverse methods of cultural analysis used by those who practice a contextual approach.

The lived experience of the particular group under consideration is the center of attention for contextual models. The process typically begins with a careful examination of the experiences of the group. Particular attention is given to action arising from analysis of the needs of the group. The method seeks to integrate action with reflection. From this action-oriented analysis of the cultural context, various themes and issues are derived, which in turn serve to reshape or even transform the group's relationship to Christian beliefs and practices. Christian communities may develop new strategies for mission in the world. Not all contextual models precisely follow this pattern; exceptions particularly occur among writers describing their models as more Bible-centered or church-centered.[13] Yet the understanding that theology is seen through the lens of cultural context is characteristic of the contextual approach.

In order to see more concretely how contextual models connect theology and practice, we next explore the relationship between liberation theology and pastoral care.

Liberationist Contextual Models and Pastoral Theology

The theology of liberation, particularly as it has developed in Latin America, has exerted a powerful influence upon the development of contextual theologies.[14] Unlike the ethnographic approaches discussed earlier, which focus upon cultural identity, liberation approaches demand social change.[15] As Schreiter summarizes the method:

> Liberation models analyze the lived experience of a people to uncover the forces of oppression, struggle, violence, and power. They concentrate on the conflictual elements oppressing a community or tearing it apart. In the midst of grinding poverty, political violence, deprivation of rights, discrimination, and hunger, Christians move from social analysis to finding echoes

in the biblical witness in order to understand the struggle in which they are engaged or to find direction for the future.[16]

As it moves from social analysis to theological reflection, liberation theology adopts a technical concept of *praxis*. This is not merely a synonym for "practice," but rather a dialectical relationship between action and reflection.[17] Beginning with action, moments of action and reflection are fully integrated into a hermeneutical circle. Bevans describes *praxis* as "reflected-upon action and acted-upon reflection—both rolled into one."[18] For theology, this approach results in the elevating of right action (orthopraxy) into dialogue with right believing (orthodoxy).

How does this method of liberation connect with the daily world of pastoral practice, particularly in places like Valleywood? Although advocacy for justice and for freedom from oppression, based on social class analysis, may fit the context of some Latin American and other third world societies, what is its relevance to pastoral care in the developed Euro-American societies? A critical examination of Stephen Pattison's attempt to respond to such concerns in *Pastoral Care and Liberation Theology* points the way to understanding and evaluation of the use of liberation approaches.[19] Pattison's rather complex method, which we summarize in the following paragraphs, adapts a four-stage "hermeneutic circle" into a five-stage "methodological spiral."

Pattison argues that the methods of the theology of liberation can be used in reorienting both the theoretical focus and the daily practice of pastoral care in the "northern hemisphere." He declares that "pastoral care needs to be liberated from its psychological and individualistic captivity."[20] Pattison's quest for such liberation relies upon his adaptation of the methodology of the Uruguayan priest and liberation theologian, Juan Luis Segundo. In particular, Segundo's understanding of "the hermeneutic circle" provides the key to Pattison's approach.[21]

Segundo's hermeneutic circle is an ongoing four-stage process that seeks to account for changes in the interpretation of Scripture caused by changing contemporary reality. The ways in which Christians experience reality, particularly due to their commitment to the struggle for liberation, creates *suspicion* that ideology has determined both social structures and ideas (stage one). This *ideological suspicion* is then applied to institutional frameworks that legitimate the current arrangements of society (known in Marxist theory as "ideological superstructure")— including the prevailing theology (stage two). This application leads to *exegetical suspicion* that present interpretations of the Bible have ignored important evidence obscured by ideology (stage three). The result is the development of a *new hermeneutic*, an interpretation of Scripture that seeks to take into account the new data uncovered by social analysis (stage four). The process continues—perhaps more like a spiral than a circle—to respond to constantly changing political, social, and cultural realities.

Pattison then takes Segundo's four-stage hermeneutic circle and proposes a five-stage "methodological spiral" that attempts to integrate the insights and methods of liberation theology into pastoral care theory and practice.[22] The "insights and methods of liberation theology" (labeled stage A) give rise to "suspicion… that pastoral care has hidden socio-political implications and biases" (stage B). The suspicion leads to "social and political analysis of [the] context of pastoral care" (stage C). This stage utilizes the "tools of suspicion," most notably Marxist class conflict analysis, with the goal of exposing injustice and social inequalities. Stage D then analyzes "the practice, theory, and theology of pastoral care … to uncover their socio-political significance and implications." The process then moves to stage E, "the reorientation of pastoral care towards socio-political awareness and commitment on the side of the oppressed." The "new insights and awareness," which result from this reorientation, continue the spiral at a new level (stage A1).[23]

The test of Pattison's rather unwieldy model lies not in its theoretical elaboration but in its power to reorient pastoral care through the illumination of a specific situation. Pattison, who has experience in mental health chaplaincy, chooses as his test case the context of pastoral care with mentally ill people in Britain. He devotes most of the book to a detailed analysis of this complex situation.

Pattison examines the sociopolitical context of mental illness in the United Kingdom. He argues that social class plays a central role in both the incidence and the treatment of mental illness in Britain. He contends that "factors within our present capitalist social order...lead to a greater incidence and prevalence of identified mental illness among working-class people."[24] In addition, "speed of recovery, quality and type of treatment facility, length of hospital stay, and long-term prospects are also inversely and negatively linked to social class position."[25] Using class conflict analysis, he offers sharply pessimistic assessments both of psychiatric hospitals and of more recent approaches to "community care."[26] In short, persons who are mentally ill are identified as "prominent among the poor and oppressed in society."[27]

Although one might hope that mental health chaplains lead the church in mounting a prophetic critique of the situation of the mentally ill and advocating social change, Pattison found this plainly was not the case. Both in their theoretical literature and in their practice, mental health chaplains unsurprisingly focused upon individual care and counseling. This individualist orientation meant that chaplains were generally unaware of the broader sociopolitical context of the mentally ill and their treatment. Consequently they played a conservative role in the political situation and were liable to the charge of silently perpetuating the oppressive status quo. Pattison observes that

> they acquiesce inaudibly to the *status quo* in the face of poor and inadequate social conditions in and outside the caring services. They thereby unwittingly ensure the perpetuation of those conditions and contribute, at least passively, to the long-term unnecessary suffering of those for whom they (sincerely) profess to care.[28]

Therefore, Pattison calls for the transformation of this inadequate and oppressive individual, psychological paradigm for pastoral care of the mentally ill.

Having used the "tools of suspicion" (stage B) derived from the insights of liberation theology (stage A) to examine both the social and political context (stage C) and the theory and practice of pastoral care of the mentally ill (stage D), Pattison proceeds to make his proposals for the sociopolitical reorientation of pastoral care (stage E). Unfortunately, this stage is where the method he proposes bogs down. In rather utopian fashion, Pattison proclaims, "meeting the needs of the world and of all people should be the aim of the church and its carers."[29]

He then proceeds to offer "six basic principles which might inform those pastors who seek to develop a socially-politically aware and committed pastoral care": (1) "thorough analysis of the sociopolitical context"; (2) "an option for the oppressed"; (3) a role for " 'organic intellectuals' of oppressed groups, [who are] exercising an educative, consciousness-changing role"; (4) "preparedness to belong to, and co-operate with, groups of all kinds seeking desirable social and political change"; (5) "an 'unfinished' model for social and political action"; and (6) "pastoral care of individuals [that is]...not...allowed to act in an ideological, reality-disguising, and oppression promoting way."[30] Pattison discusses each of these principles further, offering a brief, general application to the British mental health situation.

Despite its concrete, praxis-oriented beginnings, the method experiences difficulty in moving from general principles to the choice and advocacy of specific actions. For example, Pattison asks, "What does it mean to make a concrete option for the oppressed in the mental health sector?" He then begins his response to this crucial question quite vaguely: "The answer to the question is that it might mean all manner of things depending on who are identified as being oppressed and what their needs are."[31]

One suspects that this dramatic limitation revealed in Pattison's detailed example is inherent in the *method* he is seeking to use. If a theologian or pastor employs a method of class conflict analysis in a revolutionary situation, given the intensity of conflict, powerful actions of resistance to oppression (for example, armed protest) may emerge and seem appropriate to the situation. (Sadly, this method has led to some advocating the use of violence in the struggle of certain Christian leaders against oppression.) If, however, like the circumstances of the mentally ill in Britain, the reality of oppression does *not* create a revolutionary situation, then it becomes far more difficult for liberationist approaches to pastoral theology to find appropriate actions and to develop coalitions that sustain the momentum of resistance.

The action-reflection dynamic of *praxis* in liberation theology requires a commitment to concrete action against clearly identified oppression. Although Pattison plainly exposes the need for greater sociopolitical awareness in pastoral care, he struggles to identify precisely what concrete action this reorientation should advocate. Liberationist contextual models operate effectively when a clear-cut divide between oppressor and oppressed enables actions seeking justice to avoid the mire—or, critics would say, to ignore the reality—of political ambiguity.

Feminist and Womanist Contextual Models

The quest for equality and justice that characterizes contextual models not only involves the analysis of social class, but also arises from the contexts of race and gender.[32] The nineteenth and twentieth centuries witnessed the dramatic rise of movements for both racial and gender equality among the Western nations. Although long delayed and often resisted, these movements have begun to influence the ways in which Christians connect their beliefs and practice of ministry. Our brief examination of some recent feminist and womanist approaches to pastoral theology seeks to describe and analyze these examples of contextual models that begin theological reflection with the lived experience of women.

In "Three Decades of Women Writing for Our Lives," Kathleen Greider, Gloria Johnson, and Kristen Leslie report on a survey of books and articles written in English and published in North America by women in the fields of pastoral theology and pastoral care and counseling from 1963 to the middle of 1998.[33] Their analysis of this literature reveals that women authors have "contributed precisely and significantly" to the emergence of a "communal contextual paradigm" in these fields.[34] Greider, Johnson, and Leslie discuss seven themes that appear in the literature and serve as foci for the development of the communal contextual paradigm: (1) *ekklesia* and its ministry, (2) marginalized people and taboo topics, (3) female experience, (4) theological education, (5) soulfulness,[35] (6) violence, and (7) systems of care.

Although the authors maintain that the themes need to be considered together to characterize the paradigm adequately, they observe that "the most clearly distinctive contributions of women writing pastoral theology" center on the theme of female experience.[36] Within this theme, they organize the literature around four subthemes: (1) "what it means to be female," (2) "the significance of embodiment in human experience," (3) "the primacy of relationality," and (4) "concern for women's wholeness and care."[37] The analysis of the diverse experiences of women provides the lens through which theology is developed and ministry is perceived.

This focus upon women's experience marks a significant shift from previous male-centered (androcentric) ways of connecting theology and ministry. As Christie Neuger declares:

> Women no longer have to fit into a paradigm oriented around men's experience where women have been seen as "the other" and generally found deviant in some form. Considerable agreement exists among feminists that methodology that pays attention to women's experience for its own sake, rather than seeing it as derivative or deviant from men's experience, is of central importance. Yet considerable debate occurs around what it means to talk about "women" as a group and about a trait or quality of women that defines them as a group.[38]

The obvious diversity of women's experience raises difficulties for essentialist views, which find some characteristic that universally defines women's experience. Some feminist pastoral theologians have sought to utilize women's *embodied* experience to respond to this issue. Exploring biologically based developmental issues (for example, menarche, childbirth, and menopause) and their interaction with cultural context across the life span of women offers a framework for articulating feminist approaches to pastoral care.[39] Yet the formative role of culture in shaping and giving meaning to biological experiences moves toward a social constructivist view. Constructivism denies any defining universal traits or qualities in women's experience, instead emphasizing the ways specific cultural contexts define (socially construct) the experience.[40]

Feminist pastoral theologies that hold a social constructivist view of women's experience therefore elevate the role of cultural context in the formulation of theology.[41] Neuger contends that "theology is *always* a product of the immediate relationships and their contexts, and it is *only* within those concrete and particular realities that the nature of the human-divine relationship can be understood."[42] Adopting this view of the limits of theology could reduce all mystical theology and transtemporal spirituality to empirical explanation. To emphasize the importance of context in feminist pastoral theology does not require the rejection of theological tradition, but rather its critical retrieval and reformulation. As Pamela Couture explains:

> Feminist, womanist, and practical theologians have argued against the idea that contextual theology, or theology that reflects inductively on the here and now of human existence, is somehow second-class theology to systematic, doctrinal, or dogmatic theologies.... Instead, as contextual theologians we assume that these theologies represent the codified experience of persons in the past. When one theologizes *from* systems and doctrines *to* the lives of contemporary persons, we claim, one does so only at the risk of imposing such codes on persons whose lives are radically different from those of the past. The position does not require that we reject theological systems and doctrines as false, unhelpful, or unimportant to contemporary experience, nor does it reject the significance of theological and ecclesial tradition to contemporary people.[43]

The question of how the contemporary contexts of women's experience relate to the historical contexts of the beliefs and practices of Christian communities of the past is one of continuing debate and significance for feminist pastoral theology.[44]

Growing awareness of the limitations of the white middle-class orientation of early feminist theology in defining women's experience has led to challenges from women from diverse racial and ethnic groups.[45] The most visible of these challenges has been the rise of womanist pastoral theology. The particularity of the experiences of women of color contests the comparatively privileged perspectives and even "passive racism" of white feminists who have led in the movement.[46] As Watkins Ali asserts, "Womanist sources present an important voice that has been missing in the pastoral theological dialogue—the voice of poor African American women representing the issues of America's most needy cultures."[47] The force of this concern is magnified if one expands the horizon of womanist theology beyond North America to a global context. In prioritizing the needs of the poor, womanist and liberation approaches find common ground.

The method of praxis, described earlier in our discussion of liberationist contextual models, is commonly embraced by feminist and womanist pastoral theology.[48] The concerns for attending to marginalized perspectives and commitment to the struggle for justice are clearly visible, with a greater emphasis placed upon the role of education in transformative resistance to oppression. For example, Brita Gill-Austern, following the work of Rebecca Chopp,[49] describes the use of praxis in pedagogy:

> Emancipatory praxis. . . names and struggles against the forces, the structures, the methods, and the content of subjects that have kept women from naming their own experience, from being partners in the discernment of truth and the construction of knowledge. Emancipatory praxis will use whatever tools it has at its disposal to struggle against oppression and to further individual and social transformation.[50]

Feminist and womanist approaches in pastoral theology commonly make use of a variety of methods to challenge androcentrism and to develop theology and ministry from the perspective of the lived experience of women. For instance, although feminist theology is clearly contextual, it is not unusual to find feminist pastoral theologians utilizing revised correlational approaches. For example, Carrie Doehring blends correlational methods into her method of feminist pastoral theology.[51] She describes the relationship of contextual, feminist, and correlational theology in the following way: "A contextual approach becomes a feminist approach when feminist gender studies are used correlationally with other disciplinary perspectives in a way that allows the androcentrism of any disciplinary perspective to be critiqued."[52]

The lens of women's experience in pastoral theology has brought into focus pastoral practices different from those highlighted by pastoral care in a male-oriented, clergy-centered paradigm. For example, in the mid–twentieth century, Protestant pastoral care commonly described the ministry functions of a pastor with the categories of "healing, sustaining, guiding and reconciling."[53] Miller-McLemore has proposed "resisting, empowering, nurturing, and liberating" as modalities for "reorganizing the functions of pastoral care" from a feminist perspective.[54] Also, Watkins Ali has offered a critical assessment of Seward Hiltner's "shepherding perspective" from a womanist perspective.[55] Pastoral theology developed from the context of women's experience is seeking to transform the ways in which care is practiced by Christians.[56]

Amidst all of this flourishing contextual theology, some women's voices point to the difficulty of maintaining interconnections with Christian communities whose beliefs and practices the communal contextual paradigm originally sought to transform. As Neuger wisely observes, "The risk here is, of course, the fragmentation of postmodernism and constructivism."[57] Whether feminist and womanist pastoral theology will be able to forge and sustain life-giving connections among Christian communities, rather than merely contribute to the theological and political Balkanization of the beliefs and practices of those communities, remains a vital question.

Assessing Contextual Models

Models for connecting theology and ministry that emphasize the analysis of context are appealing in their concreteness and bewildering in their diversity. Our assessment focuses upon the theological "family resemblance" in method among the multiplicity of contexts. We begin with some general evaluation of the interrelated strengths and weaknesses of contextual approaches. Then we return to our master case study to examine ministry and theological reflection that start with an analysis of the contexts of Valleywood Church.

Critical Evaluation

Christians who seek to connect theology and ministry in pluralistic societies can understand the appeal of contextual models. The analysis of a specific context provides a clear, concrete point of departure for theological reflection. The historical particularity of each context invites a ministry anchored in powerful sociocultural indicators such as race, gender, and social class. Ministry is no longer entangled in abstract religious rhetoric or reduced to individual subjectivity. Instead, the action-reflection dialectic of praxis calls for commitment to social change.

Contextual models are ideally positioned to employ the empirical research tools of the social sciences. As we observed with correlational models, the challenge lies in avoiding the subordination of theology to the human sciences. The critical analysis of cultural contexts can uncover injustice and oppression, which commonly fuel social conflict and violence. Practitioners following contextual models use such analysis to support their advocacy for social change. Also, some contextual models seek to utilize cultural analysis to "read the signs of the times" in an effort to discern how God is at work in the world.[58]

In addition, the analysis of contextual models often reveals the sad complicity of the church—along with other social institutions—in the perpetuation of oppression. The biblical call for justice resonates with contextual approaches. Proponents often understand themselves in a prophetic role in both the church and culture.

A major limitation of contextual models derives directly from their strength of particularity. Contextual models lack the capacity for generalizability. They commonly find themselves unable to discover unity in the midst of all their multicultural diversity. As our analysis of Pattison's work revealed, the attempt to adapt a liberationist contextual model from the culture in which it was developed to another significantly different culture encounters major difficulties. Similarly, the rise of womanist theology challenges any claims of feminist theology to reflect the range of women's experience, even when only North American women are considered. The restriction of each approach to its particular cultural context raises a serious problem for Christian theology. Although contextual models carefully avoid the dangers of universal dogmatic approaches to Christian doctrine, they lack the capacity to generate theological statements that can properly claim universal or even widespread applicability. What is true for "me and my group in our context" may not be true for "you and your group in your context."

To put the critique more technically, with the inevitable abandonment of the Kantian demand for universalizability, contextual models fall victim to a loss of ethical normativity. If there are no *generalizable*[59] norms for right behavior beyond one's specific cultural context, then claims for "orthopraxy" leading to justice are suspect.[60] The analysis of oppression requires at least some generalizable preunderstanding of freedom and its limits. Otherwise, the danger of fragmentation becomes apparent.

The vacuum created by the loss of cross-cultural norms poses a great dilemma for contextual models. Sometimes the vacuum is filled by the adoption of rigid ideologies. For example, contextual models may advocate some of the ideology of revolutionary Marxists and radical feminists, who are not known for their openness to the legitimacy of the diverse range of Christian practices. Alternatively, and more typically, the vacuum is simply not filled. Then, particularly in pluralistic cultures such as contemporary

Europe and North America, contextual models may careen down the slippery slope of relativism.

Contextual models embrace the ideal of diversity. Each group is understood and valued in the framework of its own context. So, most contextual models adapt well to the assumptions of postmodernity. Religious communities are imaged as participating in a web of networks, rather than in centralized institutional forms. Contextual models typically express great openness to political and ideological differences and affirm the issues that arise out of these differences. Yet the cost of this openness is significant. The identity of the group and the needs of its specific context supersede the claims of wider loyalties, particularly to historic Christian beliefs and practices. Contextual models struggle with the danger of diffusion—or, at times, even the loss—of distinctive Christian identity.

Comparative Case Evaluation: Contextual Models and Valleywood Church

Our critical assessment of the strengths and limitations of contextual models leads now to the question of the practical application and evaluation of this approach through our master case study. Although there are many ways one could analyze the contexts of the Valleywood case, we will examine both the church and the community contexts of the case through the lenses of race and ethnicity, gender, and social class.

Race and Ethnicity

The first African Americans to live in Valleywood, Henry and Rosa Parker and their three children, experienced the oppression of active racism during the 1960s. The welcome that Valleywood Church offered the Parkers, though an affirmation of the gospel against the culture, did not have sufficient commitment and power to prevent the Parkers from being forced to move away. Although the church still vocally opposed active racism, it eventually seems to have acquiesced to the de facto racism of Valleywood's suburban life. This pattern of cultural conformity has probably weakened the congregation's capacity to use the power of the gospel to challenge and transform the culture.

Today, the Valleywood community displays much less evidence of active racism, but evidences of passive racism are still visible in the patterns of relationship between whites and the relatively few blacks who live in the community. Although Valleywood Church prides itself on racial openness, very few African Americans have ever attended. The patterns of worship and congregational life clearly reflect the white middle-class ethos of the congregation. Ministry that seeks significant social change on this issue will need to lead the congregation to move beyond the comfort zone of its own familiar patterns.

One possible avenue for some change lies in cooperative ministry opportunities with predominantly African American churches. Ministries could be mutually initiated, involving both Euro-American and African American congregations in the development process of specific ministry projects. Leaders from Valleywood Church could investigate what kinds of community ministry programs have been developed by African American congregations in the Seattle area. Perhaps ministries resembling the Christian Action Lay Ministry Program of the Apostolic Church of God, which we discussed in the previous chapter, might be located. The churches could then explore whether these community ministry programs would welcome the participation of suburban churches like Valleywood. Members from Valleywood Church who covenanted to be involved might find both their unconscious racism and their middle-class stereotypes of family life to be challenged and perhaps transformed.

The rapidly growing population of Pacific Rim Asian Americans in the Valleywood community has created a multi-ethnic environment. Although there are some open conflicts, racial prejudice against Asian Americans in the community is most commonly displayed in an attitude of passive condescension toward Asian cultures. Dale's experience with Church World Service in India has sensitized him to the dangers of these subtler forms of prejudice. His experiences should empower him to preach and teach about the power of the gospel to transform attitudes from judgment to acceptance of others who are different.

Valleywood Church has experienced tensions regarding the sharing of its facilities with First Korean Church. Conflicts over the care and use of shared worship and classroom space are particularly likely to occur. Other than the joint Christmas dinner and other occasional fellowship activities, little dialogue or sharing of ministries seems to take place between the congregations. Jackie and Dale might consider a variety of shared educational events and mission projects to build bridges of social understanding and to confront indirectly the dynamics of passive racism.

The social location of Asian Americans in Valleywood may also help to illumine the dynamics of Jenny's situation. Jenny's conflicts with her parents and with First Korean Church may be fueled by her desire to escape what she perceives as the second-class status of her upbringing. Ministry could assist Jenny to connect her current vocation with aspects of her cultural heritage. For example, Jenny could be invited to use her training in elementary education in a joint church ministry project with Korean American children.

Gender

Valleywood Church understands itself as a church that is affirming of women and open to diverse views about gender issues. The church has called women copastors, first Louisa and now Jackie, and has given them pastoral responsibility and authority. Yet a gender analysis should explore whether persistent examples of sexism still remain. For example, does Jackie notice that in public situations some church members seem to prefer Dale's leadership to hers? If so, is this because he is male? Do some members presume that Dale's ministry is more authoritative than

Jackie's? Despite the church's affirmative attitude toward women, major gender issues still underlie each of the examples of non-traditional families in the case.

The Lesbian Couple: Darlene and Sue

Both Darlene and Sue have chosen no longer to identify with the androcentric, heterosexual cultures in which they were raised and also experienced the failure of relationships. The hospitable attitudes toward gays and lesbians they discovered in the University of Washington medical culture support the continuing political movement advocating the full equality of gay and lesbian lifestyles. This movement seeks more than an end to gender-based discrimination, but genuine acceptance and endorsement of gay, lesbian, bisexual, and transgendered lifestyles in the wider culture.

Darlene and Sue seek not only Valleywood Church's welcome of their lesbian blended family, but also the church's blessing and advocacy on their behalf. Many feminist and some liberationist approaches would interpret Darlene and Sue's experience as both suffering under and struggling against patriarchal and heterosexist oppression. According to this view, Valleywood Church should not only accept Darlene and Sue's lesbian blended family, but also affirm their lifestyle, bless their union, and seek to empower Darlene and Sue in their struggle for liberation. This sociopolitical analysis commonly assumes a dichotomous "either-or" reading of the context: *Either* the church supports the full political agenda of gay liberation *or* the congregation is on the side of the homophobic oppressor. Of course, in the continuing political controversy, conservative either-or readings of context flourish as well. Since members of Valleywood Church hold diverse views on this political issue, dichotomous readings of the political context will tend to polarize the congregation rather than lead to a consensus in support of ministry.

Other readings of the context see more complexity and ambiguity instead of an either-or dichotomy. For example, some members of Valleywood Church might strongly oppose discrimination against gays and lesbians and yet not believe *the church* should endorse a gay lifestyle.[61] They would likely hold various opinions about the political issue of what society should do in regard to gay and lesbian relationships. According to one expression of this "welcoming but not affirming" view, the church's attitude toward the moral status of Darlene and Sue's long-term lesbian relationship could roughly parallel its attitude toward Jenny and Jim's long-term heterosexual cohabitation. (The obvious weakness of the parallel lies in the lack of the culturally approved option of marriage for Darlene and Sue's relationship.) Persons holding the "welcoming but not affirming" view might favor ministry that welcomes Darlene and Sue and their children but strongly resist efforts to change the church's ministry to one of activist advocacy.

The POSSLQ: Jim and Jenny

Jenny's feminism is shaped by her rejection of the patriarchalism of her Korean American culture, as expressed in both her family of origin and the First Korean Church. Jenny no longer speaks to her father, who may be viewed as the symbolic carrier of these patriarchal values. As a third-generation Korean American, she has chosen to embrace the American value of independent individualism, which stands in tension with the traditions of Korean culture.

Jenny's education at Valleyview High School and Western Washington University reinforced the emphasis on independent individualism, which particularly characterizes American culture in the Pacific Northwest. This value is also strongly expressed in her long-term relationship with Jim, which explicitly rejects the traditions of marriage. Jenny's refusal to allow her daughter, Mary, to be baptized, or even to be brought to First Korean Church, is consonant with the independence of her identity.

Unfortunately, even though Jenny understands herself as a feminist, the feminist emphasis upon collaborative communities of sisterhood seems to be absent from her experience. Members of Valleywood Church might invite Jenny to participate in a small group ministry that seeks to reconnect aspects of her identity as a feminist with the Christian community. She might benefit from a group that views the gospel and certain feminist values as mutually supportive, rather than as in irreconcilable contradiction.

The Single-in-Church Woman: Jill

The androcentric character of Jill's culture fostered the illusion that she could find her identity and fulfillment in a man who was her soul mate. Churches and Christian organizations played a major role: first in legitimating the myth and then in providing support when Jill's marriage with Michael failed.

Although Jill's second marriage, to Ed, provides more opportunity for a sense of fulfillment in a career, Jill still seems dependent upon others for identity and self-esteem. Her experience in church has been unable to assist Jill in overcoming an intensifying isolation. Ministries focused upon empowerment and transformation through the development of a mutually supportive community might offer a way for Jill to experience congregational care. Furthermore, knowing Jill's history and gifts, the pastors could suggest some specific areas of ministry in which she might become involved. Such ministry experience might lead Jill to feel more connected to the congregation and perhaps even result in an increase in her self-esteem.

Social Class

Valleywood Church is a suburban, middle-class congregation. (Marxist theorists would label it as a bourgeois institution.) Although the church's values are sometimes in tension with those of the wider Valleywood community (for example, the congregation's early emphasis upon civil rights), in general, the church's views seem to mirror those of its culture. For example, being a member of a community service club—such as the Kiwanis or Rotary—and being a member of Valleywood Church might be seen as mutually compatible and reinforcing.

Tensions that Valleywood Church experiences with First Korean Church may point not only to conflicts between Anglo and Korean traditions, but also more deeply to conflicts between settled middle-class and aspiring middle-class values. For instance, the differing parenting styles of Jim's parents, Loren and Judy, and Jenny's parents, Sam and Sung Hee, are probably rooted not simply in ethnicity, but also in social class. Tensions based on social location characterize not only the churches, but also the community of Valleywood as a whole. Even the rivalry between Jim's Valleydale High School and Jenny's Valleyview High School reflects differences in the median social class of the students.

The middle-class values of Valleywood Church may help account for some of the dynamics of the church's relation to the three nontraditional families in the case. For instance, when one seeks to analyze the underlying nature of the attraction of Valleywood Church to Darlene and Sue, as contrasted with explicitly gay congregations such as the Metropolitan Community Church, Valleywood's settled middle-class social location may play a critical role. The gospel the church proclaims may be subordinate to the social class it represents, particularly to nearby homeowners. Similarly, a powerful concern for middle-class "respectability," rather than simply a concern for Christian living according to the gospel, may explain much of the pressure on Jenny and Jim to be married. In addition, the strong, middle-class ethos of Valleywood Church may create negative dynamics for Jill. Her working-class background could contribute to her sense of isolation at church.

In summary, critical analysis of the cultural contexts of the Valleywood case study through the lenses of race and ethnicity, gender, and social class creates suspicion of the status quo. Church and community life are deconstructed by cultural critique. If the powerful analysis of contextual models is to lead to a "bridge" of action and reflection between theology and ministry, wise reconstruction is required.

CHAPTER 4

Narrative Models

Human beings naturally tell stories to describe their experiences. What some philosophers and theologians categorize as "the narrative quality of experience" implies that human nature is essentially characterized by storymaking.[1] The claim is that human experience is *inherently* narrative; experience without a story becomes less than human.[2] For example, each person possesses a "life story," no matter how tragic, fraught with contradiction, or even meaningless it may seem.

Given the central role of narratives in the Jewish and Christian Scriptures and also the primary place of the "gospel story" in Christian proclamation, one is not surprised to discover a variety of attempts to use narrative to link Christian theology and ministry. Since the rise of Romanticism in nineteenth-century Euro-American culture, the claim that each person or group has a history, and that it is "a story worth telling," has shaped the self-understanding of Western cultures. Each church or institution investigates and proclaims its "history." Whether it is a local congregation celebrating its anniversary or an ancient university celebrating its heritage, the assumption is made that this particular group has a history that is an important subject for study. Such a view of history is a thoroughly modern notion. For example, it would not even have occurred to Christian theologians of the Middle Ages, such as Bonaventure or Thomas Aquinas, that anyone would want to study or celebrate the "history" of the University of Paris!

This chapter investigates narrative models, with particular attention to the relationship between narrative theology and narrative approaches to history. Following an introductory discussion of the rise of narrative theology in the last quarter of the twentieth century, the chapter offers a sketch describing how narrative models may be used to connect doctrine and practice. Then a detailed historical example analyzing a curious affinity between Teresa of Avila and contemporary Protestant evangelical women illustrates the critical retrieval of historical narratives to inform both systematic and pastoral theology. After some general evaluation of such narrative models, the chapter concludes with some direct application and evaluation of narrative models in the Valleywood Church case.

The Rise of Narrative Theology and the Promise of Narrative Models

In the last three decades of the twentieth century, Western theology struggled to move beyond the impasses of "modern theology" based upon a foundationalist epistemology[3] and historical-critical methods.[4] The difficulty has been particularly vexing regarding the doctrine of revelation[5] and its implications for the Christian doctrine of God.[6]

One route taken by a number of Protestant and Catholic theologians has been to elevate the category of "story"—which has been utilized in Scripture and worship throughout the history of both the Jewish and the Christian communities—to the status of a master concept of Christian theology. In this context, "story" commonly is taken to imply a historylike narrative that is not fictional but true and trustworthy.[7] Theological themes such as "the gospel story" or "the biblical story"—or even, more grandly, "the Christian story"—are characterized as "the master story" upon which others depend.[8]

A parallel movement to narrative theology has been taking place in historical fields. For example, Justo González authored a widely adopted two-volume introduction to church history entitled *The Story of Christianity*, which utilized a narrative approach, both in style and content.[9] More recent, Roger Olson has published a substantial survey of the history of Christian thought entitled *The Story of Christian Theology*, which begins with the discussion "Christian Theology as Story."[10] The family resemblance between works like these and the narrative theology movement points to the possibility of using the category of narrative to build a hermeneutical "bridge" across "Lessing's ditch," which has divided history and theology since the German Enlightenment of the late–eighteenth century.[11]

Crossing the divide between theology and ministry, rather than the ditch between theology and history, is the central focus of our study. Narrative connections between belief and practice offer a direct way to include aspects of both history and biography in theological reflection upon ministry.[12] Narrative models can also offer a conceptual bridge across the separation between the classical and practical disciplines of theological study.

Narrative provides a natural connection for linking an individual's story with the master stories of the Christian faith. The practice of Christian witness or testimony makes explicit the connections between a Christian's personal experience and his or her knowledge of the teachings or traditions of the faith. This theme of witness or testimony has been the focus of significant reflection in late–twentieth-century philosophical hermeneutics and Christian theology.[13]

Narrative also provides a vehicle for including the experience of others in the circle of Christian reflection. Hearing the stories of others—whether the stories of saints in the continuing

Christian tradition of hagiography or the stories of the marginalized in recent contextual theology—expands the hermeneutical circle connecting doctrine and practice.[14]

The pastoral care and counseling movement has developed a wide range of approaches to evoke and interpret stories. Anton Boisen's work in mental health chaplaincy, which pioneered clinical pastoral education, led to the metaphor of persons as "living human documents."[15] In a fashion somewhat analogous to the way the historical documents of Scripture and the Christian tradition are interpreted in the classical disciplines of theology, human documents need to be both respected and interpreted by a pastoral theology that utilizes the tools of the human sciences. As Charles Gerkin has shown, Boisen's image of the living human document became a "paradigm" for the hermeneutical task of pastoral care and counseling.[16] Gerkin used Boisen's image to link the stories of pastoral counseling to the broader hermeneutical tradition. Many of the perspectives in hermeneutical philosophy advanced by figures such as Hans-Georg Gadamer and Paul Ricoeur were extended to shape the interpretation of clinical narratives, the stories of the self embedded in living human documents.[17]

In response to the challenge of pluralism in Western culture, Gerkin wisely sought to move beyond the middle-class individualism of much pastoral counseling. In *Widening the Horizons*, he argued for a "narrative hermeneutical practical theology."[18] He explored a variety of interpretive strategies for connecting the stories of communities with the Christian story.[19] The problem with this approach—as suggested by Gerkin's unwieldy name for it—is that the increasing experience of pluralism in postmodern Western society, particularly in urban areas, causes the cultural "center" of communities to collapse. (Ironically, Gerkin named his test case community "Centerton"![20]) Postmodern societies are increasingly structured around the privatized, interconnected web of social networks, rather than around a downtown main street lined with mainline churches. The Christian story—or the story of any religion or group of religions—cannot be at the center of a postmodern, pluralistic society simply because there is no one center. Narrative models need to gather and interpret stories from interconnected networks of communities, rather than envisioning a community structured around the "village green" or city center.

The critical-historical retrieval of the diverse stories of Christian communities offers one promising method for reconnecting doctrine and practice in a postmodern context. Ellen Charry has recently utilized such analysis of historical narratives to approach the interface of theology and ministry. Charry seeks to reestablish a connection between doctrine and practice by rehabilitating the role of virtue in the theology of Christian communities. She argues for an "aretegenic" reading of the development of Christian doctrine through careful historical examination of a variety of major figures in the tradition.[21] Christian doctrine is primarily understood through its pastoral function, rather than through its metaphysical claims. Historical narratives and the ethical concerns of diverse Christian communities are closely intertwined with the formation of Christian doctrine.

Instead of merely describing the promise of such narrative models in the abstract, we now turn to explore a concrete historical example in detail—the curious affinity between Teresa of Avila, the first woman doctor of the Roman Catholic Church, and some contemporary Protestant evangelical women.

Teresa of Avila: A Catholic Doctor for Protestant Women?[22]

Teresa of Avila (1515–82)—a Carmelite nun who founded strict observance monasteries, taught mystical prayer, and experienced spiritual levitation—does not at first glance seem to be a likely candidate to inspire conservative evangelical women.[23] The very little that Teresa knew about Protestants—all of whom she indiscriminately labeled as "Lutherans"—caused her to view them as dangerous heretics outside the saving fold of the

Catholic Church. In previous generations, even those non-Catholic scholars who were appreciative of Teresa, such as Alexander Whyte, evaluated her significance in limited terms such as the following: "Teresa performed a splendid service inside the Church to which she belonged: but that service was wholly confined to the Religious Houses that she founded and reformed."[24]

Yet recent scholarly assessments of Teresa present a strikingly different picture. As historian Gillian Ahlgren observes, the process leading to Teresa's canonization in 1622 revealed that "what Teresa [had] achieved was much less important than the virtues that she embodied and that other women could imitate."[25] The cultural anthropologist Angeles Arrien proclaims, Teresa "was a passionate advocate for young women and was committed to creating environments within her convents where women would be free to turn inward and serve in the most effective ways possible."[26]

Teaching the history of Christianity in Protestant evangelical colleges and seminaries has led me to observe an unexpected affinity between Teresa and women students. Using a narrative historical model offers a way to understand and interpret this curious connection.

A Remarkable Identification

One spring, I taught the masters-level history course "Classics of Christian Devotion" at The Southern Baptist Theological Seminary in Louisville, Kentucky. Teresa's spiritual classic, *Interior Castle*, was one of the required texts. Through both classroom discussion and student presentation, it became clear that Teresa's spiritual pilgrimage and writing engaged many of the women students in the class in a far more personal way than other classics in the course, including more contemporary ones by Protestant authors.

As class members read Teresa's work and then participated in a student-led presentation, the identification of women students with Teresa's pilgrimage was striking. Several women in the class declared that "Teresa's struggle with the male religious authorities" connected with their own quest for acceptance and recognition as "women called to ministry."[27] One woman sharply commented, "Teresa's experience with the Spanish Inquisition reminds me of what's going on in my own denomination right now!"[28] In written course evaluations at the end of the semester, the only negative feedback concerning Teresa's *Interior Castle* came from two white male students in the class.[29]

The next fall, I taught an undergraduate church history course at the Lutheran Bible Institute of Seattle, Washington (now Trinity Lutheran College). Teresa was again among the required figures for student presentation. Once more, it became apparent that many of the women in this class, across an age span from late adolescence to senior adult, engaged Teresa's life and spirituality in a more direct way than that of other male and female historical figures studied in the course.

A student presentation on Teresa was planned for the college's stained-glass illuminated chapel. Class members were instructed to remove their shoes (in imitation of the Discalced Carmelites) and follow a candlelight pilgrimage through stations representing the seven mansions of the *Interior Castle*.[30] Following the presentation, several students remained to discuss the effect of the presentation. Two women students, both of whom had returned to school after a number of years, affirmed that studying Teresa had caused them to "grow both personally and spiritually." As one asserted, "Studying Teresa has empowered me to pursue the ministry God has for me."[31] During an in-class course evaluation, the students concurred that of the ten student presentations of the quarter, the one on Teresa was clearly the most effective.[32]

What factors can help account for this remarkable identification of the Protestant women in these classes with Teresa? Certainly the external circumstances of Teresa's life would seem to make her an unlikely candidate for such identification.[33] Teresa lived as a nun in Spain during the Catholic Reformation —a period of extremely restricted opportunity for women. Teresa's work of reforming the Carmelite Order and establishing new houses for the Discalced Carmelites supported the restoration of a primitive rule of strict monastic observance. In addition, her mystical visions were politically dangerous, since women claiming such special religious experiences—known as *alumbradas*, or "illuminated ones"—were repeatedly denounced by the Spanish Inquisition.[34] Moreover, her writings even include anti-Protestant denunciations of "Lutherans"—of whose views she seems to know very little![35]

A Teacher's Dilemma

As a teacher of church history and historical theology, I strive to encourage Christian students to understand and encounter the diverse story of Christianity as their history, not simply those parts that relate to their particular tradition or reinforce their particular prejudices. I also seek to enable students to reflect theologically upon the significance of this historical study for their spiritual development and their ministries. Given many students' lack of historical background and their believed stereotypes about the irrelevance of the study of the past for contemporary ministry, the motivational aspect of the task is often critical.

For some women students, the difficulties of historical study of the Christian tradition are compounded by the androcentric ways in which the Christian past has been recorded and taught. Yet other women seem unable or unwilling to confront gender issues at all, despite faculty encouragement. So, it seems crucial to give special attention to educational opportunities that facilitate the identification of women students with the stories and struggles of women in the history of Christianity.

Educationally effective achievement of such a relationship among contemporary women students and historical figures requires maintaining a difficult and delicate balance. On the one hand, there is the danger of anachronism. Teresa of Avila is not a social activist advocating equality between the sexes, let alone a Christian feminist, in any modern sense. Identification that seeks to recreate her as such is historically false. On the other hand, there is the danger of irrelevance. Without some histori-cally warranted sense of connection with Teresa, students quickly lose interest in studies that just point out the distance between Teresa's context and their own. How does one understand a nun of the Catholic Reformation who could encourage her sisters to recognize "the great favor God has granted them in choosing them for himself and freeing them from being subject to a man who is often the death of them and who could also be, God for-bid, the death of their souls"?[36]

Therefore, in seeking to discover some themes that might account for the attractiveness of Teresa's story to Protestant women today, we need to probe beneath the circumstances of Teresa's early modern context that suggest her distance from our postmodern setting. For example, in *The Divine Romance: Teresa of Avila's Narrative Theology,* Joseph Chorpenning has taken Teresa's early reading of popular romances and used the genre to offer a unified reading of the images found in Teresa's spiritual theology.[37] A narrative historical model asks: What aspects of Teresa's story connect with the stories of present-day readers or audiences? So, in our case the question is what themes connect Teresa's very Catholic story with the stories of contemporary Protestant women. Our analysis explores virtues and patterns of behavior in Teresa's story that are mirrored in the stories of women today.

A Thematic Analysis

Recent historical studies of Teresa have highlighted several aspects of Teresa's life and theology that offer insight into our question.[38] We will examine three of these critically retrieved themes in our quest to understand how Teresa's story might speak to the stories of some Protestant evangelical women today.

Rejecting Status Inconsistency

The first theme we will consider is what Teresian scholars have labeled the "status inconsistency" of her family.[39] Although

Teresa's family was wealthy, having apparently purchased the status of nobility sometime before 1520, they belonged to a suspect class.[40] They were *conversos*, or Jews who had converted to Christianity under pressure from the church and state.[41] (The common name for *conversos* was *marranos*, meaning "pigs" or, colloquially, "sluts.") In 1485, Teresa's grandfather had done public penance before the Inquisition at Toledo in response to the accusation that he had been secretly practicing Judaism. Although officially "reconciled" to the church, it was not surprising that Teresa's grandfather and his four sons (probably the second of whom was Teresa's father, Don Alonso Sánchez de Cepeda) moved away from Toledo to Avila.

Teresa experienced strong dissonance between noble status and suspect *converso* status. So, she was attracted to monastic reforms that called persons to abandon all forms of external social rank and elaborate hierarchy in favor of a simpler community life. As Christ renounced the position of heavenly honor to take on human flesh, so Christ's followers were called to leave their concerns with worldly honor to be adopted into God's new community.

Evangelical women, particularly those who are struggling to be pioneers in the church's official ministries, experience their own "status inconsistency." This tension is particularly acute for women who are welcomed to study in all programs in seminaries but then find themselves and their ministries suspect in the churches that originally nurtured their faith.[42]

Teresa was simultaneously a person who sought to reform the church of its obsession with status and who shrewdly survived within it. The ironic culmination of her struggle with status inconsistency did not occur until 1970, when Pope Paul VI conferred upon Teresa the title of "Doctor of the Church."[43] Teresa's long journey within the church from suspected heretic to first woman "Doctor" might help account for her attractiveness to Protestant women struggling with status in their own traditions.

Surviving Ecclesiastical Authoritarianism
The second theme we will consider is Teresa's struggle with ecclesiastical authoritarianism. Teresa's religious visions and

locutions made her suspect in the eyes of her confessors and other ecclesiastical superiors, some of whom sought to convince Teresa that her religious experiences were from the devil. The latter sections of her autobiographical *Life*, beginning with chapter 23, trace her repeated sufferings in the hands of incompetent and unsympathetic confessors.

The autobiography itself became the focus of suspicion after Teresa was denounced to the Inquisition by the vengeful Princess of Eboli in 1575. The Inquisition confiscated the manuscript, and it was not released until after Teresa's death. Yet, despite these conflicts and the continual ecclesiastical negotiations that surrounded them, Teresa remained loyal to the church.

Unlike other women of her time who claimed ecstatic religious experiences,[44] Teresa managed to avoid becoming a condemned *alumbrada*—an enthusiast who put the authority of her personal religious experience before the authority of the Catholic Church's teaching.[45] Ahlgren has carefully analyzed the political challenges faced by women who sought spiritual perfection in sixteenth-century Spain:

> Unable to define "holiness" for themselves, they were often also unable to conform to male definitions of female religious behavior. Thus religious accomplishment in or out of the convent involved a tremendous amount of politicking. In a very real sense, attitude was everything. The proper attitude toward religious authority—expressed primarily through obedience to institutional policy, opinion, and superiors—was essential to survival.[46]

Teresa's context necessitated that her pursuit of holiness include wise political discernment. Ahlgren maintains that this "climate of suspicion" about the religious experiences of women led directly to Teresa's difficulties with the Inquisition.[47]

One intriguing example of Teresa's discernment is her studied imprecision in the use of Scripture. Since vernacular biblical translations were listed on the Index of prohibited books of 1559, Teresa had to exercise great caution in the ways she quoted or referred to Scripture. For example, after discussing Jacob's vision of the ladder (Genesis 28:12) in the "Sixth Mansions" of *Interior Castle*,[48] she quickly adds, "I don't know if I'm guessing right in what I say, for although I have heard this story about Jacob, I don't know if I'm remembering it correctly."[49]

Teresa not only disavows any official authority to her interpretation, but also clearly implies she is only relying upon her memory of *hearing* the Scripture, rather than reading it in one of the prohibited Spanish translations. Furthermore, any correct interpretation of Scripture that she shares with her sisters in her writings is humbly acknowledged as a direct gift from God, rather than as any expression of Teresa's own knowledge. As she wisely declares in almost Socratic fashion, "As I am so stupid in these matters, it has been no small thing that His Majesty [Teresa's title for God] should have enabled me to understand the meaning of this verse in the vernacular."[50] Teresa's disavowals of authority as a biblical interpreter point to a pattern of carefully studied biblical imprecision. This strategy allows her to explain Scripture to her sisters without claiming the forbidden role of a teacher in the church.

In a detailed study of Teresa's writing style, Alison Weber persuasively argues that "what some of Teresa's admirers have described as her irrepressible feminine 'charm' or 'coquetry' might be better understood as covert strategies of empowerment."[51] Even E. Allison Peers, the venerable English translator of Teresa in the mid–twentieth century, recognized the ironic style of Teresa's protestations that she is a "poor little woman" (*pobre mujercilla* or *mujercita*) writing under compulsion. As Peers comments, "even the most exacting critic can take lessons of one kind or another from this 'confused' writer."[52]

One aspect of Teresa's strategy of emphasizing women's weakness as a covert strategy of spiritual empowerment is her repeated focus upon physical or physiological weakness. This stereotypical portrayal of weak women obscures the explosive issue of the legitimacy of their spiritual experience. Weber observes references to women's physiological weakness especially predominate in *The Foundations* begun in 1573 and probably continued intermittently to the last year of her life. Although some of these references may simply reflect Teresa's own declining physical health, Weber contends that

> as much as her repeated references to women's "*flaqueza*" [weakness, thinness] suggest an internalization of prevailing misogynistic views, we should note that in most cases Teresa presents women's weakness as primarily physiological rather than moral or spiritual; women are physically disadvantaged in their pursuit of perfection, but they are never spiritually disqualified.[53]

Teresa's humor and humility may both be interpreted as key elements in her "survival strategy" as a woman with mystical experiences of God in the dangerously patriarchal environment of sixteenth-century Spain. As Ahlgren observes,

> Thus her self-deprecating humor is most properly understood not as internalized self-doubt but as an important part of the persona she adopted as a survival strategy. The canonization testimonies suggest that this aspect of Teresa's persona was so developed during her lifetime that it fooled many of her contemporaries.[54]

Teresa utilized a variety of approaches in her writings to underscore her humility. Ahlgren delineates three aspects of this "rhetoric of humility": (1) Teresa's colloquial style, which appears to be more like conversation than official teaching; (2) Teresa's common self-portrayal as a woman only writing under orders from her ecclesiastical superiors; and (3) Teresa's continued willingness for trained theologians to correct her teachings.[55]

Teresa walked a fine line in distinguishing her remarkable spiritual experiences from the heresy of Illuminism, the charge leveled by the Inquisitors against the *alumbrados*. Weber portrays the balancing act inherent in Teresa's many careful attitudes:

> Thus, she accepted the veneration of images but preferred to use them as an inspiration to mental prayer. She repeatedly acknowledged her dependence on the guidance or correction of the educated clergy or *letrados*, while maintaining that those

who had not practiced mental prayer were incapable of judging its orthodoxy. She accepted that contemplation was neither a necessary nor sufficient path to salvation yet urged her friends to pursue it in spite of all dangers. She did not deny the efficacy of vocal prayer, provided it was accompanied by the mental effort of sincere devotion. She avowed her obedience to hierarchical authority but placed the authority of her inner revelations above that of the Church. She acknowledged the necessary mediation of the Church and the merit of works yet professed that the divine union was ultimately gratuitous.[56]

This repeated pattern of careful distinctions imparts a dialectical tension to Teresa's spiritual theology. Teresa is neither openly rebellious against nor mindlessly conforming to the Catholic Church's hierarchical authority. She uses the "modest" language of self-deprecation to disarm the power of the church to discredit her spiritual experiences. She is a "little woman" whom God has chosen to bless with spiritual gifts.[57] Teresa provides her readers with the following self-portrayal: "In the case of a poor little woman like myself, weak and with hardly any fortitude, it does seem to me fitting that God lead me with gifts, as He does now, so that I may be able to suffer some trials He has desired me to bear."[58] Among the trials that Teresa has suffered, she ranks the continued harassment of the Inquisition—which she characterizes as "the opposition of good men to a little woman"—as one of the greatest.[59]

Therefore, Teresa is able to use ironically the submissive language of her weakness to defend the religious authenticity of her spiritual gifts. In classic Pauline fashion, God's "power is made perfect in [Teresa's] weakness" (2 Cor. 12:9).

Teresa was not always successful in her attempts to use an ironic style to avoid the sanction of the Inquisition's censors. For example, Teresa's second redaction of *The Way of Perfection* (probably completed in 1566), clearly shows her rewriting in an effort to avoid and to respond to the criticisms of the censors. Ahlgren offers the following example:

Rather than condemn the [1559 Valdés] Index itself, she reassured her Carmelite readers that if they could learn to do without spiritual books and content themselves with the most basic props of Christian spirituality [the Lord's Prayer and the Hail Mary], they could be reasonably sure that these, at least, would not be taken from them. In fact, Teresa extended this ironic commentary on censorship even to God: "Praise God, who is mighty above everyone and whom they cannot take away from you." Teresa herself removed this sentence when she prepared the second version of the *Camino* [*Way of Perfection*]. Her criticisms were not lost on the censor, who deleted "they won't take the Our Father and the Hail Mary away from you," and noted in the margin, "She seems to be reproving the Inquisitors for prohibiting books on prayer."[60]

Teresa's use of the strategy of irony required not only clever judgment, but also the virtue of constant vigilance in her writing and rewriting under the gaze of the Inquisition.

Teresa's literary strategies for surviving ecclesiastical authoritarianism were severely tested in the case of Song of Songs. Teresa sought to enable women to understand this erotic book of biblical poetry in the context of their spiritual experience, while avoiding any claim to an official right to interpret Scripture. Teresa's *Meditations on the Song of Songs* (also known as *Conceptions of the Love of God*) was written between 1566 and 1567 and then circulated privately. Teresa's interpretation fused erotic and maternal imagery in mystical reflection upon selected, rather explicit verses from the Song. For example, the famous first line of the second verse, "Let Him kiss me with the kiss of His mouth," which Bernard of Clairvaux had mystically expounded at length to his Cistercian monks, played a key role in Teresa's meditations.[61] As Teresa brings her comments on this verse to a close, she summarizes:

> Hence, my Lord, I do not ask You for anything else in life but that *You kiss me with the kiss of Your mouth*, and that you do so in such a way that although I may want to withdraw from this friendship and union, my will may always, Lord of my life, be subject to Your

will and not depart from it: that there may be nothing to impede me from being able to say: "My God and my Glory, indeed *Your breasts are better and more delightful than wine.*" [62]

Although Teresa's confessor and adviser Domingo Báñez officially approved the work in 1575, Teresa was ordered to burn her copy of the work by one of her later confessors, Diego de Yanguas, in 1580. She obediently complied. Fortunately, when Yanguas ordered Teresa's sisters in Alba to do the same, they instead made a gift of the manuscript to the Duchess of Alba, who protected it for posterity.

Given this sort of suspicious and threatening atmosphere, it is not surprising that Teresa wrote with more caution regarding the Song of Songs in *The Interior Castle* in 1577.[63] Teresa continued to make specific allusions to the Song, particularly in the "Seventh Mansions," the final stage of the spiritual journey. For instance, she observes, "These effects...are given by God when he brings the soul to Himself with this kiss sought by the bride, for I think this petition is here granted."[64] This powerful allusion, however, was immediately followed by rapid references to other biblical images that diffused its effect: "Here an abundance of water is given to this deer that was wounded. Here one delights in God's tabernacle. Here the dove Noah sent out to see if the storm finds the olive branch as a sign of firm ground amid the floods and tempests of this world."[65] By use of this covering of diverse scriptural prooftexts, Teresa sought to protect her key mystical image—the kiss of Jesus' mouth—from the Inquisitor's censure. She appeared to be a weak woman flitting from one biblical image to the next, rather than a powerful and dangerous commentator on the erotic spirituality of the Song of Songs.

Protestant evangelical women in ministry in Europe and North America today are not faced with the life-threatening vehemence of the Spanish Inquisition. Nevertheless, encountering the authoritarian opposition of a resurgent religio-political fundamentalism in many churches, they readily—perhaps too readily[66]—identify with the dynamics of Teresa's struggles with the Inquisition. Teresa's ironic use of language—including particularly her quick-witted humor—offers resources for surviving in difficult church situations. Teresa becomes perceived as the historical embodiment of Jesus' counsel to the disciples in Matthew 10:16 to "be wise as serpents and innocent as doves." In her postscript to *Interior Castle*, Teresa shrewdly frames her wise counsel as follows:

> And considering how strictly you are cloistered, my sisters, how few opportunities you have of recreation, and how insufficient in number are your houses, I think it will be a great consolation for you, in some of your convents, to take your delight in the Interior Castle, for you can enter it and walk about in it at any time without asking leave from your superiors.[67]

Becoming Friends of God

A final theme that enables Teresa's life and writings to appeal to contemporary Protestant women is her understanding of Christian community as friends of God. By grace God has made the people of God to be friends of God. So, Christians are called to live together in community, not bound by social distinction or claims to status, but as friends. As Rowan Williams observes, "in her work friendship *replaces* honor as the primary form of social connectedness."[68] God's friendship has broken down all of the barriers that prevent authentic Christian community.

Teresa's model of Christian community as friends of God resulted not only in the reform of the Carmelites, but also in the development of a spiritual theology that reflects the anguish and rapture of her personal journey toward God.[69] Teresa's theology is not simply the communication of a clever rhetoric in defense of her spiritual experience, but the articulation of the consoling and empowering presence of the grace of God in her life and communities.

Teresa's belief in the God-given gift of the freedom of human reason enables her to model for her sisters how to remain under obedience to the Catholic Church and yet be free from external control of their spiritual relationship with God. For example, in her effort to distinguish between false experiences of spiritual "absorption" (*embebecimientos*) and genuine experiences of spiritual rapture, Teresa advises:

anything that so controls us that we know our reason is not free should be held as suspect. Know that liberty of spirit will never be gained in this way. For one of the traits reason has is that it can find God in all things. All the rest is subjection of spirit and, apart from the harm done to the body, so binds the soul as to hinder growth.[70]

The experience of God's friendship transforms the attitudes of members of the community who experience persecution. In her description of the "Seventh Mansions" of the Interior Castle, Teresa describes this God-directed change,

When these souls are persecuted again, they have a great interior joy, and much more peace....They bear no enmity to those who ill-treat them, or desire to do so. Indeed they conceive a special love for them, so that, if they see them in some trouble, they are deeply grieved and would do anything possible to relieve them; they love to commend them to God.[71]

The power of such spiritual transformation in community has repeatedly enabled the reform and renewal of the Christian movement, even when institutional corruption and recalcitrance seemed at their worst. When confronted with continuing gender-based discrimination and restricted ministry opportunities within the church, Protestant evangelical women find that transformative spiritual community with God and one another (especially through the development of networks of support) affirms and sustains their calling to ministry. The monastic simplicity of Teresa's model of Christian community resonates with the biblically grounded Protestant pietism of many of these students. So, although she is neither a feminist nor a social activist, Teresa may be perceived as a wise Catholic teacher of Protestant women today.

Assessing Narrative Models

The power of stories to build bridges between past and present, between speaker and audience, between Christian teaching and ministry practice, has long been evident. Our narrative historical analysis of the connections between Teresa of Avila and some contemporary evangelical women has demonstrated the kind of transferable interpretive skills of reading and analysis that enable Christian ministers to use narrative models to connect the Christian faith to concrete situations of ministry. We have critically examined some virtues and patterns of behavior in Teresa's story that form hermeneutical bridges to the stories of women today.

Beyond the appeal of narrative models, however, lie some significant limitations and weaknesses for connecting Christian doctrine and pastoral practice. Our critical assessment of narrative models will begin with some general evaluation followed by a specific analysis of the use of a narrative model in the Valleywood Church case study.

Critical Evaluation

A major strength of narrative models lies in the way they reflect the storylike character of much human experience.[72] People commonly describe and reflect upon their lives in stories. In *The Call of Stories*, Robert Coles has powerfully portrayed and analyzed the ways in which stories may be used in Western culture to link teaching with the development of moral imagination.[73] Yet, in moving from the attraction of stories to the practicalities of action—particular service to others—one often encounters a lapse: a broken link between the moral call of stories and the practical realities of enactment. In a note in his subsequent work, *The Call of Service*, Coles admits to this difficulty: "Of course, the person being called does not always take the step from having a sense of what ought to be done to making a commitment of time and effort."[74] Although some of this difficulty may be attributed simply to individual moral weakness or failing, the nature of narrative itself accounts for part of the problem.

Stories, whether categorized as fictional or nonfictional, portray a narrative world hermeneutically connected yet always removed from the daily world in which persons live and act.[75] The degree of this removal may vary greatly from the dramatic unreality of escapist fiction to the phenomenological, experiencelike character of stream-of-consciousness narratives. Yet, no matter how "lifelike" the narrative, telling a story always creates some distance from life itself.

This distance between the "call of stories" and the demands of action creates the familiar gap in which the moral disconnection between teaching and ministry occurs. People commonly rationalize their failures to respond to the stories—even moving stories—they hear because, after all, they are "just stories." Even the sacred stories of the Bible are easily treated in this way, as any struggling church school teacher or Bible study leader can attest. Narrative models that seek to connect theology and ministry lose their effectiveness in the gap between the narrative world and the everyday world of moral action and struggle. For example, in the story of Teresa of Avila, the hagiographical idealization of "the saint," particularly in the process of her canonization, increases her distance from the moral struggles of her readers today.

In order for narrative models to function effectively in ministry, strong interpretive bridges must be built and maintained between the Christian story and the diverse stories of those participating in the ministry, including particularly the ministry leaders themselves. Anderson and Foley maintain that

> The future of faith communities depends on their capacity to foster an environment in which human and divine narratives regularly intersect. More specifically, the future of Christian communities requires that they enable the weaving together of the divine and human in the image of Jesus Christ.[76]

The vital role of witness or testimony in narrative theology, described earlier, may be understood as an ongoing effort to build and maintain the interpretive bridges between "my story" and the Christian story. Establishing and preserving such bridges often poses difficult challenges, demanding knowledge of both the traditions of Christianity and the needs of the participants in the ministry, as well as creative imagination to connect them. Such "hermeneutical labor" creates major demands on the intellectual and emotional energy of the pastoral leader. Much of the endless popular literature on "ministry burnout" and "compassion fatigue" points to the cumulative toll taken by these demands.

In addition to the attractive fit between narrative models and the narrative quality of human experience, another major strength of narrative theology lies in the way it matches the narrative character of much of Scripture and the history of Christianity. This match has been enhanced by many of the recent approaches to narrative history and theology, discussed in the first section of this chapter. Yet this strength leads directly to a major difficulty.

In contemporary Western culture, stories "speak for themselves"; they are self-authenticating. An important example of this self-authenticating character may be found in the contemporary Western belief that one's story—or, one's personal testimony—speaks for itself and cannot be refuted by argument. Due to this self-authenticating nature of narrative, limited mechanisms are available in narrative theology for internal self-criticism.[77] For example, the focus on virtue and character ethics in writers such as Stanley Hauerwas is commonly viewed by critics such as James Gustafson as tending toward the danger of moralism.[78] The prophetic critique of the church's complicity in injustice and oppression, which is so pervasive in contextual models (particularly those shaped by liberation theology), is either avoided or muted in narrative ones. Instead, narrative approaches can easily slide into a postmodern sectarianism, which seeks to isolate the church from the complex political and ideological issues of the culture.[79]

So, the clear strengths of narrative models—their attractive fit with the narrative quality of experience and their match with the narrative genres found in much of Scripture and the history of Christianity—are directly linked to their weaknesses: (1) the obvious gap between the call of the world of stories and action in the world of everyday experience; (2) the resulting, continuous demand for Christian leaders who use narrative models to build and maintain reliable interpretive bridges between the Christian story and the stories of those participating in the ministries, including themselves; and (3) the limited capacity of self-authenticating narrative models to offer appropriate self-criticism and thus avoid the dangers of moralism and sectarianism. This general evaluation of narrative models now calls for some practical evaluation of their value in our master case study.

Comparative Case Evaluation: Narrative Models and Valleywood Church

A narrative approach to ministry at Valleywood Church focuses upon first hearing the stories of the copastors and each of the three nontraditional examples, which challenge the boundaries of a ministry based upon the assumption that a family consists solely of a married (heterosexual) couple with children. A narrative model then seeks to connect these stories with the Christian story, both as experienced in the life stories of the individuals and as mediated through the specific story of the Christian community at Valleywood Church.

The Copastors: Jackie and Dale

The differences between the traditional nuclear families in which both Jackie and Dale were raised and the nontraditional examples in the case are immediately apparent. As they listen to the stories of these parishioners, Jackie and Dale experience a clash of stories. They realize that the ministries to families they have experienced make assumptions about the nature and boundaries of families that simply do not fit these people and their relationships.

One response to this realization that is frequently made in Christian ministry is simply to reassert the norm. The Christian minister holds high the "ideal" of the traditional nuclear family, yet shows the greatest possible pastoral discretion to all those who fall outside. Yet Jackie and Dale think that perhaps Christian ministry should do more than this. They are seeking greater clarity about Christian understanding and ministry to families and believe that Valleywood Church might need to reexamine some of its culturally shaped assumptions about families. Jackie's and Dale's stories point to some of the reasons for their openness to new possibilities.

Jackie's educational background in psychology provided her with tools for actively listening to, rather than judging, the stories of others. Her training in family ministry offered exposure to various forms of families and the transforming insight that the "traditional" nuclear family achieved its form only in the nineteenth century, rather than in biblical times. Jackie's CPE training initiated her into a psychodynamic view of ministry relationships, which is oriented more to process than to projects.

Like Jackie, Dale is more focused upon listening to the struggles of his parishioners than offering pastoral advice. His youth ministry experiences, particularly with young people of lower socioeconomic status, have made him more concerned about relationships and less bound to traditional patterns of worship and ministry. His work with Church World Service in India challenged his identification of Christianity with his own white, middle-class American culture.

As a clergy couple, Jackie and Dale understand their call as pioneering some new patterns for leadership in ministry. Their own division of pastoral responsibilities along lines of giftedness, rather than gender stereotypes, has enabled them to encourage others in the church to move beyond traditional role expectations both in their service at church and in their families. Moreover, the patterns of daily life that Jackie and Dale have established in their egalitarian marriage have predisposed them to see marriage in terms of shared functions, instead of ascribed gender roles.

The Lesbian Couple: Darlene and Sue

Darlene and Sue understand both sexual preference and commitment as choices people make to opt for certain kinds of experiences among a variety of options. They want Valleywood Church not merely to recognize, but to *bless* the choices they have made in their relationship. Darlene and Sue desire to be recognized as a blended family, equal to Valleywood's other families and faithfully committed to their children. They seek the church's support for the religious nurture of Harry and Tom. However, Darlene and Sue hold a view different from the majority of people at Valleywood about the primary kinds of sin and evil of which the church should teach their children to beware. Abuse, homophobia, and heterosexism rather than alcohol, pornography, and promiscuity head the list. Darlene and Sue wonder if the church will oppose the kinds of evil and sin they know from their experience.

Sue's and Darlene's stories provide the key to understanding their worldview. Darlene was an overachieving child and adolescent of great potential and significant achievements. After being betrayed in love in a heterosexual relationship, she experimented sexually and chose a new lesbian lifestyle. Sue is the survivor of abuse who seeks strength from the love and care of others. Choosing a lesbian lifestyle was both a statement of her love for Darlene and a declaration of independence from the worldview of her mother, the survivor of abandonment by Sue's father. The theme of abandonment by men thus predates and shapes Sue's abusive marriage. Darlene and Sue both experienced being wounded in a heterosexual relationship involving motherhood—Darlene by Gordon's infidelity, Sue by Frank's abuse.

Darlene's and Sue's stories illumine their deeply held ambivalence toward the church. The church, in alliance with Darlene's parents and Sue's mother, has been the channel of both approval and guilt. At times, the church has been a community offering the embrace of loving acceptance and, in Sue's case, practical assistance during crisis. Yet the church has also blessed the marriages in which they were wounded and communicated disapproval of their sexual experimentation and new lifestyle.

Darlene and Sue believe that the church should be a community offering inclusive love and supporting their long-term commitments to each other and their children. For Darlene and Sue, the inclusiveness of God's love far overshadows the holiness of God's love. They want Valleywood to be a church that proclaims that God's grace accepts us just as we are and that God blesses the choices and commitments of our hearts.

The POSSLQ: Jim and Jenny

Jim and Jenny understand their relationship as a long-term personal commitment free from both legal and ecclesiastical ties. They freely choose to love each other—and now their daughter, Mary—seeking to avoid any of the entanglements of parental, church, and societal expectations. Yet their self-described identities are clearly shaped by the cultures they reject. Their mutual resistance to the religious and cultural expectations of their parents fuels the dynamic that sustains their mutual commitment. Jim and Jenny's continued refusal to be married serves as their continuing declaration of independence from the cultures of their parents. Their resistance to Mary's baptism signals an unwillingness to enter into even a "Half-way Covenant" with the worldviews of their parents.[80]

The laissez-faire style of parenting practiced by Loren and Judy (Jim's parents) allows more opportunities for continuing interaction and communication with Jim and Jenny than the more directive style of Sam and Sung Hee (Jenny's parents). Yet, in the end, Jim is no less resistant to the hopes and expectations of his parents than Jenny. Loren and Judy are simply perceived as being more tolerant and permissive of Jim's independence than Sung Hee and especially Sam are of Jenny's.

Jenny's feminism may perhaps be perceived as more threatening to the beliefs and values of her parents than Jim's agnosticism is to his parents. Her rejection of her "authoritarian" father is directly linked to her rejection of her family's "conservative, patriarchal church." Given her family and church experience, it is difficult for Jenny to imagine a God who is not also conservative and patriarchal.

The church is thus identified negatively with the continuing struggle to develop an identity independent of one's parents, whether they are laissez-faire or more controlling. Jim and Jenny are unable to separate the truth of the Christian story from the traditions of Valleywood Church and First Korean Church. These traditions now span four generations from Jim and Jenny's grandparents to Mary. The family stories are so entwined and enmeshed with the particular traditions of these institutions that Jim and Jenny are unable to identify any divine "treasure" in the "earthen vessels" of these congregations (2 Cor. 4:7).

This failure is most dramatically revealed in Jim's experiences with the traditions of the annual Christmas dinner for Valleywood and First Korean, the place where he first met Jenny. In this event, commercial cultural values finally overwhelmed Christian tradition. Jim, the little "confused angel," accurately diagnosed the problem when he proclaimed the good news that "Santa Claus [not Jesus] is coming to Valleywood." Christmas at Valleywood has been reduced to a celebration of family traditions. The birth of Jesus has been completely assimilated into the celebration of family identity. To describe the situation in terms of Christian doctrine, the Incarnation has been attenuated.

Given this interpretation of Jim's religious experience, his atheism and subsequent agnosticism may be seen as a truthful recognition of his failure to find God at Valleywood. Although Jim and Jenny still attend Christmas dinner as members of "the Valleywood family," they do not understand themselves or their daughter as part of the family of God.

The Single-in-Church Woman: Jill

Jill's story reveals the failure of a theology that blithely interprets the story of God to mean that God has a perfect plan for one's life, including the one right spouse. This romantic interpretation of the Christian story, unfortunately, draws much more upon the "prince charming" mythology of fairy tales than upon the stories of marriage in Scripture. Betrayed and deeply wounded by Michael—the man whom she called her soul mate—Jill finds comfort and limited solace in her eventual marriage to Ed, who, though not a Christian, knows how to show kindness and support. Although both Jill and Darlene experienced the betrayal of heterosexual love, Jill finds herself alone without children. Also unlike Darlene, Jill eventually chooses a new marriage, rather than discovering a different sexual preference.

Jill's story drives her attempts to move beyond the painfully demonstrated limitations of the beliefs her mother taught her about the spiritual quest for the perfect spouse. Jill now experiences ambivalence toward the church, which unwittingly conspired in arranging and blessing the physical and theological context in which she was betrayed, yet offered useful assistance during the crisis that followed. Even greater than this difficulty, however, is the sense of spiritual isolation in church, which particularly intensifies following the death of her mother.

Anderson and Foley depict this struggle: "lonely or alienated individuals who need to find an alternative to their own experience of marginalization find instead that their isolation is intensified in the rituals and stories of a worshiping community."[81] Jill portrays herself with the image of a "fallen nun." Like a nun, like Teresa of Avila, she seeks a direct relationship with God through the only "perfect spouse," Jesus Christ. Yet she feels "fallen," not simply because of her betrayal by Michael but because of her remarriage to Ed, who, like her father and brother, has little interest in her spiritual quest. As she sits alone in church, Jill knows the truth of Hannah Arendt's piercing observation that "solitude requires being alone, whereas loneliness shows itself most sharply in company with others."[82]

Connecting Nontraditional Families with the Story of Valleywood Church

Valleywood Church began as a "family-centered but socially progressive" congregation. Yet the stories of the nontraditional families whom Jackie and Dale encounter in their ministry challenge the congregation's original assumptions regarding the nature and boundaries of families. A narrative model seeks to make connections between these stories and the church's story, as the Christian community at Valleywood has attempted to be a faithful witness to the Christian story. More precisely, a narrative model seeks the critical retrieval of themes from the history of the congregation that intersect, both positively and negatively, with the stories of the people in the case.

For example, the congregation's long history of small group ministries and the counseling focus found in the ministry of previous pastors have created a culture in which persons are encouraged to share their personal stories with others in the church, particularly with the pastors. The expectation is that persons who seek to become part of the Valleywood "church family" will blend their stories with the ongoing story of the congregation. They will find some significant connections between their stories and previous patterns of virtue and behavior in the congregation. Persons who have been part of the church family but have become separated from the life of the community are repeatedly invited, both directly and indirectly, to return and renew their connection with the church by sharing their stories with the pastors, small groups, or even the entire congregation. Sometimes this process of sharing and blending stories will succeed, and the new or returning members will become fully incorporated in the fellowship of the church. Other times, despite the congregation's intent to welcome all who come and to honor diverse views, the stories are perceived as revealing that these people "do not fit" into the life of the congregation. Then—often sadly, sometimes tragically—these persons either exclude themselves or feel excluded from the fellowship.

The pastors of Valleywood facilitate this process of narrative blending in two related ways. First, as is commonly expected, in both worship and pastoral care, they lift up themes from the Christian tradition that relate to the stories of those to whom they minister.[83] So, for instance, Jackie and Dale might use the biblical theme of God's healing grace (as in the narratives of Jesus' healings in the Gospels) to address the woundedness that Darlene, Sue, and Jill experience from their failed marriages. To take another example, the pastors might use the biblical theme of reconciliation (as in Paul's call to reconciliation in 2 Corinthians 5:18-20) to seek to move Jenny and her father, Sam, beyond their mutual alienation.

The second way Jackie and Dale can facilitate narrative blend-ing is to lift up specific strands from the history of Valleywood Church that connect with the stories of the persons to whom they minister. For instance, in response to Darlene and Sue's con-cerns about justice for gay and lesbian persons, the pastors might share the story of the church's welcome of Henry and Rosa Parker, the first African Americans who lived in Valleywood. Using this approach, they would be seeking to build a hermeneu-tical bridge from the church's historic opposition to racism to an opposition to other forms of discrimination. If such interpretive bridges can win wide acceptance in the congregation, Valleywood Church can both welcome others into its story and empower new areas of outreach.

Jackie and Dale might use the pioneering openness of Valleywood Church to women pastors and their own pastoral call as an egalitarian clergy couple to construct bridges to Jenny's fem-inism. Jenny might be able to see that her experience of her father as a conservative patriarch does not need to determine her attitude toward all of Christianity, particularly not to the current community of Valleywood Church. Furthermore, Jenny and Jim's understanding of their relationship as a freely chosen, long-term personal commitment of love without legal and ecclesiastical ties might be challenged by the model of an egalitarian Christian marriage that moves beyond companionship to vocation.[84]

Finally, an example of a hermeneutical bridge that Jackie and Dale might offer to Jill may be found in the church's past involve-ment with the house church movement. Although Jill's long involvement with the congregation entails many painful memo-ries, the home-centered, small-group patterns found in house churches, and continued in some of the congregation's ongoing support ministries, might help address Jill's experience of isola-tion in church.

Our analysis of the stories of Valleywood Church's case has illus-trated a variety of ways narrative models both deepen pastoral understanding of all of those involved in ministry and suggest prac-tical strategies for ministry. Yet narrative models lack the direct, self-critical connections with the Bible and Christian tradition that enable ministers to build reliable hermeneutical bridges with confidence. Narrative frameworks are more effective in offering ways to *understand* others than challenging them to change. The performance models for connecting theology and ministry, which we will examine next, seek to address this concern.

CHAPTER 5

Performance Models

Christian ministry in a rapidly changing, pluralistic world is often understood as a performance. For instance, conflicts concerning worship, which beset the church today, frequently involve debates over performance. This use of the term "performance" involves more than the mere execution of an action, but *presentation* to others or in company with them.[1] In Christian theology, one's performance may be offered first of all to God, as well as to other people. Models for connecting theology and ministry may rely upon images and metaphors from the performing arts, particularly music and drama, to illumine the connections between Christian beliefs and actions. Christians do not merely state religious beliefs, but "act them out" or enact them. They *perform* their faith in both word and deed.

Scholars have recently expressed renewed interest in reflecting upon the nature of specific Christian practices.[2] Those Christian practices that are enacted publicly in the life of the Christian community are commonly the focus of performance models. For example, public practices that comprise Christian worship—such as preaching, reading Scripture, the sacraments (or ordinances), and music[3]—may be viewed through the lens of performance.

The relationship between theology and the arts is highlighted in performance models. Proponents often claim that a performance expresses or creates meaning that cannot be found elsewhere. For instance, Jeremy Begbie relates the following illustration:

> When Robert Schumann was asked to explain a difficult étude [a musical study or technical exercise] he had just performed, he sat down and played it a second time. Its meaning could only be grasped in performance, by a personal, imaginative fusion of frame and story.[4]

Although our analysis will primarily focus upon examples involving musical performance, other performing arts may also be used.[5] For example, Paul Fiddes's *Participating in God* carefully develops the image of dance as a metaphor for the dynamic relations between the persons of the Trinity, known technically as *perichoresis*.[6] Fiddes uses the image of the divine dance to connect theology and pastoral care, particularly regarding the issues of intercessory prayer, suffering, bereavement, and biblical interpretation.[7]

The history of Western theology's ambivalent relationship with the arts—whether ancient, medieval, or modern—includes the contradictory patterns of condemnation of the arts as promoting pagan immorality or idolatry and of celebration of the arts as expressing the praise of God.[8] Therefore, given such ambivalence, theological reflection using artistic analogies such as performance is too often relegated to the margins.

Christians whose traditions affirm the arts, often out of a creation-focused theology, find themselves more comfortable with performance models. To take one prominent example, the Anglican tradition, with its heritage of natural theology and its liturgical emphasis, has often fostered both theological reflection upon the arts and ministry utilizing the arts. Also, Christians whose theology tends to view God as changing through God's interaction with the world are attracted to performance models. For example, the dynamic view of God advocated by process theology fits well with analogies of artistic performance.[9]

The analysis of performance models in this chapter first examines the analogy between musical performance and biblical interpretation. Frances Young's development of the analogy, as she historically describes various "performances" of the church's interpretation of Scripture, receives particular attention in relationship to our concern for connecting theology and ministry. Then Gordon Lathrop's approach to pastoral liturgical theology is briefly explored. Next, a detailed example investigates the relationship between theology and song among Protestant Christians in nonliturgical traditions. Some historical and theological warrants are presented for the case that "the law of singing is the law of believing."[10] Then the chapter turns to evaluation of the strengths and limitations of performance models. After some general critical evaluation, we return to the Valleywood Church case and apply a performance model.

The Analogy of Performance

The challenges of authentic performance in the arts provide some striking parallels to the challenges of authentic performance in ministry. Although there are, of course, obvious differences between the worlds of theology and the performing arts, it is the points of resemblance that form the basis for the analogy. Since authentic performances involve the major task of interpretation— often starting from a script or score—the idea of "performing the Scriptures" provides a point of departure for our comparison.

Performing the Scriptures

Nicholas Lash uses the phrase "performing the Scriptures" to develop the analogy between the artistic interpretation of a text in performance and Christian interpretation of Scripture.[11] Employing the score of a Beethoven string quartet and the script of Shakespeare's *King Lear* as examples, Lash observes that for some kinds of texts, performance is "the fundamental form of interpretation."[12] He then argues that this characterization applies to the Christian interpretation of Scripture. The "life, activity and organization of the Christian community" is thus "construed as performance of the biblical text."[13]

Lash's dynamic understanding of the performance of Scripture utilizes "patterns of human action" to connect the life and sufferings of Jesus and his disciples with Christians today.[14] These patterns enable his understanding of performing the Scriptures to be extended easily to the performance of ministry. Although Lash offers the ecclesiastical "in-house" examples of the liturgy of the Word and the celebration of the Eucharist, others have extended the performance of the Scriptures to contexts beyond the institutional "walls" of the church.

For example, in *The Word on the Street*, seminary professors Stanley Saunders and Charles Campbell include street preaching and street theater in ministry to the homeless in Atlanta.[15] The sermons and essays arising from their volunteer ministry at The Open Door Community reflect a dramatic tension between patterns of middle-class Protestant church life and the social realities of ministry among the urban poor. Through the themes of "worship, Word, solidarity, and space" used to organize the book, the authors connect their ministry experience and theological reflection. Saunders and Campbell declare that

> in this community we have discerned a virtuoso performance of Christian Scripture, and we have been blessed by the small roles we have been given among the Open Door's company of actors. All of the words that follow are merely footnotes to this community's primary performance of Scripture; our reflections grow out of this performance and seek to point back to it.[16]

The practice of performing the Scriptures is not confined to a few social locations or to culturally restricted forms of church life.

Like the gospel it proclaims, the performance of Scripture may flourish in diverse contexts.

The analogy of performance can be used to illumine the history and current dilemmas of the interpretation of Scripture. Frances Young's development of the analogy between musical performance and biblical interpretation in *Virtuoso Theology* points to a number of thought-provoking parallels.[17] Young describes music as possessing two natures: the physical and the spiritual. For example, though music clearly moves through time, we commonly speak of time standing still when we are caught up in listening.[18] The meaning of music cannot be simply translated into words; if music is to communicate fully, it must be interpreted and performed.[19] Similarly, the Scripture is both human words and the Word of God, " 'incarnate' in a time-bound text and yet eternal, transcending the limits of human language and culture."[20] Any performance of Scripture presupposes interpretation.

Good performance requires skill that results from long years of disciplined practice. Musical performance demands a certain precision in rhythm and harmony, which parallels the linguistic precision demanded of the competent biblical interpreter.[21] Yet no two performances are exactly alike. Technical competence must be complemented by inspiration for authentic performance to occur. The place of historical reconstruction is vigorously contested in discussions concerning the criteria for authentic performance of classics (for example, period instruments and older performing styles).[22] In the midst of these continuing debates, "the constraints of the score," "beliefs about the composer's intentions," and "an understanding of the proper content of musical communication" shape the performer's grasp of the music.[23] Similar factors affect the authentic performance of Scripture in the midst of continuing debates about its history and interpretation. To cite one important example, the conventional patterns of typology and allegory written into biblical texts shape the spiritual interpretation of Scripture in a manner resembling the "conventional 'signs' and 'motifs' " in a musical score.[24]

In addition, the context of a performance plays a vital role in its effectiveness. The reception and response of the hearers to a musical performance, though often changeable and difficult to specify, are an indispensable part of authentic artistic communication. Similarly, attempts to analyze the contexts of both performers and hearers (readers) in the past and present communication of biblical texts characterize contemporary biblical interpretation.[25]

Tradition plays a key role in the development of Young's musical performance analogy. She emphasizes the place of performance traditions in classical music, even while admitting they sometimes must be challenged. She then asserts that "tradition rather than the text itself provides the canons of classic performance."[26] This high view of tradition, supported by Young's reading of Irenaeus, raises a debate with the Bible-centered view of Christian theology shaped by the Reformation.

Young uses the analogy of performance to illumine the relationship between the Bible and early Christian doctrine. For example, she portrays Tertullian's use of biblical texts to move towards the doctrine of the Trinity as resembling a trio sonata.

> What Tertullian was working towards, with the complex evidence of the Gospels as his most convincing material, was something like a Trio Sonata, a musical statement "grounded" in the bass or "continuo" played on cello and harpsichord, but gloriously elaborated in the interweaving melodies of two superimposed instruments, the whole being a perfect unity yet all three parts being distinguishable by the attuned ear. God the Father, the one God of all the monotheisms derived from the Jewish scriptures, is the ground or bass common to all doctrinal systems; but Christian tradition hears that bass as underlying the melodies played by the Word and the Spirit, the whole comprising the "content" of the biblical revelation.[27]

Young also employs the analogy of a contrapuntal duet[28] to describe the use of Scripture in the christological controversies, which led to the doctrinal view of Christ as possessing divine and human natures.[29] In both cases, she argues that even if the ancient exegetical arguments are no longer completely convincing, these analogies offered "patterns of performance" that continue to shape Christian doctrine.[30]

Finally, Young's musical performance analogy develops the idea of improvisation. Using the example of a cadenza to a classical concerto,[31] Young describes improvisation as both "integrated" with its elaboration of the musical score and yet shaped for a particular audience at a specific place and time. Young maintains that "the performer is a kind of bridge between the 'classic' work and the audience" and argues that the connection must be flexible, as "a rigid bridge will crack under pressure."[32] Young then applies this analogy to the performance of the Scriptures through preaching. She declares:

> It is no good simply replaying the old cadenzas, because each generation has to appropriate the themes anew, and the renewal alone can effect communication. In order to improvise these essential new cadenzas, which will inevitably be somewhat ephemeral, the preacher needs...philological skills, hermeneutical theories, imaginative insights, and a lot of sensitivity to context. The bridge has to be flexible.[33]

Young's use of improvisation points to some limitations of her performance analogy. Although improvisation can usefully point to a variety of ways Scripture may function authoritatively in preaching, it also reduces the authority of Scripture if one describes its performance in preaching as mere improvisation. The virtuoso performer, rather than the message of the music, can all too easily become the focus of attention and authority. Furthermore, the rather fixed constraints of improvising a classic cadenza are certainly not the only way musicians can improvise! The notion of improvisation can lead in theological directions that go far beyond performing the Scripture. As Carolyn Bohler has shown, jazz improvisation may even be used to portray the interaction between humanity and God, imaged as a "jazz band leader":

> God does lead; in fact, God is the most persuasive member of the band....Yet, God is playing, too, alongside us....God nods to us, to take our turns, to slow down, to give others their turns. As Jazz Band Leader, God guides each band member

individually, but simultaneously guides the group as a whole....God has themes (beauty, peace, love?) which God wants to evoke, yet God enjoys improvisations upon those themes which come from our creativity. Unlike the Orchestra Conductor, the Jazz Band Leader has no complete score towards which the band members are lured.[34]

Finding a balance between freedom and faithfulness is a difficult task for performance models such as Young's. The analogy of performance may be pressed too hard in one direction or the other. Then theologically false alternatives—such as the exaltation of the performer's identity or the wooden repetition of the mantras of tradition—replace the biblically grounded practices of the Christian faith. The performance of ordered worship instead seeks to offer Christians in liturgical traditions a balanced way to connect their faith and ministry.

Pastoral Liturgical Theology

Gordon Lathrop's approach to liturgical theology provides an example that includes practical pastoral concerns.[35] Lathrop seeks to relate liturgical theology to specific problems in both the local church and society. The final third of his *Holy Things: A Liturgical Theology* is devoted to what he identifies as "pastoral liturgical theology," which seeks to make concrete, reforming applications of liturgical reflection. Lathrop's Lutheran identity plays a vital role in shaping his pastoral reflections in this final section.[36]

Lathrop argues that liturgy offers a "remedial norm" that can guide local congregations beyond the limitations of either-or approaches. As he maintains,

> The liturgy offers us a way through false alternatives in the present. It is neither a retreat into the group and a refusal of social-critical action nor a conversion of the faith into a social program. It is neither "groupthink" nor individualism. It is neither pure biblical criticism nor biblical fundamentalism. It

does not gather us around a lecture on the critical interpretation of a biblical book nor into an exercise of communal con-
victions regarding biblical inerrancy. Rather, the liturgy inserts
us into the rich dialectic of the biblical word.[37]

So, for instance, the hearing together of diverse words of Scripture,
which support and create tension with one another, challenges
both relativistic and one-sided ideological readings of Scripture.[38]

The key to this process is the recovery of the basic ritual order-
ing and shape of the liturgy—known as the *ordo*—of Christian
worship. Lathrop is concerned not merely with the written directions and schedules for worship, but rather with the patterns and
presuppositions that lie behind the structures of worship.[39] For
example, what does the pattern of scheduling worship on Sunday
in juxtaposition with the cycle of the seven-day week imply
about biblical patterns of the dawning of the new creation and
Christianity's relationship with the faith of Israel?[40]

The basic actions of worship leadership are rituals performed in
dialogue with the community.[41] For instance, preaching is not
telling one's story or choosing one's text, but speaking of Jesus
Christ in dialogue with the community. The community of faith
is responsible to evaluate the use of ritual leadership.[42]

Lathrop maintains that, as "broken ritual," the *ordo* dialecti-
cally connects liturgy and society.[43] The ritual retains the old, yet
speaks the new. Lathrop illustrates this dynamic:

> the *ordo* of Christian worship establishes the strongest possible
> signs at the center of the meeting and yet breaks those signs to
> the meaning of the mercy of God, making the ritual circle per-
> meable and accessible to as wide a group as possible. The *ordo*
> engages us in the meaning of place, enabling us to believe in
> location and order again, yet it points us away from here,
> toward Christ with the poor.[44]

This paradoxical dynamic enables performance of the liturgy to
become a force for reform in both church and society, rather than
a traditionalist reinforcement of the status quo. An emphasis in
worship on inclusion and a preference for the marginalized can

not only recover biblical patterns, but also reshape the church's social ministry.

Lathrop contends that through the "transformed symbols" of the liturgy, the church can stimulate alternatives to the present situation. For example, although a properly reformed liturgy will not mandate a particular agenda for addressing environmental issues, it can encourage a variety of programs for protecting the environment. Lathrop sees the possibility for change through the performance of the liturgy itself, rather than through the creation of issue-focused special services.[45]

Despite Lathrop's concern for reform and his commendable desire to avoid univocal ideologies, his pastoral liturgical theology struggles to identify practical strategies for action in ministry. For example, on the question of environmental reform, he leaves the reader with "many diverse agendas" and a reformed liturgy that "will simply say, 'Earth matters, earth is dear.'"[46] A large part of this difficulty stems from his "applications" view of the pastoral dimension, which seeks to move from the reflection of liturgical theology to specific questions of reform in church and society. If his pastoral view could have examined the lived experience of particular communities engaged in the current debates over reform, more concrete strategies of action may have emerged.

The appeal of performance models to Christians in liturgical traditions is a direct one. Liturgical emphasis upon tradition and ritual fits smoothly with the analogy of performance. This raises the question of whether performance models can also be useful and historically warranted for Christians from nonliturgical traditions.[47] Our exploration of some ancient historical roots for the relationship between theology and the practice of singing in evangelical and free church Protestant traditions sheds some light on this question.

"The Law of Singing Is the Law of Believing"[48]

Protestants in the free church (for example, the Baptist church) and evangelical traditions have learned much of their theology not from a formal liturgy,[49] but from singing songs of faith.[50] In

North America and Britain, the gospel hymns of revivalism played a major role in shaping the ways free church and evangelical Christians learned to understand and express their piety and engage in ministry. African American churches developed their own distinctive style of gospel hymnody.[51] Similarly, the performance of "contemporary Christian music" reveals the attempt to adapt Christian ministry to present contexts of popular culture. Christian ministry in these nonliturgical traditions has found itself grounded and sustained by the practice of singing.

This pattern of Christian practice suggests that the standard liturgical slogan *"lex orandi, lex credendi"* ("the law of praying is the law of believing") needs to be modified for evangelical and free church Christians. These Christians have learned their theology not from the words of liturgy ("the law of praying"), but from song.[52] So, their slogan should declare *"lex cantandi, lex credendi"*: "the law of singing is the law of believing." What are the historical warrants for such a theological view of song? Is the "law of singing" merely a modern innovation, or, like the law of praying, does it represent the ancient wisdom of the Christian faith?

The "law of singing" is not simply a modern expression of evangelical Protestantism. Rather, historical precedents for this theological significance of song may be discovered in the life of the early church in liturgical and nonliturgical settings. Both the practice of singing and the imagery of song provide examples for our investigation. In particular, we discover some historical roots for the law of singing in the writings of Augustine of Hippo. Before turning directly to Augustine, we will first briefly examine the formulation of the liturgical "law of praying" in the work of Prosper of Aquitaine and then quickly survey the relationship between theology and song in some other early Christian writings before Augustine.

The Law of Praying: Prosper of Aquitaine

The axiom *lex orandi, lex credendi* is reversible in Latin. Not only is public prayer a norm for what is believed, but also the law of belief is a norm for prayer. Worship and doctrine mutually shape each other.[53] This theological principle that the law of praying is the law of believing has been the focus of much debate in Roman Catholicism during the modern period, as well as in recent discussion among liturgically centered Protestant churches.[54]

The slogan *lex orandi, lex credendi* developed from an ancient liturgical formulation of Prosper of Aquitaine, *legem credendi lex statuat supplicandi* ("let the law of prayer establish the law of belief").[55] Prosper's formula appears in the "pseudo-Celestine chapters," written between 435 and 442. These chapters, which were appended to a letter by Pope Celestine I (422–432) and so attributed to the pope, offer arguments attacking semi-Pelagianism and supporting Augustine's theology of grace.

Prosper's claim is that the New Testament command to *pray* for all humanity (cf. 1 Tim. 2:1-4) entails the obligation to *believe* with the church that from beginning to end all faith is entirely dependent upon God's grace. The key passage from chapter 8 of the "pseudo-Celestine chapters" maintains:

> In addition, let us look at the sacred testimony of priestly intercessions which have been transmitted from the apostles and which are uniformly celebrated throughout the world and in every catholic church; so that the law of prayer may establish a law for belief [*legem credendi lex statuat supplicandi*].[56]

Wainwright argues that Prosper's formula follows a pattern of liturgical examples to support Christian doctrine. The pattern is well established in Augustine and traceable back to earlier church fathers.[57] We now survey some patterns in the relationship between theology and song in the early Christian church before Augustine.[58]

Theology and Song in the Early Church

Ralph Martin proclaims, "The Christian Church was born in song."[59] Martin points to three lines of argument to support his assertion: (1) the expectation that the "upsurge of spiritual fervor and power," which accompanied the acceptance of the gospel, should lead to "an outburst of hymnody and praise to God"; (2) Old Testament and other Jewish antecedents (for example, the hymns of Qumran); and (3) Jewish-Christian hymnic fragments found in the New Testament (for example, in Revelation 4:8), as well as specifically Christian New Testament hymns (Eph. 5:14, 1 Tim. 3:16, Phil. 2:6-11, Col. 1:15-20, Heb. 1:3).[60] Song provides a vehicle for the church to confess the mysteries of faith in a fashion that makes its theology readily available to ordinary Christians.[61]

Théodore Gérold observes that significant early church writers such as Clement of Alexandria and Chrysostom explicitly use classical Greek philosophical terminology that connects music with character formation.[62] According to Gérold, what distinguishes the Christian teachers from the classical philosophers in their use of music in moral education is that the Christian teachers focus almost exclusively upon sacred songs and chants. The significance of the *texts* of religious songs, rather than the musical melodies, is the critical difference.[63] As Johannes Quasten describes,

> The earliest of the Church Fathers frequently emphasized the beauty and euphony of the human voice...in contrast to the cultic music of the pagans. Instruments were considered lifeless and soulless, whereas the human voice was a living means of glorifying God.[64]

Early Christian preachers contrasted the pagan use of instrumental music during meals with the Christian employment of psalms and hymns.[65] Singing, as opposed to "playing," comes symbolically to characterize the lifestyle of pious Christians. This portrayal would encourage the receptivity of early Christians toward the doctrinal teaching embodied in the texts of the psalms and hymns carefully chosen by their leadership.

Similarly, the polemic of Christian writers against secular songs focuses upon their texts, particularly those with immoral associations and the names of pagan gods.[66] Christians instead substitute their own compositions: "In place of the hero-songs... there appeared songs about martyrs, while hymns to God replaced love songs."[67]

Early Christian writers commonly used the imagery of singing to God in one voice. For example, Ignatius of Antioch (c. 35–c. 107) offers some of the earliest evidence for the ideal. In his letter to the Ephesians, after he describes how the presbytery is "attuned to the bishop as strings to a cithara," Ignatius declares, "Jesus Christ is sung in your unity of mind and concordant love. And... you make up a chorus, so that joined together in harmony and having received the godly strain in unison, you might sing in one voice through Jesus Christ to the Father."[68] The imagery developed further to picture Christians singing their praise to God in unison with the hosts of heaven. For example, Cyril of Jerusalem (c. 315–386) declares that "this theology of the seraphim" (viz., the threefold "Holy, holy, holy" of Isaiah 6:3) was revealed in Scripture so that Christians could sing it in unison with the heavenly host![69]

When early Christians sang, they believed that they were inspired or filled with the Holy Spirit. The Spirit had transformed them and enabled them to be joined with God as participants in the New Song of Jesus Christ. Clement of Alexandria (c. 150–215) develops this extended metaphor of the New Song in his *Protrepticus* (often translated as "The Exhorter" or "Exhortation to the Greeks").[70] In contrast to the legendary minstrels of ancient Greece, Christ the Logos sings the New Song:

> He who is from David, yet before him, the Word of God, scorning the lyre and cithara as lifeless instruments, and having rendered harmonious by the Holy Spirit both this cosmos and even man the microcosm, made up of body and soul—he sings to God on his many voiced instrument and he sings to man, himself an instrument.... This is the New Song, the shining manifestation among us now of the Word, who was in the beginning and before the beginning.[71]

The mighty New Song brings life to those who are spiritually dead.[72] Christ the Savior employs a "polyphony" of methods for the purpose of redeeming humanity.[73] Furthermore, the "melodious order" of the Logos brings into harmony the discordant ele-

ments of the universe.[74] Clement's New Song imagery finds
echoes in Origen (c. 185–c. 254), who connects it with spiritual
regeneration,[75] and later in Eusebius of Caesarea (c. 260–c. 340),
who ties it to the proclamation of the gospel—the New
Covenant of salvation—to all the nations.[76]

Yet strong opposition to the practice of singing also existed in
the early church, particularly in some of the more stringent forms
of Eastern monasticism. For example, in *Sayings of the Fathers*—a
collection of Egyptian desert fathers and mothers from the fourth
and fifth centuries—Abbot Pambo denounces a young brother's
desire to sing *troparia*—hymns written in poetic prose with accen-
tuated patterns:

> Woe to us, my son! The days have come when monks turn
> away from the enduring nourishment which the Holy Spirit
> gives them and surrender themselves to singing. What kind of
> contrition is that? How can tears come from the singing of
> *troparia*?...See, I tell you, my son, the days will come when
> Christians will destroy the books of the holy Evangelists, the
> holy Apostles and the inspired Prophets, and they will rip up
> the Holy Scriptures and compose *troparia* in their place.[77]

Intense moralistic polemic against the practice of singing created
serious tension and conflict with those advocating the positive
Christian uses of song. Thus, the choice of early church leaders,
including Augustine, to embrace the practice of singing was not
decided without conflict and some struggle with ascetic moral
reservations.[78]

We now focus more sharply our quest for historical roots for
the relationship between theology and song by turning to
Prosper's theological mentor, Augustine.

The Law of Singing: Augustine of Hippo

The writings of Augustine (354–430), which shaped so dramatically the development of Christian doctrine in the West,

provide the key sources in the search for historical warrant for "the law of singing."

Rather than becoming mired in the abstract issues and technical details of Augustine's early treatise on music,[79] which sheds little light on the role of song in his life and ministry, we begin with a passage in Augustine's magisterial *City of God*. After seeking corroboration of the place of singing in two of his well-known letters, we then examine the place of song in his Christian experience. Various texts from Augustine's spiritual classic, *Confessions*, point towards the powerful presence of music in both the formation of his Christian identity and his understanding of worship.

City of God

Augustine describes the "order of the ages" as a "most beautiful song" in chapter 18 of Book 11 of the *City of God*.[80] He asserts that, given God's foreknowledge of humanity's evil future, God would not create any humans—not to mention angels—if God did not likewise know that God could turn them to good uses.[81] Therefore, the good and evil of the universe serve as rhetorical "antitheses" in the text of a poem or song. Through contrast, they enhance the beauty and power of the course of history.

As H. I. Marrou describes Augustine's musical analogy:

> St. Augustine liked to imagine the course of history as an exquisite song....This was not simply a way of expressing his optimistic judgment on the world and its future with the use of an aesthetic image: it is a close comparison....The meaning of a piece of music, its very being, is finally established only when the last movement of the fugue has been played, the last chord struck; when the last cadenza has died away. Until then the melody can always arise again, be modulated, develop in a new direction, take on a new vitality and be enriched with new harmonies....History can with truth be compared to an immense concert conducted by the all-powerful hand of God. Only he knows where it is going....Like the piece of music it can

always rise again and be renewed. It will only possess its full meaning once it has come to an end.[82]

The remarkable analogy between the pattern of human song and the pattern of divine providence causes one to wonder if there may not be other resemblances between the ways Christians sing—both in the words and process—and the contents of Christian beliefs about God. For instance, by singing through their tears at a funeral, some Christians might confess their faith in the constancy of God's care.[83] Augustine hints at a response to the question with his example of antitheses. As he observes, the "most beautiful song" is "enhanced by what might be called antitheses."[84] Augustine emphasizes later in the same chapter that there is good scriptural precedent for this poetic use of antitheses. He quotes 2 Corinthians 6:7-10 and Ecclesiasticus 33:14-15 as illustrations.

The language of poetry and song does not suffer the limitations of philosophical and theological argument in expressing and celebrating the mystery of God.[85] For example, Christian thinkers have struggled with the paradox of reconciling good and evil in the world with the nature of God.[86] When one sings, the alternatives of the paradox can be poetically juxtaposed. The tension of the paradox not only is expressed within the song, but also enhances its beauty.[87] Thus, through the use of antithesis, the celebration of God's mystery in song—like the celebration of God in the poetry of liturgy—provides an opportunity for Christians to move beyond the limitations of "logical arguments" both in the expression of their faith and in their spiritual development.

Letters

This role of song in expressing the mystery of the faith not only is found in Augustine's *City of God*, but also appears in two of his letters.[88] In Letter 138 to Marcellinus, written in 412, Augustine is dealing with the question of why the sacrifices of the Old Testament are no longer fitting for the current Christian era.

Seeking to apply the principle that altered circumstances demand a change in that which is right to do, Augustine asserts:

> The sacrifice which God had commanded was fitting in those early times, but now it is not so. Therefore, He prescribed another one, since He knew much better than man what is suitably adapted to each age, and being the unchangeable Creator as well as Ruler of the world of change, He knows as well what and when to give, to add to, to take away, to withdraw, to increase, or to diminish, until the beauty of the entire world, of which the individual parts are suitable each for its own time, swells, as it were, into *a mighty song of some unutterable musician [magnum carmen cuiusdam ineffabilis modulatoris]*, and from thence the true adorers of God rise to the eternal contemplation of His face, even in the time of faith.[89]

A rising song of praise to God articulates the response of the faithful worshipers. Across the changing eras God, "Ruler *[moderator]* of the world of change," is contemplated through mighty and mysterious song.

In Letter 166, "On the Origin of the Human Soul," which was written to Jerome in 415, Augustine extends the role of song a step further. Augustine is wrestling with the pastoral-theological dilemma of the souls of infants who die before they are baptized. He takes refuge in the mystery of God's providence and turns to music for illustration and comfort. In this epistle, not only does song celebrate God's providence in the midst of changing events, but also the process of skillfully composing a song becomes an extended metaphor for God's providential regulation of creation. Augustine develops this comparison in the following manner:

> Hence, if a man who is skilled in composing a song *[faciendi artifex carminis]* knows what lengths to assign to what tones *[vocibus]*, so that the melody *[quod canitur]* flows and progresses with beauty by a succession of slow and rapid tones, how much more true is it that God permits no periods of time in the birth and death of His creatures ... to proceed either more quickly or more slowly than the recognized and well-defined law of

rhythm requires, in this wonderful song [*mirabili cantico*] of succeeding events.[90]

Thus, the rhythmic art of composing a song offers a parable,
which enables one to glimpse the mystery of God's wise distribu-
tion of "time in the birth and death of His creatures." The law of
singing opens a new window onto the great mystery of God's
providence.

Confessions

The use of musical imagery to describe the process of understanding Augustine's theology is by no means restricted to conservative "ecclesiastical" scholars such as Marrou. For example,
in her proposal of a new reading of Augustine's *Confessions* as a
"text of pleasure," Margaret Miles observes, "Necessarily discussed seriatim, text, context, and subtext must subsequently be
mixed, as the separate instruments on different soundtracks are
mixed, if the music of the text is to be heard in its full strength
and beauty."[91] To take another recent example, Gillian Clark
resorts to musical imagery to describe the rich complexity of the
text of *Confessions*: "This is 'polyphonic discourse,' not a clear
melodic line."[92]

In the famous events in the garden at Milan that climax in
Augustine's conversion to Christianity, the child's chanting voice
dramatizes the role of song. Not only does song serve as a musical
model and metaphor of the mystery of God, but also the practice
of singing teaches and transforms Christians. As Augustine nar-
rates his experience:

> So I was speaking and weeping in the most bitter contrition of
> my heart, when, lo!, I heard from a neighboring house a voice,
> as of a boy or girl, I know not, chanting, and often repeating,
> "Take up and read; take up and read." Instantly my counte-
> nance altered and I began to think most intently, whether
> children were wont in any kind of play to *sing such words*

[*cantitare tale aliquid*], nor could I remember ever to have heard the like.[93]

Augustine's initial exposure to hymn singing in worship occurred through his involvement in Ambrose's congregation.[94] As Don Hustad explains, "Ambrose...countered the Arian hymns with his own doctrinally pure [i.e., Nicene Trinitarian] texts."[95] A classic example of such theologically weighted hymnody is the famous text attributed to Ambrose, *O lux beata trinitas*:

> O Trinity of blessed light,
> O Unity of princely might,
> The fiery sun now goes his way;
> Shed Thou within our hearts Thy ray.
>
> To Thee our morning song of praise,
> To Thee our evening prayer we raise;
> Thy glory suppliant we adore
> Forever and forever more.
>
> All laud to God the Father be;
> All praise, eternal Son, to Thee;
> All glory, as is ever meet,
> To God the holy Paraclete.[96]

Thus, as early as Ambrose (c. 340–397), hymns are being used in worship in the West to articulate complex Christian doctrine for the common people.[97]

Reflecting on the experience of singing these Ambrosian hymns[98] also provides Augustine with insight into the philosophical dilemma of time and its relation to narrative.[99] Gillian Clark lucidly expounds Augustine's view of the process as found in Book 11 of *Confessions*:

> As I sing one of Ambrose's hymns...I move from one sound to
> the next, remembering what I have just sung and expecting

what I shall sing next. I am stretched between what I have done and what I shall do; I measure the long and short syllables, but I cannot measure their duration until they are over, and then they are no longer there to be measured. I cannot explain what I am doing, and what is true of singing a hymn is also true on a larger scale of human life, so that existence in time disintegrates as I try to make sense of it.[100]

So, in contemporary philosophical terms, Augustine's reflection upon the phenomenology of his experience of singing offers a model for the paradoxical relationship between time and eternity. Musical time becomes the paradigm for theological time.

Clark offers another intriguing observation about Augustine and church music in *Confessions*. In Book 10, after Augustine has completed the narrative of his conversion and its immediate aftermath, the reader is naturally curious to know something about his present life as bishop. As Clark notes, "The one thing we learn . . . is that he worries about music in church—it encourages the faithful, but does it distract their fallible bishop from the content of the service?"[101]

Augustine is acutely aware of the subtle power of the beautiful singing voice both to enhance worship and to distract from the words of worship. (Many Christians today may recognize this tension in their own experiences of worship.) So, Augustine is torn between endorsing and expressing concern regarding the singing of psalms in worship. On the one hand, he declares,

when I remember the tears I shed at the Psalmody of Thy Church, in the beginning of my recovered faith; and how at this time I am moved, not with the singing, but with the things sung, when they are sung with a clear voice and a modulation most suitable, I acknowledge the great use of this institution.[102]

On the other hand, he agonizes, "Yet when it befalls me to be more moved with the voice than with the words sung, I confess to have sinned penally, and then had rather not hear music."[103]

Therefore, whether as a catechumen struggling towards conversion or as a bishop concerned about worship, Augustine encounters the transformative power of song. The "law of singing" both influences and challenges his Christian identity and vocation.

A Contemporary Epilogue

Richard Mouw has recently argued that theologians have much to learn from engaging the popular piety of contemporary Christians.[104] Mouw advocates the adoption of a "hermeneutic of charity" toward the religious expressions of theologically uneducated but sincere Christians. Taking his theological point of departure from John Henry Newman's classic essay "On Consulting the Faithful in Matters of Doctrine," Mouw contends,

> So it is fair to interpret Newman as saying that there resides, deep in the bosom of Christ's mystical body, a profound practical *theological* wisdom. Laypeople possess an important share of this discerning power, and no account of what is *theologically* true or false is adequate without taking into consideration the laity's prudent sense of how our doctrines are to be lived out in the concrete realities of practical existence.[105]

This call for caring discernment of the wisdom found in the piety and practices of faithful Christians applies to the law of singing. As an illustration of this practical wisdom, the following testimony from a contemporary Baptist church newsletter can be cited: "Music has been my teacher since I was a little girl. Through singing, I have learned theology, Jesus' life, death and resurrection, scripture, prayer, and more."[106] Is such testimony merely a pious endorsement of the religious status quo? Or does the possibility for personal and social transformation become available through singing the language of those songs?

Many singing Christians would testify that on the wings of song they have experienced the power of the gospel for both spiritual emancipation and social justice. The role of the songs of African American Christianity in the civil rights movement in the United States offers a dramatic example of this emancipatory connection. As Cheryl Kirk-Duggan explains, "the Black church grew as an agency of social control and justice; the Black preacher was a catalyst for change; Jesus was a refuge and means of liberation; and song held them all together."[107] Both the ancient wisdom of the early church and the contemporary wisdom of faithful Christians concur: *lex cantandi, lex credendi.* The law of singing is the law of believing.

Our examination of some historical warrants for the relationship between theology and the practice of singing in the early church has sought to legitimize the extension of performance models beyond formal liturgical contexts. The ancient wisdom of Christianity can inform the practice of both liturgical and non-liturgical Christian communities. Performance models offer one way to utilize the resources of the Christian heritage in the practice of contemporary ministry.

Assessing Performance Models

Performance models are built upon an analogy. So, our assessment will begin with some critical evaluation of the interrelated strengths and weaknesses of the analogy of performance in illumining the connections between theology and ministry. Following this general evaluation, we return again to the case of Valleywood Church and explore the application of a performance model.

Critical Evaluation

Analogies, like metaphors, depend upon both similarity and difference for their effectiveness.[108] Although an analogy formally highlights the similarity between its terms, if the terms are not to be identical, dissimilarity must necessarily be present. To take a classic example of this characteristic, *pastoral* ministry is both similar to and dissimilar from the practice of actually herding sheep.[109] (As some pastors might declare, contemporary ministry is more like herding cats!) Cross-disciplinary analogies—like performance—can creatively illumine Christian faith and practice. Yet these analogies are inherently restricted by the terms of the comparison. For example, in Frances Young's work, which we discussed earlier in this chapter, the "performance" of contemporary ministry is both similar to and dissimilar from the "'authentic performance' of classics."[110] Ignoring or de-emphasizing the dissimilarity creates the danger of a forced analogy, where the analogy of performance might confuse or misdirect ministry rather than illumine it. For instance, debates over the use of period instruments in authentic classical musical performance should not be used to direct what instruments are appropriate for contemporary Christian worship. A rough parallelism should not be allowed to become a forced analogy. The *dissimilarity* between the terms of the analogy must be taken into account as well.

The public nature of performance points to another interrelated strength and weakness of these models. The strength lies in the opportunity for ministry to enter and engage the wider arenas of culture. For example, consider the experience of ministers who *perform* wedding ceremonies for persons who are not actively practicing Christians. The pastoral and theological issues involved in planning and performing the service (for example, the selection of music, readings, and vows) commonly engage Christian doctrine with various currents of the public culture. Yet the weakness of performance models is simultaneously made visible. The public nature of performance models leads to the danger of the loss of personal authenticity of faith. As the critics of such weddings might charge, they are "*only* a performance." One possible response to this charge might be to stress the presence and activity of God in the service—perhaps even claiming that God is the performer. Yet this raises a host of concerns regarding how one discerns (rather than simply asserts) God's presence and activity among those who are reluctant or doubtful.

The evocative nature of performance models reveals an additional set of interrelated strengths and weaknesses. On the one hand, since performance has the capacity to evoke emotions of great depth and power, these models can forge connections between Christian beliefs and actions. Spirit-filled performance can point to a spirituality linking theology and ministry. Yet, on the other hand, the evocative nature of performance easily leads to an overreliance on notoriously variable aesthetic judgments. The emotions evoked by the same performance may be evaluated by different groups as Spirit-filled, demonic, delusional, or even irrelevant. Furthermore, the performer may become the center of attention, rather than a vehicle for communicating the message.

Finally, the worship-centered focus of most performance models has the great strength of promoting a clear Christian identity in continuity with Christian tradition. Performing the Scriptures or liturgy or Christian song in worship can locate the identity of a Christian community in a well-defined way. Yet this clear focus simultaneously makes difficult the extension of performance models to include other areas of ministry. How does the community understand and evaluate ministries that have at best only indirect connections to worship, if any are visible at all?[111] Furthermore, the sharp conflicts over styles of worship—colloquially known as "worship wars" in North America—clearly reveal the difficulty of maintaining sufficient consensus even at the congregational level to ground a worship-centered performance model linking theology and ministry.

Comparative Case Analysis: Performance Models and Valleywood Church

Before Jackie and Dale came to Valleywood Church as pastors, their internship year in a large Presbyterian church in the San Francisco Bay area raised their awareness of the centrality of worship in shaping effective pastoral ministry. They participated in ministry that developed a mutually supportive interaction between worship and pastoral care. The performance of worship helped preserve the transcendent, spiritual dimension that can so easily be obscured amidst the experience and issues of daily life. Bringing the day-to-day realities of pastoral care into worship not only allowed worship to remain connected to the concerns of the congregation, but also enabled worship itself to function as a form of pastoral care. Jackie and Dale want this positive dynamic between worship and pastoral care to characterize the ministry at Valleywood Church. Five years of pastoral ministry have revealed some of the opportunities and difficulties of extending this worship-centered vision to meet the challenges of pastoral care with nontraditional families in the congregation.

The Performance of Worship and Pastoral Care at Valleywood Church

Valleywood Church has a history of openness to innovations and experiments in worship. The congregation participated in the "house church" movement in the 1960s and 1970s and later in experimental worship under the leadership of Pastors Jon and Louisa. Through these experiences, the church has sought to connect its traditions of worship to themes and trends in American culture in the Pacific Northwest (for example, the early rise of ecological consciousness), which were influencing the lives of its members and their families. This heritage has given the congregation the flexibility to adapt its worship to the needs of the rapidly changing Valleywood community.

Yet Valleywood's history of experimental worship risks the loss of distinctive Christian identity, if the church accommodates the message of the gospel too closely to the culture. Jim's childhood declaration in the Christmas pageant humorously voices the danger: "Behold I bring you good tidings of great joy. Santa Claus is coming to Valleywood!" One is not surprised to discover that as young adults, Jim and his partner, Jenny, still attend Christmas dinner and other social functions but will not attend worship services. Their Christian identities faded, as Jim and Jenny assimilated into secular culture. Jackie and Dale have struggled unsuccessfully to develop new forms of worship that will provide an opportunity for Jim and Jenny to encounter the gospel again.

Darlene and Sue welcome the church's openness to experimental forms of worship. They find that in the services they have opportunities to express many of their concerns and needs, as well as those of their sons, Harrison and Tom. Yet their advocacy for their lesbian blended family raises serious questions among members of the congregation. The experimental forms of worship at Valleywood are often so inclusive that they seem to give approval and blessing to a broad range of alternative lifestyles. Jackie and Dale wonder whether—and, if so, how—the words of worship should distinguish between genuine acceptance of Darlene and Sue and endorsement of their lifestyle. They have similar questions regarding Jim and Jenny's alternative lifestyle.

The authentic performance of the Scriptures might offer a way for Jackie and Dale to lead Valleywood Church to respond pastorally to these dilemmas raised by nontraditional families without falling into the bitter rhetoric of ideological debate over alternative lifestyles. Performing Scripture as a whole to proclaim the working of God in the midst of *all kinds of families* (each with its own struggles and sinfulness) reflects the saving witness of the Bible. The Scriptures repeatedly show God's actions in the world as involving diverse forms of family structure.[112] Performing the Scriptures to declare the saving grace of God, while acknowledging the realities of individual and corporate sin, could enable the congregation to maintain a perspective on difficult moral issues.

Furthermore, the Lord's Supper (or Eucharist) can be frequently performed at Valleywood in a way that emphasizes Christ's invitation to all to receive God's grace. The visual and material symbolism of the Supper, pointing to the sacramental presence of Christ, can communicate a message of reconciliation that goes beyond words. So, worship through word and sacrament can focus the congregation's ministry on performing and thereby embodying the gospel message.

Although Jill's experience is not that of an alternative lifestyle, her divorce from Michael and subsequent marriage to Ed (the kind non-Christian) reveals the brokenness of relationships to which the gospel speaks. Performance in community may convey more clearly the mercy and grace of God. Worship that emphasizes the communal performance of the Scriptures and the Lord's Supper might enable Jill to see herself as no longer alone at church, but in a company of pilgrims and strugglers.[113] Jill's need for community perhaps can be more deeply addressed through *communion* in worship than through further fellowship activities.

The Performance of Sacraments and Rituals for Nontraditional Families

Darlene and Sue's desire to have their union officially blessed by the church and Mary's grandparents' desire for her to be baptized (despite the lack of consent from her parents) both point to the continuing social and religious power of Christian sacraments and rituals. The performance of church rituals recognizing nontraditional families has created significant conflict within and between Christian communities, sharply raising questions of the authority for and legitimacy of these practices.

In Darlene and Sue's case, Jackie and Dale are caught up in the continuing controversy in their denomination over the issue of homosexuality. No matter how tactfully or neutrally worded, the performance of an official blessing of Darlene and Sue's union is interpreted as a political statement in favor of gay and lesbian marriage. As American society moves toward increasing recognition of gay and lesbian domestic partners, the pressure increases upon churches such as Valleywood to embrace uncritically one side or the other of the political issue. The performance of church ritual, instead of uniting a congregational community, may then easily divide it. Wise pastoral discernment, which takes into account the various "audiences" for the performance of church rituals, is desperately needed in these conflicts.

In Mary's case, Jackie and Dale are faced with issues of generational family conflict. The performance of the sacrament of baptism at Mary's age would not be welcoming her into the covenanted family of God, but manipulating her in opposition to her parents. The underlying conflict is between Mary's parents and grandparents over Jim and Jenny's refusal to become officially married. Therefore, Jackie and Dale are probably wise to follow their denomination's polity requiring the session's decision regarding parental consent for Mary's baptism, not allowing themselves to be maneuvered into performing the sacrament in response to social pressure.[114] Disciplined integrity is required for the performance of the art of ministry.

CHAPTER 6

Regulative Models

R egulative or rule-based models for connecting Christian doctrine and pastoral practice are new alternatives in pastoral theology. The cultural-linguistic approach to Christian doctrine developed by George Lindbeck provides a distinctive perspective that can be used to connect theology and ministry. Based upon an understanding of Christian doctrine that seeks a new way beyond the polarities of conservative propositional theology and liberal symbolic theology, regulative models are particularly attractive to Christians who describe themselves as "postliberal." Christians whose communities hold a high view of Scripture that is open to critical study may also find particular appeal in regulative models. The shape of Christian ministry guided by a regulative model is still in the formative stages.[1]

Regulative models are closely connected with the performance models we examined in the last chapter. Both types of models construct cross-disciplinary analogies, which connect theology and the practice of Christian communities. For example, the theme of Christian communities "performing the Scriptures" is central to both approaches. Yet, unlike models that emphasize the performing arts (for example, the analogy between theology and musical performance), Lindbeck's approach constructs an analogy between understanding Christian doctrine and the practice of learning a new language. This chapter carefully examines Lindbeck's analogy and its implications for connecting theology and ministry. As we shall see, Lindbeck's functional view of the nature of theology sets a regulative approach apart from other models that emphasize Christian practices.

We begin by offering a general introduction to some key themes in Lindbeck's cultural-linguistic approach to Christian doctrine, particularly emphasizing its methodological distinctiveness from other types of Christian theology. Next, we examine some ways in which a regulative model focused on practice might be especially valuable to pastoral theologians and Christian ministers involved in pastoral care and ecumenical worship. This is followed by a case study that connects the pastoral care of a student who hears voices and the doctrine of revelation. Lindbeck's approach is adapted and extended to interpret the case. Then our assessment of regulative models offers some critical evaluation of their strengths and weaknesses. The chapter concludes with the application of a regulative model to our master case study of Valleywood Church.

Describing Lindbeck's Cultural-Linguistic Approach[2]

In *The Nature of Doctrine*, George Lindbeck constructs an analogy between understanding Christian doctrine and learning to speak a new language.[3] One may perhaps recall struggling to master the rules for French or Spanish verbs or German declensions—or maybe even just learning parts of speech in a high-school English class. In any case, what was the purpose of all those rules? Wasn't the goal to learn to speak, read, write, and, yes, perhaps even think fluently in the new language? The sign of mastering the new language was not that one could recite all the rules, but that he or she could speak grammatically. The rules were the means, not the goal.

Most people do not learn the rules of a language in order to become grammarians, but in order to speak grammatically, so they can communicate coherently and effectively with the language. In fact, one of the signs that a person can speak grammatically is that she or he no longer consciously has to think of the rules while speaking. Many people who speak grammatically cannot recite all the rules they use. Indeed, the natural way to master a new language is not to take language courses that study grammar formally, but to immerse oneself in a community of competent speakers of the language. The rules, then, become internalized. For example, a fluent English speaker should not consciously need to think about whether her or his subjects and verbs agree in number. If the rules achieve their purpose, they will recede into the background.

Lindbeck maintains that Christian doctrine works in a similar fashion. The purpose of Christian doctrine is to enable members of the Christian community to speak correctly about the teachings and mysteries of their faith. Indeed, the natural way to learn the language of Christianity is not to take courses that study the history of Christian doctrine formally, but to immerse oneself in a community of knowledgeable and committed Christian disciples who practice Christianity on a daily basis. So, learning to speak correctly about the faith and practicing it are united in the life of Christian communities. When Christians violate the rules of doctrine—the grammar of their faith—they may end up speaking not only ungrammatically or incorrectly about the faith, but perhaps even incoherently. The language of doctrine is second-order language; it provides boundaries or negative guidelines around the mysteries of the faith.

For example, the rules of the doctrine of the Trinity do not explain the mystery of the nature of God. They simply sketch out or bound an area of discourse within which Christian theology can speak grammatically. So, on the one hand, the rule of doctrine called monotheism states that it is incorrect to think of the God whom Christians worship as three separate gods. (Such a view would be tritheism or polytheism.) On the other hand, the three-ness of the Trinity implies that it is also incorrect to think of the God whom Christians worship as a monolith. (Such a view would be monarchianism.) Within these boundaries, any of a great variety of ways of combining God's threeness and God's oneness may be not only acceptable and coherent, but also orthodox.

Obviously, Lindbeck's regulative approach to doctrine differs from the ways in which earlier Christian theologians—both conservatives and liberals—have conceived of the nature of Christian doctrine. Lindbeck carefully distinguishes his view of doctrine—which he labels the "cultural-linguistic" approach—from two other ideal types.[4] The first type is "cognitive-propositional." This approach views doctrines as providing information and making truth claims about "objective realities." Doctrines are propositions that summarize the facts of the Christian faith. Christianity's truth claims primarily concern realities that lie in the external world. The cognitive-propositional view of doctrine contains theologies both that seek to verify the facts of the Bible in the external world (for example, Protestant biblical literalists who argue that the world was created in six days) and that seek to make truth claims that go beyond the details of the biblical text (for example, Roman Catholics who claim that the Virgin Mary was herself immaculately conceived).

The second type of approach to doctrine from which Lindbeck distinguishes his own view is the "experiential-expressivist" model. This approach understands doctrines as symbolizing inner feelings and experiences. For example, in some kinds of Protestant pastoral theology shaped by the German liberal tradition of Friedrich Schleiermacher the valuable method of describing contemporary lived experience becomes elevated into the primary criterion for evaluating the truth of Christian doctrine.[5] What matters most in this type is the internal world of psychological and spiritual experience. Doctrine offers a way in which the inner realities of faith may be symbolized publicly.

So, in contrast to both cognitive propositions and expressed experiences, Lindbeck argues that doctrines are best understood to function as rules. The rules of doctrine work something like grammar in guiding the ways in which Christians speak of their faith.

Perry LeFevre insightfully observes that Lindbeck's proposal enables differing groups "not only to engage in dialogue, but [also] to agree where they have disagreed."[6] This characterization of Lindbeck's approach points to the possibility that postliberal theology may offer a new path for ministry to take account of doctrinal differences and development. Rather than continuing the polemical polarities that have divided theological liberals and conservatives since the nineteenth century, there may be a third way—the postliberal way.[7]

According to Lindbeck's approach, doctrines primarily function as neither cognitive assertions about ontological reality (the literal "conservative" view) nor symbolic expressions of personal and communal religious experience (the stereotypical "liberal" view). Instead, doctrines simply work like rules. Doctrines are the grammar that guides the ways in which religious stories are told.

Lindbeck's cultural-linguistic approach reverses the relationship between the text of the Bible and cultural categories of the contemporary world found in other types of theology. Instead of "translating" the Scripture into contemporary categories, Lindbeck speaks of the text of Scripture "absorbing" the world. As Lindbeck explains, "Intratextual theology redescribes reality within the scriptural framework rather than translating Scripture into extrascriptural categories. It is the text, so to speak, which absorbs the world, rather than the world the text."[8] The process is not so much focusing *on* Scripture as focusing *through* Scripture to encounter the changing world.[9] This movement contrasts with apologetic theology, which seeks to transpose Scripture into contemporary categories and thought forms.[10] For example, Stanley Hauerwas and L. Gregory Jones sharply depict the difference between Lindbeck's proposals and some kinds of contemporary liberal Protestantism by comparing *The Nature of Doctrine* to Harvey Cox's *Religion in the Secular City*. As Hauerwas and Jones explain:

> Cox's approach remains a liberal accommodation to modernity. Cox assumes that there is an identifiable "modern world"

to which various groups are reacting, and then modifies his understanding of the task of theology on the basis of his reading of the present situation. Lindbeck, on the other hand, concentrates on the actual outlook and practice which constitute a particular religious tradition in which an evaluation of present experience can meaningfully take place.[11]

Yet, while reversing the direction of movement (or, more technically, the pattern of conformation) between the text of Scripture and the world, Lindbeck explicitly and carefully avoids the danger of relapsing into some sort of precritical view of Scripture, which ignores the problems and issues of the contemporary world.[12] For instance, Hauerwas and Jones emphatically differentiate Lindbeck's approach from fundamentalism and religious right conservatism:

> In contrast to...religious conservatism...Lindbeck is not advocating a precritical stance toward scripture. Rather, he shifts the locus of criticism from proposition to practice, and calls for renewed attention to the stories and texts which form the basis for Christianity, because only then will we know what it is we believe.[13]

Thus, Lindbeck's cultural-linguistic approach to Christian doctrine offers an alternative for relating Scripture and the world that seeks to move beyond the liberal-conservative polarities of modern theology. We next examine the possibility of connecting Lindbeck's regulative model of Christian doctrine with the ministries of pastoral care and worship.

Connecting a Regulative Model with Pastoral Care and Worship

Lindbeck's regulative view of doctrine develops as reflection in the midst of the practice of Christian communities. Lindbeck does not first create an abstract theory of doctrine that then may be (secondarily) applied to practice. Rather, both the language of doctrine and theological reflection upon it take shape in the context of the life and conflicts of specific historical and contemporary Christian communities. As Lindbeck describes this practice-based focus, "The theory that is relevant to practice is not first learned and then applied, but rather is chiefly useful as part of an ongoing process of guarding against and correcting errors while we are engaged in practice."[14]

The emphasis upon the priority of practice offered by Lindbeck's regulative approach might be particularly valuable to those pastoral theologians and ministers who would describe themselves as "practitioners" of care. Although Lindbeck's approach is not clinical, it employs the kind of detailed cultural description that may be of assistance to those seeking to move pastoral care beyond one-to-one psychotherapeutic modalities into congregational and other group contexts.

Lindbeck's view of doctrine focuses upon empirical communities, not upon ontological metaphysics[15] or individual "religious affections."[16] Doctrine is inextricably bound to the beliefs and practices, both historical and contemporary, of clearly identifiable communities of faith.[17] If holding a doctrine is more like "obeying a rule" rather than "interpreting a truth," then pastoral caregivers can help those receiving care to discern different ways of following the rule appropriate to different contexts and circumstances.[18]

Persons are formed and deformed by the religious communities in which they participate.[19] Pastoral theologians and Christian ministers need to understand the connections between community beliefs and the practices that embody these beliefs for good or for ill. Despite the myths of North American religious individualism, both healthy religious identity and destructive religious abuse are shaped by group processes linking the beliefs and actions of religious communities. The patterns of life fostered by religious communities demand the best critical attention of theologians and ministers, who seek to understand the web of cognitive, affective, and behavioral dimensions of human religious life.[20]

Lindbeck's regulative model is especially compatible with recent sociological and anthropological approaches to religion that focus upon cultural practices, rather than on individual psychology.[21] Since Lindbeck's view of doctrine developed in the context of his own intensive involvement in ecumenical discussions, dialogue about the practice of worship in uniting or dividing churches plays a vital role.[22] Michael Root has offered a practical application and extension of Lindbeck's proposal in determining criteria for developing a "consensus sufficient for unity" (or alternatively, a "church-dividing difference") in current ecumenical discussions.[23] Root proposes three specific tests for determining whether sufficient unity exists in a religious group for the ecumenical performance of a practice essential to the community's religious identity (for example, a practice such as the Lord's Supper). The tests are that the practice may be performed: (1) "together," (2) "regularly," and (3) "in a comprehensive range of situations."[24]

Those responsible for the leadership and theological evaluation of worship might adapt Root's criteria to analyze the situations of ecumenical or interfaith worship in which they are engaged. So, for example, although the participants at such events (such as ecumenical chapel services at a Christian college or seminary) typically do not all share a common theology of worship, the practices they observe in worship together might be such that they could all agree on performing them "without violating [any member's] understanding of the identity of the church."[25] As Root declares,

> One may think the action in question is unnecessary, inappropriate, or foolish. One may contend that if one were compelled to perform it, such compulsion would violate one's understanding of the identity of the church. But if agreement can be reached on how it *can* be performed together without violating one's understanding of the identity of the church, then the differences that remain, however significant, cannot be church-dividing.[26]

To explore another example, ecumenical worship in the context of a seminary classroom offers a significant arena in which pastoral theologians and theological students may seek to modify and extend Root's criteria. A regulative approach based in practice rejects any attempt to ignore or cover over differences of belief among members of the class. Instead, a postliberal view of doctrine explicitly encourages class members to seek to articulate and explore doctrinal differences in the context of specific worship practices. Since doctrines function as rules, then articulating and agreeing to rules for the class's participation in worship practices—rather than debating whose tradition or experience contains the "best" account of the mystery—becomes the focus of discussion.

A postliberal view avoids lowest common denominator approaches to worship. Instead, prior to performance in class, worship practices are described in their cultural particularity. Members seek to determine whether, without violating the understanding of church and classroom in their diverse faith communities, they will be able to participate (1) together and (2) regularly in worship (3) across the range of traditions represented in the class. Even if the class discovers that it is unable to meet these three tests for ecumenical worship, the educational experience gained through the articulation of students' own traditions in regard to specific worship practices and the encounter with different boundaries may be both spiritually and theologically formative.

Having examined the natural fit between the practice of ecumenical worship and a regulative model based upon Lindbeck's cultural-linguistic view of doctrine, we now turn to the more challenging question of whether Lindbeck's model may be extended to the practice of pastoral care with individuals. The following exploratory case study seeks to adapt aspects of Lindbeck's approach to a pastoral care situation involving the doctrine of revelation.

Darrel's Voices and the Doctrine of Revelation[27]

Darrel[28] was a quietly intense, African American undergraduate at Yale University, where I served as Baptist chaplain. I met Darrel initially at the beginning of his first year, when, at my invitation, he politely stopped by my office for an introductory chat. Although I attempted to maintain some contact with Darrel following the visit by letter, phone, and the usual host of invitations to campus ministry events, he never expressed any interest in further conversation or participation.

Then one winter afternoon in the middle of his sophomore year, Darrel suddenly appeared at my office. He asked if he could talk with me immediately about something. Sensing his anxiety, I invited him to sit down and share whatever he wished.

After some brief preliminaries, Darrel arrived at the concern that had caused him to come. He had been hearing voices. As he walked alone around campus, he heard quiet voices emerging from those massive stone buildings. They were whispering his name. They were calling to him. What were they trying to say to him? What did they mean?

Further conversation with Darrel quickly revealed that he had already gone to the Department of University Health with his concerns. He was already meeting regularly with one of Yale's carefully selected psychiatric residents to explore his experience psychologically. He had sought me out to explore the *religious* meaning of his experience. Could it be possible that God was speaking to him through these voices? Were these voices revelation?

Regretfully, I must confess that nothing in my divinity school education and nothing in my introductory CPE experience prepared me to respond adequately to Darrel's request. I was fairly experienced in short-term informal counseling with college students, and I knew how to refer. Darrel, however, was not seeking these skills. He wanted a chaplain to help him evaluate his experience in *religious* categories. He hoped I might be able to help him sort out whether there was any *revelation*—and not just hallucination—in these experiences. Was it possible that God was trying to speak to him through these voices, or was it merely self-delusion—or perhaps even something evil?

Distinguishing among kinds or types of revelation based on how they function offers one fruitful way of responding to the pluralistic perplexity of Darrell's voices and the possibility of revelation. George Lindbeck argues in *The Nature of Doctrine* that theology should analyze doctrines based on how they function within the life of religious communities,[29] rather than on some external and supposedly universal standard of truth.[30] In accordance with Lindbeck's view of doctrine,[31] I suggest that we distinguish at least three types of revelation, which I am tentatively proposing to label simply Revelation 1, Revelation 2, and Revelation 3.[32]

Revelation 1 is revelation as individual subjective appropriation. A person shaped by the traditions of her or his culture (including religious traditions) experiences revelation. This revelation may be something as dramatic as hearing voices or seeing visions, or it may be something as simple as experiencing the presence of God while praying or meditating. The degree to which specific religious traditions mediate the experience may be clearly manifest (for example, in singing a hymn or reciting a Scripture) or much less explicit (as in hearing one's name whispered among stone buildings).[33] In any case, the individual involved personally appropriates the revelation in her or his experience.

Revelation 2 is revelation as illumination through communal tradition. Revelation of this type may refer to a historical experience (for example, Israel experiencing God in the Exodus) or a present experience (your church experiencing God's presence during worship last Sunday). Community members may be engaged in a variety of communally authorized religious practices—worshiping together, participating in a Bible study group, protesting for human rights—when they experience a revelation of the presence of God. Like the disciples with the resurrected Jesus in Emmaus, suddenly their eyes are opened and they recognize God (cf. Luke 24:31). Of course, Revelation 2 is not restricted to events or practices that are institutionally connected to the church and its ministry. Community members commonly believe that God can use anything in the world to reveal Godself. What distinguishes Revelation 2 from Revelation 1 is that these events are interpreted *communally* as revelation through the lens of tradition. Revelation 2 is communally discerned.

Revelation 3 is revelation as recognition of authoritative community traditions and practices. Whether the Bible, the Torah and Talmud, the Koran, the declarations of the Magisterium, or the pronouncements of some religious leader, a body of tradition is privileged as normative revelation for community members. Disputes among members are commonly expressed, if not resolved, by appealing to this commonly held authoritative tradition.

Obviously the boundaries between these different types of revelation are fluid. They blend into one another. For example, revelation experienced through the practice of studying scripture such as the Bible or Koran could be classified as belonging to any of the three categories, depending on how the studying *functions* for the individual or community involved. Yet, within each type of revelation, the functions described are recognizably different and sometimes in tension with one another. For instance, the statement "I was reading random passages in the Bible [or Koran] last night and God spoke to me" is quite different from "While studying the Scripture, our group experienced the presence of God." In turn, both of these differ significantly from "Our church or tradition teaches that through Scripture God has spoken to us, saying...."

Adopting a functional approach that seeks to distinguish between types of revelation would do much to clarify the approach that pastoral theology takes to describing revelation in lived human experience. The rough, simple categories of Revelation 1, 2, and 3 offer ways for pastoral theologians to signal how revelation functions in the living human documents and communities under study. Is revelation used to refer to individual subjective appropriation (Revelation 1), illumination through communal tradition (Revelation 2), recognition of authoritative community traditions (Revelation 3), or something beyond these rough categories?[34]

Now we turn again to the narrative of Darrel's visit. Using the rough types of revelation—Revelation 1, Revelation 2, and Revelation 3—as a rule to analyze the narrative might help clarify Darrel's request for pastoral care. This sort of theological analysis of Darrel's story could also enable pastoral caregivers to explore the dynamic in Darrel's relationship with God, rather than simply to offer competent psychological diagnosis. The rough types of revelation can provide a vehicle for connecting the first-order religious language of Darrel's experience with the second-order language of theological reflection.[35] The language of experience is "absorbed" into the world of biblical and theological reflection.

Darrel reported hearing voices, which were calling his name and which he believed might be revelation. If Darrel was experiencing revelation here, it was clearly Revelation 1—revelation as individual subjective appropriation. Darrel was struggling with the question of whether to and how to appropriate this experience. Skillful pastoral conversation might not only assist Darrel in recognizing and articulating his struggle but also offer some useful categories for thinking through his response.

The category of Revelation 1 points to the intensely individualistic focus of Darrel's perceived present relationship with God. The dramatic change of social location that accompanied his move from his African American community of origin to the Ivy League campus of Yale University intensified the focus on the self that commonly occurs in the beginning years of college education in the liberal arts.[36] The possibility of some form of mystical or ecstatic experience needs careful consideration, along with concerns regarding psychopathology.

Darrel's faith had been nurtured in an African American Baptist community that frequently and publicly reported many instances of Revelation 2—revelation as illumination through communal tradition. In Darrel's home church, individual experiences of God's call (Revelation 1) are nurtured, interpreted, and evaluated by the traditions of the community (Revelation 2). Darrel's isolation from the ongoing life and practices of his faith community during his college years may perhaps be reflected in his experience of Revelation 1 apart from Revelation 2. When engaged in communally authorized religious practices, whether alone or in groups, members of Darrel's faith community of origin commonly testified to recognizing God's revelation in their lives.

Therefore, Darrel sought out a Baptist chaplain for assistance in interpreting his experience. Although he might have been better served by a chaplain or pastor of his own ethnicity (both of whom were readily available at Yale), Darrel chose to visit an official representative of his denominational tradition, who presumably had received a calling and professional training in the interpretation of Revelation 3—authoritative community traditions and practices. Perhaps Darrel expected "the Baptist Chaplain at Yale" might be able to speak with some authority regarding the fine line between spiritual reality and religious illusion. In any case, Darrel was hoping that my knowledge of God—both through experiences of Revelation 2 and the interpretation of Revelation 3—might help him explore and evaluate the possible religious meaning of his experience.

The question of God's presence amidst Darrel's voices still remains. Yet pastoral theological reflection on revelation has perhaps enabled us to glimpse a bit more clearly the mystery of God's presence in the "dim mirror" of human experience (cf. 1 Cor. 13:12).

Assessing Regulative Models

Regulative models explicitly highlight the significance of Christian doctrine in the midst of practice. Thus, much of our critical evaluation examines the theological adequacy of the new understanding of Christian doctrine the models advocate. Following an assessment of some of the strengths and weaknesses of this new approach for pastoral theology, we then examine our master case study of Valleywood Church from the perspective of a regulative model.

Critical Evaluation

Regulative models for connecting Christian doctrine and pastoral practice have the significant strength of valuing the resources of Scripture and tradition in ministry while allowing for gradual change. Christian ministry both focuses on community practices and participates in a dialogue with enough common language for participants at least to "agree on where they disagree."

Yet a survey of the extensive discussion among theologians of Lindbeck's cultural-linguistic approach to Christian doctrine reveals concerns about its approach to the truth claims of Christian doctrine. A number of critics, including both conservative Protestants and Catholics, have voiced their fears that Lindbeck's approach would lead to religious relativism. Lindbeck's functional approach to the nature of Christian doctrine, which bypasses questions of ontological reference, is perceived as relativizing the truth of doctrine. For example, in the journal *Catholica,* Armin Kreiner, of the Institute of Fundamental and Ecumenical Theology in Munich, declares, "The christological and trinitarian statements were in no way only understood as 'grammatical' rules, but also as ontological statements."[37]

It is striking to compare that pronouncement from a venerable German Catholic professor with the following comment by American evangelical Alan Padgett, formerly pastor of San Jacinto United Methodist Church. In a review of Lindbeck's book in the *Theological Students Fellowship Bulletin*, Padgett declares, "The adoption of *just* an ethical-functional approach to religious language short-circuits the basic question of truth in religion, and leads in the end to religious relativism."[38] So, although the language may be different between a South German Catholic and a Southern California evangelical, the fear is the same. The adoption of a regulative view of doctrine will inevitably lead to the slippery slope of relativism.[39]

Bruce Marshall, one of Lindbeck's students, has strongly argued that this fear of the slippery slope of relativism misunderstands Lindbeck's proposal.[40] Although Lindbeck's emphasis upon performative language (the way language functions) does not judge a statement true or false,[41] it instead creates the conditions "under which one can state a sentence is a true proposition."[42] Therefore, Lindbeck's cultural-linguistic view of doctrine does not rule out or ignore the need for Christian communities to make historically grounded judgments on the truth or falsity of Christian teachings. It simply seeks to interpret the reality that at different times and places these judgments may *change*, without compromising the integrity and Christian identity of the communities involved.

Thus, for example, without compromising their integrity or their church's identity, Lutheran theologians may today affirm that recent Catholic interpretations of the doctrine of justification are true. This obviously marks a dramatic change from their sixteenth-century Lutheran forebears, who labeled the teaching of the Catholic Church on justification as that of the Antichrist! This ecumenical reconciliation is a shift in the development of Western Christian doctrine that Lindbeck's proposal can account for without evoking accusations of "lowest common denominator theology" or lack of doctrinal integrity. In other words, Lindbeck's model enables theology to make sense of the reality of changing Christian teachings without denying the truth of historic doctrinal formulations. In summary, it seems fair to conclude that, although Lindbeck's functional view of doctrine may result in a de-emphasis upon the truth claims of doctrine, the dangers of religious relativism are not necessarily inherent in his approach.

Beyond the debates regarding doctrinal truth claims, regulative models for connecting doctrine and practice are also subject to two other weaknesses. The first is that regulative models may advocate an intratextual reading of Scripture to such a degree that other ways of connecting the Bible and the world are either ruled out or ignored.[43] This can result in the unintentional return to a precritical reading of Scripture, rather than a postcritical one. The Bible then "absorbs the world" in an anachronistic way, which leads to a ministry that is unable to connect with the postmodern experience of the persons to whom the church is seeking to minister.

The second significant weakness is the tendency of regulative models to support the institutional power arrangements of the church against prophetic challenges from dissenters. Here, contextual models have much to teach regulative ones. Regulative models can show only limited openness toward theological innovations arising out of contemporary political and ideological issues. Demands for peace and justice and theological innovations arising from the margins of Christian communities are too often subordinated to the traditions of the community. Ordered change and gradual transition, rather than prophetic challenge and revolutionary struggle, characterize regulative models. Change in the church and society is primarily sought through practice-centered dialogue, rather than through nonviolent resistance. Regulative models are better at guiding ministry in situations of gradual reform rather than of radical revolution.

Comparative Case Analysis: Regulative Models and Valleywood Church

Pastors Jackie and Dale, following a regulative model, plan to lead Valleywood Church to focus more intentionally on church teachings and practices that connect Christian faith and family life. Greater awareness of these spiritual roots will guide the congregation in its response to the challenges raised by nontraditional families. Jackie and Dale believe that the "grammar of faith" should play a central role in shaping the church's ministry to families.

Learning the "Grammar" of Faith and Family Life at Valleywood Church

The heritage of "family-centered yet socially progressive" ministry at Valleywood Church could be grounded more deeply in Scripture and theology. For instance, the congregation can identify specific biblical and theological warrants that both undergird and challenge its ministry with families.[44] Similarly, the church's continuing opposition to racism could be explicitly grounded in

Scripture and doctrine. Through teaching in both worship and Christian education, Jackie and Dale can lead the congregation to discover and deepen scriptural perspectives on faith and family life. Although Christian teaching should be fully cognizant of contemporary social issues in family life—such as Darlene and Sue's concerns about homophobia—patterns of Scripture shaped by the rules of doctrine should guide the teaching in the congregation's Christian education program.

Newcomers to the congregation, such as Darlene and Sue and their children, Tom and Harrison, can first be invited to "overhear" the church's faith-based conversations on the nature and practices of Christian family life. Then, once the newcomers have learned and adopted the grammar of Christian faith as spoken in the congregation, they are welcome to play significant roles in the ongoing process of discerning how Christian faith and family life should be understood and lived out at Valleywood Church.

An important consequence of this regulative perspective on ministry is the way in which the language of present experience is reduced in its authority through absorption into the categories of the biblical and historical traditions of Christianity. For example, Sue's desire "to experience the blessing of carrying a child supported by Darlene's love and care" through artificial insemination by a donor invites broader Christian ethical discussion and scrutiny. Similarly, Jim's assertion of the sufficiency of his and Jenny's "long-term commitment to each other" as a cohabiting heterosexual couple with a child is challenged by various Christian understandings of the place of marriage in family life.

The inadequate "soul mate" theology of marriage, originally held by Jill and her mother, vividly reveals some sad consequences of the church's failure to teach effectively a wise approach to marriage and family life. When Michael abandoned Jill to marry Kathy, Jill painfully experienced the bankruptcy of her previous theological understandings of herself and her marriage. Despite her earnest and prayerful seeking for a soul mate, Jill did not find identity fulfillment in her marriage to Michael. Jill's post-divorce pastoral counselors had the difficult responsibility of assisting her in beginning the process of learning a different and viable theological grammar of marriage. Developing such an understanding, grounded in Scripture and the historical wisdom of Christian communities, represents a major priority both for Christian education and for pastoral care at Valleywood. Applying a regulative model to the Valleywood Church situation involves more than enabling the congregation to learn the grammar of Christian faith in regard to family life. Rather, it also entails the difficult process of redescribing family life practices, especially in light of the challenges brought to the congregation by nontraditional families.

Redescribing the Practices of Family Life at Valleywood Church

Darlene and Sue are invited to engage in biblical and theological dialogue regarding the practices of their lesbian blended family. Their desire for the church to change traditional sexual norms is subject to theological analysis, rather than simply to the demands of personal and social experience. As Lindbeck observes:

> A postliberal might argue, for example, that traditional sexual norms should be revised because the situation has changed from when they were formulated or because they are not intratextually faithful—but not, as some liberals may be inclined to argue, on the grounds that sexual liberation is an advance toward the eschatological future. Postliberalism is methodologically committed to neither traditionalism nor progressivism, but its resistance to current fashions, to making present experience revelatory, may often result in conservative stances.[45]

Possibilities for new ritual practices, such as Darlene and Sue's request to have their union blessed by the church, are evaluated primarily by biblical and theological argument, rather than as responses to urgent personal needs or contemporary cultural practices. Valleywood Church seeks to provide caring pastoral attention to Darlene and Sue's expressed needs through the church's ongoing dialogue concerning how Scripture and theology redescribe family life practices.

Jim and Jenny's continued refusal to be married relies solely upon their personal experience of a committed relationship, as opposed to the legal and social norms of marriage. The situation reflects Jim and Jenny's critique of their parents' marriages, especially Jenny's rejection of her mother's traditional role as a submissive wife. Jackie and Dale could point Jim and Jenny to other egalitarian models of Christian commitment in marriage. For example, Jackie and Dale's own marriage models an understanding that is different from both Sam and Sung Hee's (Jenny's parents') hierarchical view and from Loren and Judy's (Jim's parents') permissive one.

The conflicts over Mary's baptism can be redescribed as the need for reconciliation of persons in both Jim's and Jenny's extended family systems. Jackie and Dale can use their opportunities to minister in this situation to point the families involved to both the compelling demand for and the possibility of reconciliation with one another through the gospel. Although the need for reconciliation is most sharply revealed in Jenny's broken relationship with her father, the conflict reveals the need for the healing and restoration of the entire network of family relationships. The difficult process of pointing these families toward reconciliation with God and with one another might begin with a scriptural and theological redescription of current conflicts.

Finally, Jill's "single-in-church" loneliness at Valleywood could be redescribed to reflect a biblical understanding of the human condition. Jill's loneliness can perhaps be converted into solitude. Involving Jill in the practice of spiritual disciplines, taught and fostered by discipleship groups in the congregation, might offer one way to encourage this spiritual transformation.

Conclusion

We have explored five types of theological models used by contemporary Christians, particularly in Europe and North America, to make connections between Christian doctrine and pastoral practice. In response to Cheryl's tenacious questions in the first chapter, we have journeyed through a wide range of models connecting theology and ministry. Each of these models has its own validity and its distinctive strengths and weaknesses.

This study has proceeded on the assumption that there is no "one best model" for all Christians to follow, but that we can learn from critical analysis of a diversity of approaches. Christians can draw from these resources to develop their own working theology of ministry in the particular communities and contexts they serve. The following reflections examine further some ways to use the theological models already presented to shape wise approaches to Christian ministry. This process seeks to assist Christian ministers such as Cheryl in integrating their theology and ministry.

We begin with a brief review comparing the strengths and weakness of the five types of theological models. In this condensed summary, we make some specific comments regarding the application of different types of models to the Valleywood Church master case. Then we offer several practical suggestions about an intentional process of blending models, which avoids the dangers of "potpourri" ministry. Finally, we point toward the mystery of God in ministry—a presence that transcends the rational approach of theological models.

Comparing Models: A Summary Review

Each of the five types of models we have examined has significant value for making connections between theology and ministry. Since no one approach can persuasively claim to be universal—the "best one" in every circumstance—comparison of the distinctive strengths and weaknesses of each type assists ministers in crafting theologically informed approaches to ministry appropriate to their particular situation.

Correlational models—the first type examined in chapter 2—have the great strength of enabling insights from theology and the human sciences openly to engage one another. For example, at Valleywood Church, biblical understandings of the church as a community of forgiveness have been correlated with psychological insights about nonjudgmental acceptance and the dynamics of family systems. Yet, over time, correlations tend to unravel, as the presuppositions and analysis of one discipline tend to subordinate the other. Valleywood's conflicts over nontraditional families reveal the limitations of psychological and theological correlations about the nature of families and the demands of social justice, which were forged in the civil rights era.

Correlational models also promote openness to dialogue with current cultural themes and trends but risk the subordination of culturally critical aspects of the gospel. For example, the application of a correlational model to the Valleywood case sharply reveals differences and invites dialogue between the majority of members at Valleywood and the lesbian couple, Darlene and Sue, and likewise between the majority of members of First Korean Church and Jenny. Yet the prophetic capacity of the Christian faith to analyze these contemporary cultural conflicts and challenge them with the power of the gospel seems attenuated. A correlational model experiences difficulty in guiding pastors Jackie and Dale toward specific action, as hermeneutical preunderstandings tend to control the outcome of conflicted situations. Jackie and Dale wonder if they should follow, resist, or somehow compromise with the patterns and trends shaping family life in contemporary North American culture. The praxis-based analysis of contextual models or the cultural-linguistic analysis of regulative models offers a clearer basis for pastoral action

Contextual models, which we explored in chapter 3, reveal the strength of cultural particularity, which enables the sort of empirical analysis that uses the tools of the social sciences to advocate social change. The critical analysis of the contexts of the Valleywood case using the lenses of race and ethnicity, gender, and social class uncovers examples of oppression that need to be met with resistance and, ultimately, liberation through the power of the gospel. Yet the lack of capacity for generalizability limits contextual models, especially with the loss of cross-cultural norms for ethics. The polarization of the church and community contexts of Valleywood, which can result from the application of contextual models, makes building an effective consensus for ministry quite difficult.

Contextual models celebrate diversity and express great openness to political and ideological differences. Yet their hermeneutic of suspicion can lead to a relativism that diffuses distinctive Christian identity. The deconstruction of church and community life at Valleywood by the cultural critique of contextual models needs to be balanced by reconstruction that preserves Christian identity. The concern for Christian identity in narrative models and the focus upon Christian practices in both performance and regulative models provide stronger approaches to renewing the identity of the Valleywood congregation.

Narrative models, which we discussed in chapter 4, fit naturally and attractively with the narrative quality of human experience. So, a narrative analysis of the Valleywood case produces a rich, multilayered account of the stories of individuals and groups, which are mediated through the story of the local Christian community. Yet narrative models struggle with the gap between the call of the world of stories and the demands of action in the world of everyday experience. As the Valleywood case poignantly demonstrates, *understanding* the stories of nontraditional families is often painfully removed from *action* in ministry that effectively includes them within the ongoing life of the congregation.

Narrative models also have the great strength of matching the narrative character of Scripture and the history of Christianity. Thus, the stories of Scripture and (as the Teresa of Avila case illustrates) critically retrieved stories of the history of Christianity may be powerfully connected to contemporary stories of individuals and communities. This method results, however, in a continuous demand for Christian leaders to build and maintain reliable interpretive bridges between the Christian story and contemporary stories in their ministry (including their own stories). For example, the difficulties of effective narrative blending in the Valleywood case vividly point toward the danger of diffusion or even loss of Christian identity. Without critical interpretation, stories may become culturally assimilated and confused; the good news at Christmas becomes "Santa Claus [not Jesus] is coming to Valleywood." Performance models and regulative models both seek to address directly this concern. Furthermore, the self-authenticating character of narrative limits the capacity of narrative models to offer appropriate self-criticism, which in the situation of Valleywood Church might challenge a self-satisfied, middle-class moralism. Contextual models, focusing upon social location, provide opportunity for a more self-critical approach.

Performance models, which we explored in chapter 5, utilize a cross-disciplinary analogy to connect theology and ministry. For example, the application of the analogy of performance to the Valleywood case illuminates some connections between experimental worship and pastoral care. Since analogies require both similarity and dissimilarity between their terms, a close interrelationship between the strengths and limitations of performance models is not surprising. The public nature of performance enables ministry to engage wider arenas of culture, as Valleywood's openness to experimental worship illustrates. Yet the public nature of performance simultaneously leads to the danger of the loss of personal authenticity of faith. For example, in refusing to be married or to grant permission for Mary's baptism, Jim and Jenny could appropriately characterize the possibility of their participation in such rituals as just "inauthentic performance." In addition, the evocative nature of performance points to a spirituality linking theology and ministry. Jackie and Dale desire to facilitate such Spirit-filled performance of worship at Valleywood. Yet, as the worship wars painfully reveal, the evocative nature of performance easily leads to conflict over notoriously variable aesthetic judgments.

Performance models, particularly those with a worship-centered focus, possess the significant strength of promoting a clear Christian identity in continuity with the Scriptures and Christian tradition. Yet the extension of worship-centered performance models to include other areas of ministry is difficult. In the Valleywood case, the possibility of such a worship-shaped Christian identity contrasts with the fragmentation and loss of Christian identity evident in both the nontraditional families and in the culturally assimilated faith of the congregation. Both correlational models and contextual models more naturally support ministry beyond the experiences of worship.

Regulative models—the last type we examined in the previous chapter—explicitly value the resources of Scripture and tradition in ministry, while allowing for gradual change. Although some critics fear that their practice-centered view of doctrine may lead to religious relativism, the de-emphasis upon the truth claims of doctrine enables regulative models to account for doctrinal change without denying continuity with the historic confessions of the church. The Valleywood case analysis shows that the congregation's heritage of family-centered yet socially progressive ministry, including its historic opposition to racism, needs to be grounded more deeply in Scripture and theology. Gradual change that is biblically and theologically warranted could enable Valleywood Church to deal responsibly with the challenges posed by the nontraditional families.

Regulative models utilize an intratextual reading of Scripture, which is liable to be misinterpreted in a precritical, rather than a postcritical, way. Instead of biblically redescribing the practices of family life at Valleywood, a precritical reading could lead to a closed, legalistic view of the challenges posed by the nontraditional families in the case. Furthermore, regulative models tend to support the institutional power arrangements of the church against prophetic challenges from dissenters. Using a regulative model to analyze the Valleywood case portrays gradual reformation, rather than Spirit-driven revolutionary transformation. Contextual models, particularly those advocating emancipatory praxis, offer greater openness to demands for peace and justice from the margins of the community.

Blending Models: Some Practical Suggestions

Following such a condensed summary of our assessments of the five types of models, readers—especially theology students and ministers in training—may appreciate a few practical suggestions as to how to proceed in using all of this analysis of theological models.

Self-critical reflection upon one's personal theology of ministry is valuable for both pragmatic and spiritual reasons. Christian leaders who are reflective about their methods of ministry are better able to draw upon and shape the resources of the faith into an effective strategy for ministry in a specific context. Ministers called into a difficult situation too often find themselves overwhelmed or, less dramatically, at a loss for words and action. So, relying upon "fire engine religion," they tend to grasp at whatever comes to mind. Implicit theology controls their inadequate response, and frequently a magical view of the presence of the Holy Spirit is invoked to avoid responsibility.

Instead, prayerful theological reflection upon one's ministry enables the formation of spiritually discerning ministers. As our case studies demonstrate, when thoughtful examination of models of ministry is placed into theological dialogue with challenging ministry situations, insightful spiritual leadership can develop.

Ministers should be encouraged to move toward a "wise eclecticism" in their choices, rather than an indiscriminate "potpourri"! Ministers who intentionally and carefully reflect upon the ways they connect theology and practice are far more likely to be faithful and useful than those who do whatever seems right at the moment and seek to justify it by whatever model comes to hand. Theological models for connecting theology and ministry are vehicles for faithful action and reflection, not rationalizations for unreflective or self-justifying behavior. One strategy for blending models responsibly rather than indiscriminately— developing a "planned hybrid," rather than a "random potpourri"—entails choosing *one* primary model and then thoughtfully supplementing it with others. We will briefly suggest some criteria for choosing a primary model and then sketch out a process for blending it with others.

Christian ministers developing a working theology of ministry might consider at least three dimensions of "fit" for the primary model they choose. By including each of these dimensions in the process of their choice, ministers can make a balanced decision that includes their particular Christian traditions, their personal faith and practice, and their local community of service.

First, the model can be appropriate to their particular *theological tradition*, particularly its distinctive ways of thinking about and proclaiming the Christian faith. For example, as we observed in the second chapter, persons in traditions that tend to emphasize an "analogy of being" between God and creation are often attracted to correlational models. More obviously, as we saw in chapter 5, Christians in worship-centered traditions tend toward performance models. Ministers can learn to articulate ways in which their models of ministry both are shaped by and publicly represent their faith tradition.

Second, the model can fit the particular ways in which a minister *personally* appropriates and practices the faith. For example, ministers who understand their faith primarily through story would likely be attracted to narrative models, though those who relate strongly to Christian faith through the arts might tend toward performance models. Through self-examination and the feedback of trusted others, ministers can select a model that authentically matches their personal and pastoral identities.

Finally, the model can fit the *local community*, or communities, in which the minister serves. For example, communities that emphasize Christian teaching might find regulative models particularly valuable, even though communities that emphasize political and social action might find contextual models to be especially attractive. A model that is appropriate to its local Christian community and its surrounding context can generate vision and energy for spiritual growth and ministry action.

Having made a choice—at least a tentative one—of a primary model, ministers can intentionally utilize it to guide both action and reflection in their pastoral practice. The various examples and case studies in this book seek to offer some snapshots of a variety of ways of applying models to specific ministry settings. Since no model is a perfect fit and each model has its characteristic strengths and weaknesses, ministers would predictably want to highlight the strengths and compensate for the weaknesses of their particular choice. The following three-step process illustrates one possible way to blend models in a supplementary way.

First, the minister can reflect upon pastoral practice to identify the specific strengths and weaknesses of the primary model. The many tools and techniques of contemporary ministry studies— such as verbatim interviews, critical incidents, role-plays, case studies, and survey research—can be employed to assist the honest, prayerful reflection at the heart of the process. Concrete, context-specific results are sought in this evaluation. For example, an assessment such as "When I heard Jenny's stories of her childhood experiences at First Korean Church and those of Sam and Sung

Hee, I was better able to understand Jenny's alienation from her parents, but was unable to suggest any concrete actions that might lead to reconciliation or improve the situation for parents and children in the congregation" is far more helpful than "When I use a narrative model in my ministry, understanding is separated from action." Identifying context-specific weaknesses provides specific tests to evaluate the effectiveness of other models.

Second, the minister can choose a supplementary model or models to compensate for the specific weaknesses identified. The summary review in the previous section offers a number of comparisons that might point to supplementary choices. For instance, contextual models provide more opportunities for a self-critical approach than do narrative models. So, one possible way to respond to the example of Jenny's alienation from her parents might be to supplement a narrative model with a contextual one.

Third, the minister can blend the models by applying the supplementary models to the identified areas of weakness in the primary one. Therefore, to continue our example, the situation of Jenny and her parents and that of other families at First Korean Church could be analyzed through the lenses of race, gender, and social class. Such analysis might expand the horizons for ministry to include actions seeking social justice for Koreans living in Valleywood that could be embraced by both Jenny and her parents, thus creating a possible channel for reconciliation. The achievement of some concrete ministry outcome like this might serve as a practical test for the effectiveness of blending a supplementary contextual model with a primary narrative one. The skillful blending of supplementary models with a primary one can do much to enhance the integration of theology and practice in ministry.

Beyond Models: The Mystery of God in Ministry

At the close of this study, we pause to remind ourselves of aspects of the calling of ministry that transcend our investigation.

Christian ministry is more than the skilled implementation of thoughtful connections between theology and practice. It involves standing with persons in community before the mystery of God. The presence of God always points beyond our wise action and our deepest reflection. As Paul testified to the conflict-laden congregation at Corinth:

> For it is the God who said, "Let light shine out of darkness," who has shone in our hearts to give the light of the knowledge of the glory of God in the face of Jesus Christ. But we have this treasure in clay jars, so that it may be made clear that this extraordinary power belongs to God and does not come from us. (2 Cor. 4:6-7)

The models for connecting theology and ministry that we have examined provide a variety of valuable ways to analyze, assess, and guide our ministry. Theological reflection upon ministry is a way to school or discipline our thought and action in service to God. Methods of reflection are vital for the ongoing life of the Christian community and its mission to the world. Yet praise of the mystery of God revealed in Jesus Christ always transcends our most sophisticated, disciplined attempts to understand the works and ways of God amid the brokenness and suffering of our world.

Notes

Preface

1. Charles J. Scalise, *Hermeneutics as Theological Prolegomena: A Canonical Approach* (Macon, Ga.: Mercer University Press, 1994).
2. Charles J. Scalise, *From Scripture to Theology: A Canonical Journey into Hermeneutics* (Downers Grove, Ill.: InterVarsity Press, 1996).

1. Models for Making Connections

1. This chapter is a significantly revised and expanded version of a workshop paper presented to the annual conference of the Society for Pastoral Theology in June 1999. I would like to thank Kerry Dearborn of Seattle Pacific University for her assistance as I developed the workshop presentation and Bonnie Miller-McLemore of Vanderbilt University for feedback following the initial presentation. The material was revised and presented in January 2000 to the Fuller Seminary School of Theology Faculty Forum on theological reflection, supported by the Lilly Foundation.

2. By "doctrines," I simply mean the historic teachings of the Christian faith. Obviously, these vary in significant ways among various Christian faith traditions, denominations, and local communities. I assume (along with much contemporary ecumenical discussion), however, that there is a central group of teachings that may be identified as basic for continuing Christian identity. For further discussion, see especially George A. Lindbeck, *The Nature of Doctrine: Religion and Theology in a Postliberal Age* (Philadelphia: Westminster Press,

1984). For ecumenical efforts to identify a common "core" of Christian beliefs, see Commission on Faith and Order, World Council of Churches, *Confessing One Faith: Towards an Ecumenical Explication of the Apostolic Faith as Expressed in the Nicene-Constantinopolitan Creed (381)*, Faith and Order Paper 140 (Geneva: World Council of Churches, 1987).

3. William C. Placher documents some of the origins of this process in *The Domestication of Transcendence: How Modern Thinking about God Went Wrong* (Louisville, Ky.: Westminster John Knox Press, 1996). Further discussion of this theme is pursued in conjunction with the test case of a regulative approach to the doctrine of revelation in chapter 6.

4. For a historical and theological examination of the use of case studies for critical reflection upon ministry in North American contexts, see my "Historical 'Snapshots' of Ministry: The Changing Language of Case Studies," *Review and Expositor* 96, no. 3 (Summer 1999): 423-40.

5. See Clifford Geertz's advocacy of "thick description" in cultural anthropology in his classic essay, "Thick Description: Toward an Interpretive Theory of Culture," in Clifford Geertz, *The Interpretation of Cultures* (New York: Basic Books, 1973), 3-30. Geertz understands culture as a *context*, not as an abstract symbol system. One can truly understand a culture only by developing a specific acquaintance with many small matters in that culture, which are intelligibly described by an interpreter in "thick" detail. Geertz originally borrowed this term from the philosopher Gilbert Ryle. (Ryle's essays "Thinking and Reflecting" and "The Thinking of Thoughts," found in the second volume of his *Collected Papers*, are cited by Geertz, *Interpretation of Cultures*, 6ff.) For the application of this term to contemporary theology, see Lindbeck, *Nature of Doctrine*, especially 115-16.

6. The details of this case study have been drawn from the experience of a number of students I have known at Fuller Theological Seminary on both the Seattle and Pasadena campuses. Cheryl's name and other identifying features have been altered to protect pastoral confidentiality.

7. In "The Human Web: Reflections on the State of Pastoral Theology" (*Christian Century* 110, no. 11 [April 7, 1993]: 366-69), Bonnie Miller-McLemore proposes that Anton Boisen's classic metaphor of the "living human document" (in *The Exploration of the Inner World: A Study of Mental Disorder and Religious Experience* [New York: Willett, Clark & Co., 1936; reprint New York: Harper & Brothers, 1952; and Philadelphia: University of Pennsylvania Press, 1971]) be altered to the "living human web." This shift not only reflects the advent of a more communal approach to pastoral care and counseling in North America, but also signals a new emphasis upon the congregational context of pastoral care. A revised and expanded version of Miller-McLemore's article documents the argument further ("The Living Human Web: Pastoral Theology at the Turn of the Century," in *Through the Eyes of Women: Insights for Pastoral Care*, ed. Jeanne Stevenson Moessner [Minneapolis, Minn.: Fortress Press,

1996], 9-26.) See also James Newton Poling, *The Abuse of Power: A Theological Problem* (Nashville: Abingdon Press, 1991), especially 126-28), which understands community as a "web of relationships," drawing upon the work of process theologians Bernard Loomer (in "On Committing Yourself to a Relationship," *Process Studies* 16, no. 4 [1987]: 255-63, especially 257) and Bernard Eugene Meland (in *Essays in Constructive Theology: A Process Perspective* [Chicago: Exploration Press, 1988]).

8. For a discussion of the connections between theology and the practice of the Christian life during the early church period, see Stuart George Hall, *Doctrine and Practice in the Early Church* (Grand Rapids, Mich.: Eerdmans, 1992). For a historical analysis of some of these issues, see Hans von Campenhausen, *Ecclesiastical Authority and Spiritual Power in the Church of the First Three Centuries* (Stanford, Calif.: Stanford University Press, 1969).

9. Richard John Neuhaus, ed., *Theological Education and Moral Formation* (Grand Rapids, Mich.: Eerdmans, 1992); the book offers both historical and contemporary reflection on this topic for theological education. See especially Rowan A. Greer, "Who Seeks for a Spring in the Mud? Reflections on the Ordained Ministry in the Fourth Century," 22-55.

10. See E. Brooks Holifield, *A History of Pastoral Care in America: From Salvation to Self-Realization* (Nashville: Abingdon Press, 1983). For a survey of this theme of integration, particularly among evangelical Protestants, see J. D. Carter, "Integration of Psychology and Theology," in *Dictionary of Pastoral Care and Counseling,* ed. Rodney J. Hunter (Nashville: Abingdon Press, 1990), 584-85. For an introduction to some early evangelical discussion, see John D. Carter and Bruce Narramore, *The Integration of Psychology and Theology: An Introduction* (Grand Rapids, Mich.: Zondervan Publishing House, 1979). I have also contributed a brief, theologically focused definition of this theme in my article "Integration," in *The New Dictionary of Pastoral Studies,* ed. Wesley Carr (Grand Rapids, Mich.: Eerdmans, 2002), 179-80.

11. For standard insiders' historical studies of the Clinical Pastoral Education movement, see Robert C. Powell, *Fifty Years of Learning Through Supervised Encounter with Living Human Documents* (New York: The Association for Clinical Pastoral Education, 1975); and, more recently, Charles E. Hall, *Head and Heart: The Story of the Clinical Pastoral Education Movement* (Decatur, Ga.: Journal of Pastoral Care Publications, 1992). For a more critical view, see Holifield's *History of Pastoral Care in America.* Using William McLoughlin's research on revivals and social reform, the American religious historian Robert Fuller has sought to characterize the purpose of the clinical education movement as a desire "to 'jolt the church' into a decidedly new mode of spirituality" ("Rediscovering the Laws of Spiritual Life: The Last Twenty Years of Supervision and Training," *Journal of Supervision and Training in Ministry,* 20 [2000]: 13-40).

12. For example, see Dorothy C. Bass, ed., *Practicing Our Faith: A Way of Life*

for a Searching People (San Francisco: Jossey-Bass Publishers, 1997); and Craig Dykstra, Growing in the Life of Faith: Education and Christian Practices (Louisville, Ky.: Geneva Press, 1999). For a practical discussion of the role of time in Christian observances—particularly sabbath-keeping—see Dorothy C. Bass, Receiving the Day: Christian Practices for Opening the Gift of Time (San Francisco: Jossey-Bass Publishers, 2000).

13. See, for example, Jack Rogers, Claiming the Center: Churches and Conflicting Worldviews (Louisville, Ky.: Westminster John Knox Press, 1995); and Thomas Sine, Cease Fire: Searching for Sanity in America's Culture Wars (Grand Rapids, Mich.: Eerdmans, 1995), and Mustard Seed vs. McWorld: Reinventing Life and Faith for the Future (Grand Rapids, Mich.: Baker Book House, 1999).

14. For my hermeneutical critique of the unreflective use of biblical proof-texts (dicta probantia), see From Scripture to Theology: A Canonical Journey into Hermeneutics (Downers Grove, Ill.: InterVarsity Press, 1996), especially 85-87.

15. Ian G. Barbour, Myths, Models, and Paradigms: A Comparative Study in Science and Religion (New York: Harper & Row, 1974), 6. Other important earlier treatments of the role of models in the philosophical dialogue between religion and natural science include that of Max Black (Models and Metaphors: Studies in Language and Philosophy [Ithaca, N.Y.: Cornell University Press, 1962]) and Ian T. Ramsey (Models and Mystery [London: Oxford University Press, 1964]). Taken together, these works formed the foundation for the work of Avery Dulles on models in theological discourse, discussed below.

16. For example, Kirk E. Farnsworth has advocated a model of "process integration" from an evangelical perspective ("Models for the Integration of Psychology and Theology," Journal of the American Scientific Affiliation 30 [March 1978]: 6-9).

17. For detailed discussion of the use of metaphor, with its "like-unlike" dialectic, in philosophy and literature, see Paul Ricoeur, The Rule of Metaphor: Multidisciplinary Studies of the Creation of Meaning in Language, trans. Robert Czerny (Toronto: University of Toronto, 1977); and Janet Martin Soskice, Metaphor and Religious Language (Oxford: Clarendon Press, 1985).

18. Avery Dulles, Models of Revelation (Garden City, N.Y.: Doubleday, 1983; reprint Maryknoll, N.Y.: Orbis Books, 1992;), 30. See also Dulles's discussion "The Use of Models in Ecclesiology," in his Models of the Church ([Garden City, N.Y.: Doubleday, 1974; expanded edition 1987], 13-30 in the 1974 edition] and his analysis and defense of the use of models in theology in his essay "The Problem of Method: From Scholasticism to Models" in his book The Craft of Theology: From Symbol to System (New York: Crossroad, 1992). For Protestant and evangelical readers, it may be helpful to note that, as Dulles is a Catholic theologian trained in the scholastic system, his use of the term "artificially constructed" does not necessarily connote any opposition to nature or organic metaphors. I would prefer to use the term "socially constructed" to avoid this

difficulty. In both Dulles's view and my own, there is always a place for the mystery of the faith.

19. In *Models of the Church*, Dulles analyzes the Church as: "institution," "mystical communion," "sacrament," "herald," and "servant" (pp. 31-82 in the 1974 edition). In the later, expanded edition of the book, he added the hybrid model "community of disciples" (pp. 204-26).

20. Stephen B. Bevans, *Models of Contextual Theology* (Maryknoll, N.Y.: Orbis Books, 1992), 27. Bevans's typology differs from mine in that it is focused upon kinds of *contextual* theology: translation, anthropological, praxis, synthetic, and transcendental models: "Each model presents a different way of theologizing which takes a particular context seriously" (p. 27). Bevans begins with the assumption that "every authentic theology has been very much rooted in a particular context in some *implicit* or real way" (p. 3, italics mine). Although this is true (perhaps trivially so), it results in minimizing the real *differences* between contextual and other types of theology. So, for example, Bevans claims, "theology of the sixteenth and seventeenth centuries, both Protestant and Catholic, was nothing if not contextual!" (p. 4). Any definition of "contextual theology" that views the propositional theology of Protestant Orthodoxy and the Catholic Reformation as "contextual" has broadened the term so that it is no longer useful for making comparisons. If *all* "authentic theology" becomes contextual, then "contextual" should no longer be used as a qualifying adjective.

21. For my earlier discussion of Dulles's work on models of revelation, see *Hermeneutics As Theological Prolegomena: A Canonical Approach* (Macon, Ga.: Mercer University Press, 1994), 4nn. 13-14; and 28.

22. Since the publication of Thomas S. Kuhn's *The Structure of Scientific Revolutions* (Chicago: University of Chicago Press, 1962), the use of the term "paradigm" has become commonplace in Euro-American theological discussion. It points to a process of both scientific and cultural change that proceeds on the basis of new "standard examples," which purport to describe "reality" while replacing older ones that have become manifestly inadequate. Barbour defines "paradigm" as "a tradition transmitted through historical exemplars" (*Myths, Models, and Paradigms*, 9).

23. Dulles, *Models of the Church*, 26.

24. Such "eclecticism" should be sharply distinguished from "relativism." Although this study clearly assumes that the contemporary historical horizon is now that of "postmodernity," the advocacy of wise eclecticism in pastoral ministry could even be compatible with views that still maintain an Enlightenment-based "consilience"—the interconnection of inductive causal explanations across disciplines as the test of universal truth. For an articulate defense of this traditional epistemology, see Edward O. Wilson, *Consilience: The Unity of Knowledge* (New York: Random House, 1998), especially 8-14. For a classic hermeneutical challenge to objectivism, see Hans-Georg Gadamer, *Truth and Method*, 2nd rev. ed., trans. Joel Weinsheimer and Donald G. Marshall (New

York: Crossroad, 1989), in which the "truth in a work of art" is contrasted to the scientific and historical objectivism.

25. In the early 1960s, Ian Ramsey argued for the superiority of using more than one model to illumine complex situations involving social relations: "Circumstances might be so complex they would best be gripped by not one model but two, and then both models, despite their diversity would be held together by the insight in which both are fulfilled. Each would then be related in its characteristic way to the situation they both claim in different ways to understand" (*Models and Mystery*, 40).

26. Although the persons and communities described in this case study are modeled upon composites of actual individuals and groups, I have significantly altered identifying data to protect confidentiality and prevent any possibility of identification. So, strictly speaking, Valleywood Church and its community are fictitious.

27. See, for example, the emphasis upon the minister as "pastoral director" in H. Richard Niebuhr, *The Purpose of the Church and Its Ministry: Reflections on the Aims of Theological Education* (New York: Harper & Bros., 1956), 79-94, particularly 79-80. For a detailed examination of the changing impact of the clinical education movement upon pastoral care, see Holifield, *History of Pastoral Care in America*.

28. For practical discussion of the relationship between congregational size and numerical church growth, see Alice Mann, *The In-Between Church: Navigating Size Transitions in Congregations* (Bethesda, Md.: Alban Institute, 1998).

29. See Paul Tillich, *Systematic Theology*, 3 vols. (Chicago: University of Chicago Press, 1951–63), especially 1:59-66. Tillich extended this method particularly in his writings about theology of culture: for instance, in *Theology of Culture*, ed. Robert C. Kimball (New York: Oxford University Press, 1959) and *Writings in the Philosophy of Culture*, ed. Michael Palmer (New York: De Gruyter; Berlin: Evangelisches Verlagswerk, 1990). For an insightful discussion of Tillich's important influence upon American pastoral theology, see Holifield, *History of Pastoral Care in America*, especially 324-42.

30. Tracy's work has been particularly influenced by the philosophical hermeneutics of Hans-Georg Gadamer, with its critique of historicism and the subject-object dichotomy of Cartesian knowing. Instead, Gadamer uses the model of truth arising from a work of art as a guide to hermeneutical consciousness.

31. Tracy claims that "this general understanding of theology as the 'mutually critical correlation of the meaning and truth of an interpretation of the Christian fact and the meaning and truth of an interpretation of the contemporary situation' serves as a general rubric informing all forms of authentically theological reflection" ("The Foundations of Practical Theology," in *Practical Theology*, ed. Don S. Browning [San Francisco: Harper & Row, 1983], 65). For

further methodological discussion, see David Tracy, *Blessed Rage for Order: The New Pluralism in Theology* (Chicago: University of Chicago Press, 1996), and *The Analogical Imagination: Christian Theology and the Culture of Pluralism* (New York: Crossroad, 1981). For Tracy's practical application of this method to global issues, see his "Practical Theology in the Situation of Global Pluralism," in *Formation and Reflection: The Promise of Practical Theology*, ed. Lewis S. Mudge and James N. Poling (Philadelphia: Fortress Press, 1987), 139-54.

32. Don S. Browning, *A Fundamental Practical Theology: Descriptive and Strategic Proposals* (Minneapolis, Minn.: Fortress Press, 1991). My preliminary review of Browning's book was published in *Review and Expositor* 90, no. 3 (Summer 1993): 445-46.

33. Diana R. Garland, *Family Ministry: A Comprehensive Guide* (Downers Grove, Ill.: InterVarsity Press, 1999).

34. See Robert J. Schreiter, *Constructing Local Theologies*, rev. ed. (Maryknoll, N.Y.: Orbis Books, 1997) for an example of the use of Catholic missions data from Africa in the development of a culturally shaped contextual theology.

35. See James Cone, *God of the Oppressed* (New York: Seabury Press, 1975) for a systematic study; and Edward P. Wimberly, *Counseling African American Marriages and Families* (Louisville, Ky.: Westminster John Knox Press, 1997) for a practical pastoral care perspective.

36. For one historically informed example, see Justo Gonzaléz, *Mañana: Christian Theology from a Hispanic Perspective* (Nashville: Abingdon Press, 1990).

37. For some pioneering work in this area, see Kósuke Koyama, *Waterbuffalo Theology* (Maryknoll, N.Y.: Orbis Books, 1974), and *Mount Fuji and Mount Sinai: A Critique of Idols* (Maryknoll, N.Y.: Orbis Books, 1985).

38. For the classic introduction to Latin American liberation theology, see Gustavo Gutiérrez, *A Theology of Liberation: History, Politics, and Salvation*, trans. and ed. Caridad Inda and John Eagleson (Maryknoll, N.Y.: Orbis Books, 1973).

39. For pastoral theology, see Bonnie J. Miller-McLemore and Brita L. Gill-Austern, eds., *Feminist and Womanist Pastoral Theology* (Nashville: Abingdon Press, 1999); Christie Cozad Neuger, ed., *The Arts of Ministry: Feminist-Womanist Approaches* (Louisville, Ky.: Westminster John Knox Press, 1996); and Jean Stevenson Moessner, *Through the Eyes of Women: Insights for Pastoral Care* (Minneapolis: Fortress Press, 1996), and *In Her Own Time: Women and Developmental Issues in Pastoral Care* (Minneapolis: Fortress Press, 2000). As feminist critiques of Western theology have argued, much of classical Western theology, although claiming to discuss the God of all humanity, primarily reflects the experience of Caucasian male Christian leaders.

40. For one example, see Anne Primavesi, *From Apocalypse to Genesis: Ecology, Feminism, and Christianity* (Minneapolis: Fortress Press, 1991).

41. Among Catholic pastoral theologians, the twentieth-century develop-

ment of their Thomistic heritage often plays a significant role in interpreting *praxis*. Some of this group particularly rely upon "transcendental" modifications of Aristotelian categories. For example, in his discussion of "the transcendental model," Stephen Bevans points to "Pierre Rousselot, Joseph Marechal, Karl Rahner, and Bernard Lonergan, all of whom attempted to interpret... Thomas Aquinas in terms of modern subjectivity and historical consciousness" (*Models of Contextual Theology*, 97-98). On a less metaphysical level, one might notice the role of "insight" in a practical work like that of Patricia O'Connell Killen and John de Beer (*The Art of Theological Reflection* [New York: Crossroad, 1994], especially 20-45).

42. The origins of the movement have been traced back to H. Richard Niebuhr, *The Meaning of Revelation* (New York: Macmillan, 1941, 1962), especially the section "The Story of Our Life" (pp. 43-90).

43. For a discussion of this crisis, see Ronald F. Thiemann, *Revelation and Theology: The Gospel As Narrated Promise* (Notre Dame, Ind.: University of Notre Dame Press, 1985). See also George Stroup's helpful introduction, *The Promise of Narrative Theology: Recovering the Gospel in the Church* (Atlanta: John Knox Press, 1981), especially "The Hermeneutics of Christian Narrative" (pp. 199-261). I have offered my own recounting of the crisis over the doctrine of revelation in "Revelation and Pastoral Theology: Historical and Methodological Reflections," *Journal of Pastoral Theology* 9 (1999): 89-103.

44. Terrence Tilley's positive response to the narrative theology movement is appropriately entitled *Story Theology* (Wilmington, Del.: Michael Glazier, 1985).

45. James W. McClendon, Jr., *Systematic Theology: Doctrine* (Nashville: Abingdon Press, 1994), especially 41ff. McClendon's first volume in this series, which uses biographical narratives to embody theological reflection, is appropriately entitled *Systematic Theology: Ethics* (Nashville: Abingdon Press, 1986). On the one hand, the work of Stanley Hauerwas in Christian ethics is commonly cited as endorsing a narrative perspective (for example, *Christian Existence: Essays on Church, World, and Living in Between* [Durham, N.C.: Labyrinth Press, 1988], especially "I. The Practice of the Church's Story," [pp. 23-97]). Yet, on the other hand, Hauerwas's identification with Lindbeck's antifoundationalism (cf. the chapter "Regulative Models" in this study) may be clearly seen in his *Against the Nations: War and Survival in a Liberal Society* (Minneapolis, Minn.: Winston Press, 1985), especially 1-9.

46. The universal foundationalism assumed in the Enlightenment legacy has been rejected by many postmodern scholars. See in particular Alasdair MacIntyre's provocative study *After Virtue: A Study in Moral Theory*, 2d ed. (Notre Dame, Ind.: University of Notre Dame Press, 1984), especially chapters 5 and 6, "Why the Enlightenment Project of Justifying Morality Had to Fail" and "Some Consequences of the Failure of the Enlightenment Project."

47. Critical historical studies such as Ellen Charry's *By the Renewing of Your*

Minds: The Pastoral Function of Christian Doctrine (New York: Oxford University Press, 1997) offer some helpful resources for addressing this concern.

48. The case study in chapter 3 represents a significantly revised and expanded version of that in my "Teresa of Avila: Teacher of Evangelical Women?" which first appeared in *CrossCurrents: The Journal of the Association for Religion and Intellectual Life* 46, no. 2 (Spring 1996): 244-49. All rights reserved.

49. Ralph P. Martin, *Worship in the Early Church* (Grand Rapids, Mich.: Eerdmans, 1964), 39. For a detailed survey of historical evidence in the early church period, see Johannes Quasten, *Music and Worship in Pagan and Christian Antiquity*, trans. Boniface Ramsey (Washington, D.C.: National Association of Pastoral Musicians, 1983). For a useful compilation of literary evidence translated into English, see James McKinnon, ed., *Music in Early Christian Literature* (New York: Cambridge University Press, 1987).

50. Frances Young, *Virtuoso Theology: The Bible and Interpretation* (Cleveland, Ohio: Pilgrim Press, 1993). The book was originally published as *The Art of Performance: Towards a Theology of Holy Scripture* (London: Darton, Longman and Todd, 1990). Young points to the similar use of a performance analogy for Scripture in Nicholas Lash, *Theology on the Way to Emmaus* (London: SCM Press, 1986); and in Brian Jenner, "Music in the Sinner's Ear?" (*Epworth Review* 16 [1989]: 35-38).

51. Young, *Virtuoso Theology,* 21.

52. This analysis in chapter 5 represents a significant expansion of my "*Lex Cantandi, Lex Credendi*: Theology and Hymnody," in *Baptist Reflections on Christianity and the Arts: Learning from Beauty: A Tribute to William L. Hendricks,* ed. David M. Rayburn, Daven M. Kari, and Darrell D. Gwaltney (Lewiston, N.Y.: Edwin Mellen Press, 1997), 129-40.

53. A "regulative" approach is based upon "rules" that function like grammatical rules—rules that "regulate" discourse (cf. *regula fidei*—"rule of faith"). It should be clearly distinguished from a legalistic approach.

54. See Lindbeck, *Nature of Doctrine.* Also see Lindbeck's essay, "Scripture, Consensus, and Community," in *Biblical Interpretation in Crisis: The Ratzinger Conference on Bible and Church,* ed. Richard John Neuhaus (Grand Rapids, Mich.: Eerdmans, 1989), 74-101.

55. See for example Stanley Hauerwas's discussion of Lindbeck in the section entitled "On Trying to Be a Performer" (*Against the Nations,* 1-9). Hauerwas confesses, "I do not know if I am a posttraditional or postliberal thinker, but I do know I want to be the kind of performer Lindbeck describes" (p. 1).

56. For an introductory description of this analogy and Lindbeck's application of it to types of theology, see my article "Agreeing on Where We Disagree: Lindbeck's Postliberalism and Pastoral Theology," *Journal of Pastoral Theology,* 8 (1998): 43-49, especially 44-45.

57. Wittgenstein's famous remark is: "Grammar tells what kind of object anything is. (Theology as grammar.)" See Ludwig Wittgenstein, *Philosophical*

Investigations, trans. G. E. M. Anscombe (Oxford: Basil Blackwell, 1953) 1:373. I have discussed the significance of Wittgenstein's remark for theological hermeneutics in *Hermeneutics As Theological Prolegomena*, 33-35.

58. My article "Agreeing on Where We Disagree" (*The Journal of Pastoral Theology* 8 [1998]: 43-49) offers further elaboration of this argument.

59. For further development and illustration of these claims, see my article "Revelation and Pastoral Theology." I also expressed earlier some of my own criticisms and reservations regarding Lindbeck's approach in *Hermeneutics As Theological Prolegomena* (pp. 108-12).

60. For further development of this notion, see my article "Developing a Theological Rationale for Ministry: Some Reflections on the Process of Teaching Pastoral Theology to M.Div. Students," *Journal of Pastoral Theology* 1 (1991): 53-68.

61. Irenaeus, *Adversus haereses*, 4.20.7.

2. Correlational Models

1. For discussion and analysis of this term, see Donald A. Schön, *The Reflective Practitioner: How Professionals Think in Action* (New York: Basic Books, 1983).

2. Tillich's influential Terry lectures entitled *The Courage to Be* (New Haven: Yale University Press, 1952) use this method to survey in broad strokes the history of theology.

3. Paul Tillich, *Systematic Theology*, 3 vols. (Chicago: University of Chicago Press, 1951–63), 1:62. For Tillich's introductory discussion of his method, see especially 1:59-66.

4. Cf. Tillich, *Systematic Theology*, 2:125-35, "The New Being in Jesus as the Christ as the Conquest of Estrangement."

5. Hiltner called for "a two-way street" in the relationship between theology and culture in his *Preface to Pastoral Theology* (Nashville: Abingdon Press, 1958), 223.

6. For Tracy's proposal of this hermeneutical method, see David Tracy, *Blessed Rage for Order: The New Pluralism in Theology* (Chicago: University of Chicago Press, 1996) and *The Analogical Imagination: Christian Theology and the Culture of Pluralism* (New York: Crossroad, 1981). Tracy discusses the application of his method to practical and pastoral theology in "The Foundations of Practical Theology," in *Practical Theology: The Emerging Field in Theology, Church, and World*, ed. Don S. Browning (San Francisco: Harper & Row, 1983), 61-82. Werner Jeanrond provides a helpful introductory overview in "Correlational Theology and the Chicago School," in *Introduction to Christian Theology: Contemporary North American Perspectives*, ed. Roger A. Badham (Louisville, Ky.: Westminster John Knox Press, 1998), 137-53.

7. Tracy's approach here is directly indebted to the philosophical

hermeneutics of Hans-Georg Gadamer. In *Truth and Method*, 2nd rev. ed. (trans. Joel Weinsheimer and Donald G. Marshall [New York: Crossroad, 1989]), Gadamer shows that a classic text develops through a long series of historical horizons of meaning.

8. For example, Lewis S. Mudge and James N. Poling in "Editors' Introduction" to *Formation and Reflection: The Promise of Practical Theology* (Philadelphia: Fortress Press, 1987), use Tracy's method as a framework for interpreting all of the contributions to this volume (pp. xiii-xxxvi).

9. Don S. Browning, *A Fundamental Practical Theology: Descriptive and Strategic Proposals* (Minneapolis, Minn.: Fortress Press, 1991). See especially pp. 44-47 for Browning's discussion of his adaptation of Tracy's revised correlational approach. See also Don S. Browning, "The Past and Possible Future of Religion and Psychological Studies," in *Religion and Psychology: Mapping the Terrain*, ed. Diane Jonte-Pace and William B. Parsons (New York: Routledge, 2001), 165-80. Jonte-Pace and Parsons have compiled a useful survey of much of the contemporary diversity in the field of religion and psychological studies.

10. Browning, *Fundamental Practical Theology*, 105-9. For Browning's earlier work in developing this five-level model, see especially his *Religious Ethics and Pastoral Care* (Philadelphia: Fortress Press, 1983).

11. In chapter 6 of *Fundamental Practical Theology*, Browning offers his "descriptive theology" of the Wiltshire Church in dialogue with a number of social scientific studies of the congregation.

12. In chapter 9, Browning offers his "strategic practical theology" of the Church of the Covenant in dialogue with a variety of contemporary models of Christian education.

13. Browning, *Fundamental Practical Theology*, 244.

14. Ibid.

15. Ibid., 245.

16. Ibid., 254.

17. Ibid., 261.

18. Ibid., 257.

19. Ibid., 266.

20. More specifically, Browning uses a view of Niebuhr's ethic of equal regard, which is reconstructed through the work of the Catholic moral theologian Louis Janssens. Earlier in the book (pp. 158-64), Browning summarizes the details of this view, which downplays the role of love as self-sacrifice in Niebuhr in favor of the Catholic tradition of love as *caritas*, interpreted as mutuality and equal regard.

21. Browning, *Fundamental Practical Theology*, 266, my emphasis. The following discussion offers some evidence of the pastor's suspicion of the liberal Protestant ethic that underlies Browning's interpretation.

22. Ibid., my emphasis.

23. Browning is particularly dependent upon David Gutman's research in

comparative anthropology and evolutionary biology to support his views of life cycle theory (*Fundamental Practical Theology*, 273-77).

24. Ibid., 277.

25. Ibid., 261.

26. As Browning admits, "There was no honest way to study this church without becoming more conscious of the preunderstandings I brought with me" (Ibid., 267).

27. Elaine L. Graham, *Transforming Practice: Pastoral Theology in an Age of Uncertainty* (London: Mowbray, 1996), 91.

28. For a detailed historical analysis of cultural factors influencing American evangelicalism, see George M. Marsden, *Fundamentalism and American Culture: The Shaping of Twentieth-Century Evangelicalism, 1870–1925* (New York: Oxford University Press, 1980).

29. For example, see Gary R. Collins with H. Newton Malony, *Psychology and Theology: Prospects for Integration* (Nashville: Abingdon Press, 1981). William A. Sanderson's "Christian Empiricism As an Integrating Perspective in Psychology and Theology" (*Christian Scholars Review* 8 [1978]: 32-41) offers a different evangelical perspective. For a critical response to Sanderson's view, see David L. Wolfe, "Reflections on Christian Empiricism: Thoughts on William Sanderson's Proposal" (*Christian Scholars Review* 8 [1978]: 42-45).

30. Leland Virgil Eliason, "A Critique of Approaches to Integrating Psychology and Theology Within Selected Evangelical Seminaries" (Th.D. diss., Boston University Graduate School, 1983). Eliason surveyed all professors of pastoral care and counseling in fifty-one evangelical seminaries in the United States and Canada. Forty-two responses (including eleven incomplete) to Eliason's four-page questionnaire were received from the eighty-two professors surveyed.

31. Perhaps the most visible and outspoken advocate of this view is the very conservative, Reformed counselor Jay E. Adams, who advocated "nouthetic counseling." Adams originally set forth his controversial method in *Competent to Counsel* (Nutley, N.J.: Presbyterian and Reformed Publishing Co., 1970).

32. Eliason, "Critique of Approaches," 63, emphasis added. Among a wide range of writers included in this category, Eliason particularly focuses upon the popular work of Gary Collins, who offers a detailed account of his approach in *Christian Counseling: A Comprehensive Guide* (Waco, Tex.: Word Books, 1980).

33. Eliason, "Critique of Approaches," 65-67.

34. Hilner's *Preface to Pastoral Theology* advocates an "operation-centered" approach to "Christian shepherding."

35. Eliason, "Critique of Approaches," 73-86. Among the diverse members of this category, Eliason pays particular attention to the work of three Baptist professors of pastoral care: Wayne E. Oates, Edward Thornton, and C. W. Brister.

36. Diana R. Garland, *Family Ministry: A Comprehensive Guide* (Downers Grove, Ill.: InterVarsity Press, 1999).

37. Ibid., 52-82. For a recent application of an ecosystemic model of family to pastoral care and counseling, see E. Wayne Hill and Carol Anderson Darling, "Using the Family Ecosystem Model to Enhance Pastoral Care and Counseling," *The Journal of Pastoral Care* 55, no. 3 (2001): 247-57.

38. Garland, *Family Ministry*, 55.

39. Ibid., 50.

40. Ibid.

41. Ibid., 299-364.

42. Ibid., 154. The study Garland cites is M. S. Forgatch, "Patterns and Outcome in Family Problem Solving: The Disrupting Effect of Negative Emotion," *Journal of Marriage and the Family* 51 (1989): 115-24.

43. Garland, *Family Ministry*, 163. The quotation cited is taken from I. C. Heyward, *The Redemption of God: A Theology of Mutual Relation* (New York: University Press of America, 1988), 44. The social scientific study Garland cites is B. F. Moss and A. I. Schwebel, "Defining Intimacy in Romantic Relationships," *Family Relations* 42, no. 1 (1993): 31-37.

44. Of course, the process of "weaving," by its nature, involves the selection of a relatively few possibilities from the range of resources offered in both Scripture and the human sciences.

45. Garland, *Family Ministry*, 96-109.

46. Ibid., 102.

47. E. Brooks Holifield, *A History of Pastoral Care in America: From Salvation to Self-Realization* (Nashville: Abingdon Press, 1983).

48. Purpose Statement of the *Journal of Pastoral Theology* 8 (1998): 88, my emphasis.

49. Rebecca Chopp, "Practical Theology and Liberation," in Mudge and Poling, eds., *Formation and Reflection*, 120-38, especially 121, 128. In her critique of the bourgeois liberalism of these correlational approaches, Chopp is following the liberation theology of Johann Baptist Metz, especially *The Emergent Church: The Future of Christianity in a Postbourgeois World*, trans. Peter Mann (New York: Crossroad, 1981).

50. Critiques of correlational models, both from liberation theologians and from the conservative religious right, sound this challenge from different directions. In addition, advocates of a Barthian approach to pastoral care offer a revelation-centered opposition to correlation. For a classic, though dated, exposition of a Barthian approach, see Eduard Thurneysen, *A Theology of Pastoral Care*, trans. Jack A. Worthington and Thomas Wieser (Richmond, Va.: John Knox Press, 1962). Thurneysen's famous dictum proclaims, "Pastoral care exists in the church as the communication of the Word of God to individuals" (p. 11). More recently, Deborah van Deusen Hunsinger's *Theology and Pastoral Counseling: A New Interdisciplinary Approach* (Grand Rapids, Mich.: Eerdmans, 1995) seeks to offer a Barthian perspective of pastoral counseling informed by psychoanalytic theory.

51. It should be emphasized that it is not the intention of this research to stake out and defend a position in these debates. Rather, this research seeks to evaluate the usefulness of various theological models for ministry in a specific case study.

3. Contextual Models

1. For example, Loren Townsend has recently suggested a contextual method for pastoral care supervision based in liberation theology ("Theological Reflection, Pastoral Counseling, and Supervision," *The Journal of Pastoral Theology* 12, no. 1 [2002]: 63-74). Townsend also very briefly examines correlational approaches and "formational motifs."

2. See, for example, Justin's *First Apology*, chap. 46, and *Second Apology*, chap. 13.

3. See particularly Clement's *Stromateis*, for example, 1.5.28.

4. Tatian's rigorist *Address to the Greeks* makes a bitter attack against Greek culture.

5. Tertullian's *On the Prescription of Heretics*, chap. 7, contains the most famous statement of this view.

6. See especially Friedrich Schleiermacher, *Speeches on Religion to Its Cultured Despisers*, trans. John Oman (New York: Harper and Row, 1958).

7. The term "masters of suspicion" is Paul Ricoeur's. See his essay "Psychoanalysis and the Movement of Contemporary Culture," trans. Willis Domingo, in Paul Ricoeur, *The Conflict of Interpretations: Essays in Hermeneutics*, ed. Don Ihde (Evanston, Ill.: Northwestern University Press, 1974), 121-59, especially 148-50. See also *Paul Ricoeur, Freud and Philosophy: An Essay on Interpretation*, trans. Denis Savage (New Haven, Conn.: Yale University Press, 1970), 32-36.

8. Stephen B. Bevans, *Models of Contextual Theology* (Maryknoll, N.Y.: Orbis Books, 1992), 6.

9. Among evangelical Protestant missiologists, see Charles H. Kraft, *Christianity in Culture: A Study in Dynamic Biblical Theologizing in Cross-Cultural Perspective* (Maryknoll, N.Y.: Orbis Books, 1979); and David J. Hesselgrave and Edward Rommen, *Contextualization: Meanings, Methods, and Models* (Pasadena, Calif.: William Carey Library, 2000). Kraft's work is often cited as an example of a "translation" approach to cross-cultural theology.

10. Robert J. Schreiter, *Constructing Local Theologies* (Maryknoll, N.Y.: Orbis Books, 1985).

11. Vincent K. Donovan, *Christianity Rediscovered*, 2nd ed. (Maryknoll, N.Y.: Orbis Books, 1982). For an assessment of the strengths and weaknesses of Donovan's "adaptation approach" to Christian mission, see Schreiter, *Constructing Local Theologies*, 11-12.

12. See, for instance, Carroll A. Watkins Ali, "A Womanist Search for

Sources," in Bonnie J. Miller-McLemore and Brita L. Gill-Austern, eds., *Feminist and Womanist Pastoral Theology* (Nashville: Abingdon Press, 1999), 51-64.

13. For a Catholic church-centered example that rejects this pattern, see George H. Tavard, *A Theology for Ministry* (Wilmington, Del.: Michael Glazier, 1983), particularly chap. 3, "Culture as Context." For examples of evangelical, biblically centered approaches that reject this pattern, see Hesselgrave and Ramen, *Contextualization*.

14. Given the abundance of material on Latin American liberation theology available in English, I will simply recommend Philip Berryman's *Liberation Theology: Essential Facts about the Revolutionary Movement in Latin America—and Beyond* (Philadelphia: Temple University Press, 1987) for readers who seek a balanced, brief introduction. For an introduction that complements Berryman with a more theological focus, see Leonardo Boff and Clodovis Boff, *Introducing Liberation Theology*, trans. Paul Burns (Maryknoll, N.Y.: Orbis Books, 1987).

15. Schreiter makes and develops this distinction in *Constructing Local Theologies*, 12-16.

16. Ibid., 15.

17. Besides the Hegelian and Marxist concepts of dialectic, other possible antecedents for the understanding of *praxis* in liberation theology include the critical hermeneutics of the Frankfurt School and the writings of Paolo Freire.

18. Bevans, *Models of Contextual Theology*, 65.

19. Stephen Pattison, *Pastoral Care and Liberation Theology* (New York: Cambridge University Press, 1994).

20. Ibid., 12.

21. See Juan Luis Segundo, *The Liberation of Theology*, trans. John Drury (Maryknoll, N.Y.: Orbis Books, 1976) for Segundo's treatment of the hermeneutic circle. Pattison's description of Segundo's work may be found in *Liberation Theology* (pp. 51-52).

22. Pattison, *Liberation Theology*, 59. Pattison describes and defends his method on pp. 60-79.

23. Ibid., 60-62.

24. Ibid., 102.

25. Ibid., 103.

26. Ibid., 150-63.

27. Ibid., 164.

28. Ibid., 203.

29. Ibid., 217.

30. Ibid., 222-23.

31. Ibid., 234. For another dramatic example of this difficulty, see Pattison's response to the sixth principle, which concludes, "Again, it all depends on who a pastor wants to identify with and be useful to" (p. 238).

32. Elaine Graham offers a detailed treatment of the category of gender in the

social and human sciences and its relation to theology in *Making the Difference: Gender, Personhood, and Theology* (Minneapolis, Minn.: Fortress Press, 1996).

33. Kathleen J. Greider, Gloria A. Johnson, and Kristen J. Leslie, "Three Decades of Women Writing for Our Lives," in Miller-McLemore and Gill-Austern, *Feminist and Womanist Pastoral Theology*, 21-50. As the authors observe (pp. 49-50 n. 2), not all of these women writers would identify themselves and their method as "feminist" or "womanist," although these perspectives have certainly predominated among women writing professionally in pastoral theology and pastoral care and counseling.

34. Ibid., 22. The authors adopted the phrase "communal contextual paradigm" from John Patton's *Pastoral Care in Context: An Introduction to Pastoral Care* (Louisville, Ky.: Westminster John Knox Press, 1993).

35. This indistinct category is meant "to signal our assessment that the discipline utilizes theological methods and categories to the extent that they are adequate to the needs of human souls searching—personally and collectively—for God" (Greider, Johnson, and Leslie, "Women Writing," 40).

36. Ibid., 33.

37. Ibid., 33-35.

38. Christie Cozad Neuger, "Women and Relationality," in Miller-McLemore and Gill-Austern, *Feminist and Womanist Pastoral Theology*, 117.

39. For example, see Jeanne Stevenson-Moessner, ed., *In Her Own Time: Women and Developmental Issues in Pastoral Care* (Minneapolis: Fortress Press, 2000), in which eighteen women writers examine a diverse range of topics across the life span of American women.

40. For a discussion of the debates between essentialism and constructivism in regard to relationality, see Neuger, "Women and Relationality," 119-21. Neuger seeks to modify the relativism inherent in pure constructivism by advocating Linell Cady's "historicist construal of identity," which locates identity in a bounded but changing sociohistorical context (p. 128).

41. For some international discussion of the cultural context of feminist theology, see Denise M. Ackermann and Riet Bons-Storm, eds., *Liberating Faith Practices: Feminist Practical Theologies in Context* (Leuven: Peeters, 1998). The articles in this volume developed out of a conference of the International Academy of Practical Theology.

42. Neuger, "Women and Relationality," 131-32, my emphasis.

43. Pamela D. Couture, "Pastoral Theology as Art," in Miller-McLemore and Gill-Austern, *Feminist and Womanist Pastoral Theology*, 175-76.

44. Rosemary Radford Ruether offers some important initial discussion of this question in "Feminism and Religious Faith: Renewal or New Creation?" *Religion and Intellectual Life* 3, no. 2 (Winter 1986): 7-20.

45. As Bonnie Miller-McLemore and Brita Gill-Austern promise, "We await eagerly to hear more from the voices of African American, Hispanic American, and Asian American sisters emerging on the horizons of our field, as well as our

sisters in other parts of the world not represented in this volume" (*Feminist and Womanist Pastoral Theology*, 19).

46. See Marsha Foster Boyd and Carolyn Stahl Bohler, "Womanist-Feminist Alliances: Meeting on the Bridge," in ibid., 189-209, especially pp. 195-97.

47. Watkins Ali, "Womanist Search," 64.

48. For example, see the essays in Christie Cozad Neuger, *The Arts of Ministry: Feminist-Womanist Approaches* (Louisville, Ky.: Westminster John Knox Press, 1996).

49. Rebecca S. Chopp, *Saving Work: Feminist Practices of Theological Education* (Louisville, Ky.: Westminster John Knox Press, 1995).

50. Brita L. Gill-Austern, "Pedagogy Under the Influence of Feminism and Womanism," in Miller-McLemore and Gill-Austern, *Feminist and Womanist Pastoral Theology*, 151.

51. Doehring characterizes her feminist perspective as "poststructuralist," "contextual," and "pragmatic." In Carrie Doehring, "A Method of Feminist Pastoral Theology," in Miller-McLemore and Gill-Austern, *Feminist and Womanist Pastoral Theology*, 101-2.

52. Ibid., 102.

53. The first three of these categories of pastoral function were developed by Seward Hiltner in *Preface to Pastoral Theology* (Nashville: Abingdon Press, 1958), with the fourth added in the work of William A. Clebsch and Charles R. Jaekle, *Pastoral Care in Historical Perspective* (New York: J. Aronson, 1964; reprint, Englewood Cliffs, N.J.: Prentice Hall, 1983).

54. Bonnie Miller-McLemore, "Feminist Theory in Pastoral Theology," in Miller-McLemore and Gill-Austern, *Feminist and Womanist Pastoral Theology*, 81.

55. Watkins Ali, "Womanist Search," 53-54, 61-63. This article reflects research from her 1998 doctoral dissertation at the University of Denver and Iliff School of Theology.

56. Another insightful essay that seeks to reconceptualize care from a feminist perspective is Kathleen D. Billman, "Pastoral Care as an Art of Community," in *Arts of Ministry*, 10-38.

57. Neuger, "Women and Relationality," 128. For example, the ideological pursuit of identity politics in postmodernity can obscure the aspects of *common* humanity (e.g., humanity created in the image of God), which are essential to the message of the gospel. This idea used to be called "human nature" and included the *Imago Dei*.

58. This description especially characterizes Roman Catholic models shaped by the new perspective on the church's role in the world proclaimed by Vatican II. See *Pastoral Constitution on the Church in the Modern World (Gaudium et Spes)* (7 December 1965): especially paragraph 4. Cf. Pope John XXIII's earlier use of the "signs of the times" theme in the famous encyclical *Pacem in Terris* (11 April 1963): especially paragraphs 126-29.

59. It is significant for this argument to note that a norm may be *generalizable* without necessarily having to be *universal*.

60. Feminist theologians might respond to this criticism by arguing for a contextual determination of justice. Rather than a "one-size-fits-all" type of justice, they could claim that justice *will be determined* through the struggle to achieve it in specific contexts of oppression. This view assumes that justice, though always incomplete, is in the process of being "birthed." I am indebted to conversations with Lisa McCullough for the insights of this counterargument.

61. For a well-informed and articulate evangelical statement of this view, see Stanley J. Grenz, *Welcoming But Not Affirming: An Evangelical Response to Homosexuality* (Louisville, Ky.: Westminster John Knox Press, 1998).

4. Narrative Models

1. See the classic essay of Stephen Crites describing and defending this view, "The Narrative Quality of Experience," *Journal of the American Academy of Religion* 39, no. 3 (September 1971): 291-311. Crites's musical analogy offers an experiential point of connection between narrative models and performance models. For an introductory explanation of Crites's rather technical prose, see Terrence Tilley, *Story Theology* (Wilmington, Del.: Michael Glazier, 1985), 23-26.

2. In Crites's terminology our human experience *is* "an incipient story" (Crites, "Narrative Quality," 297).

3. In the philosophical study of the nature of knowledge (epistemology), the term "foundations" refers to universal beliefs and experiences, which are assumed to be certain in themselves and upon which other knowledge depends in a system of beliefs. For a helpful introduction to nonfoundationalism and its implications for theology, see John E. Thiel, *Nonfoundationalism*, Guides to Theological Inquiry Series (Minneapolis, Minn.: Fortress Press, 1994). A critique of the failure of the foundationalist "Enlightenment project" in moral philosophy is provided in Alasdair MacIntyre, *After Virtue: A Study in Moral Theory*, 2nd ed. (Notre Dame, Ind.: University of Notre Dame Press, 1984).

4. For a somewhat overdrawn statement of this struggle in biblical studies, see Gerhard Maier, *The End of the Historical-Critical Method*, trans. Edwin W. Leverenz and Rudolph F. Norden (St. Louis, Mo.: Concordia Publishing House, 1977). For a useful survey of twentieth-century theology from an evangelical perspective, see Stanley J. Grenz and Roger E. Olson, *20th-Century Theology: God and the World in a Transitional Age* (Downers Grove, Ill.: InterVarsity Press, 1992).

5. Ronald Thiemann helpfully illustrates the problem across a spectrum of Protestant theology in *Revelation and Theology: The Gospel as Narrated Promise* (Notre Dame, Ind.: University of Notre Dame Press, 1985), especially 9-46.

6. See William Placher's historical tracing of this problem in *The*

Domestication of Transcendence: How Modern Thinking About God Went Wrong (Louisville, Ky.: Westminster John Knox Press, 1996).

7. For analysis of the "historylike" character of biblical narratives, see Hans W. Frei, *The Eclipse of Biblical Narrative: A Study of Eighteenth- and Nineteenth-Century Hermeneutics* (New Haven, Conn.: Yale University Press, 1974).

8. For helpful introductions to the early years of the narrative theology movement, see George Stroup, *The Promise of Narrative Theology: Recovering the Gospel in the Church* (Atlanta: John Knox Press, 1981) and Tilley, *Story Theology*. For a more recent rendering of narrative theology in a "baptist" mode, see James W. McClendon Jr., *Systematic Theology: Doctrine*, vol. 2 (Nashville: Abingdon Press, 1994) and *Systematic Theology: Witness*, vol. 3 (Nashville: Abingdon Press, 2000).

9. Justo González, *The Story of Christianity*, 2 vols: Vol. 1, *The Early Church to the Dawn of the Reformation*, and Volume 2, *The Reformation to the Present Day* (San Francisco: Harper & Row, 1984).

10. Roger E. Olson, *The Story of Christian Theology: Twenty Centuries of Tradition and Reform* (Downers Grove, Ill.: InterVarsity Press, 1999), 13-23.

11. Gotthold Ephraim Lessing declared that there was an "ugly ditch" between "the accidental truths of history" and "the necessary truths of reason" in his essay "On the Proof of the Spirit and of Power" (1777), in *Lessing's Theological Writings*, ed. Henry Chadwick (Stanford, Calif.: Stanford University Press, 1956), 51-56.

12. See James W. McClendon, Jr., *Biography As Theology: How Life Stories Can Remake Today's Theology* (1974; reprint, Philadelphia: Trinity Press International, 1990). I include the writing of critical biography as a subset of historiography, despite an awareness of the limitations of the "great men and women of history" approach frequently promoted by "historical biography."

13. For example, see Paul Ricoeur, "The Hermeneutics of Testimony," trans. David E. Stewart and Charles E. Regan, in Paul Ricoeur, *Essays on Biblical Interpretation*, ed. Lewis S. Mudge ([Philadelphia: Fortress Press, 1980], 119-54), and McClendon, *Witness*. For an examination of the place of testimony as a Christian practice, see Thomas Hoyt, Jr., "Testimony," in *Practicing Our Faith: A Way of Life for Searching People*, ed. Dorothy C. Bass (San Francisco: Jossey-Bass Publishers, 1997), 91-104.

14. The term "hermeneutical circle" refers here to the pattern of mutual interaction between a text (or other piece of Christian tradition) and a ministry situation. In circular fashion the text interprets the situation and the situation illumines the text. Friedrich Schleiermacher developed the idea of the hermeneutical circle to refer to the interaction between a text and a reader, but later philosophical hermeneutics has expanded the discussion to refer to a wider range of interpretive activity. For a discussion of the hermeneutical circle from the perspective of Hans-Georg Gadamer's hermeneutics, see David Couzens

Hoy, *The Critical Circle: Literature, History, and Philosophical Hermeneutics* (Berkeley: University of California Press, 1978).

15. Boisen developed the metaphor to describe the educational task of theology students whom he brought to work in the hospital. In *The Exploration of the Inner World: A Study of Mental Disorder and Religious Experience* (New York: Willett, Clark & Company, 1936; reprints, New York: Harper & Brothers, 1952, and Philadelphia: University of Pennsylvania, 1971). Boisen declares, "I was much concerned that theological students should have the opportunity to go to first-hand sources for their knowledge of human nature. I wanted them to learn to read human documents as well as books" (p. 10).

16. Charles V. Gerkin, *The Living Human Document: Re-Visioning Pastoral Counseling in a Hermeneutical Model* (Nashville: Abingdon Press, 1984), especially chap. 2, "The Living Human Document: Boisen's Image as Paradigm" (pp. 37-54).

17. Gerkin also discusses nineteenth-century contributions to hermeneutics by Friedrich Schleiermacher and Wilhelm Dilthey (*Living Human Document*, 40-44), making particular use of Dilthey's idea of a "hermeneutical detour" through reflection.

18. Charles V. Gerkin, *Widening the Horizons: Pastoral Responses to a Fragmented Society* (Philadelphia: Westminster Press, 1986), 22.

19. Gerkin (*Widening the Horizons*, 43-48) adopts Michael Goldberg's typology for narrative theology: "structuring the story," "following the story" and "enacting the story" (Michael Goldberg, *Theology and Narrative: A Critical Introduction* [Nashville: Abingdon Press, 1982], chap. 5).

20. Gerkin, *Widening the Horizons*, 76-97. The community that Gerkin chose was rather homogenous—"approximately 13,000 people in a somewhat mountainous area of a southeastern state" (p. 76).

21. Ellen T. Charry, *By the Renewing of Your Minds: The Pastoral Function of Christian Doctrine* (New York: Oxford University Press, 1997). Charry coins the term "aretegenic" based upon the Greek term for virtue or goodness. She examines Paul (and also Ephesians), Matthew (especially the Sermon on the Mount), Athanasius, Basil, Augustine, Anselm, Aquinas, Julian of Norwich, and Calvin. Her critical historical studies go beyond the more biographical approaches of other narrative theology.

22. A previous version of this case study appeared as "Teresa of Avila: Teacher of Evangelical Women?" *Cross Currents: The Journal of the Association of Religion and Intellectual Life* 46, no. 2 (Spring 1996): 244-49. The article has been significantly revised and expanded for this chapter.

23. For reliable English translations of Teresa's writings, see Kieran Kavanaugh and Otilio Rodríguez, trans., *The Collected Works of St. Teresa of Avila*, 3 vols. (Washington, D.C.: Institute of Carmelite Studies, 1976, 1980, 1985). I have also consulted the recent Spanish edition, (Teresa de Jesús, *Obras Completas*, ed. Maximiliano Herráiz [Salamanca: Ediciones Sigueme, 1997]), which contains Teresa's extensive extant letters.

24. Alexander Whyte, *Santa Teresa, An Appreciation* (Edinburg and London: Oliphant Anderson & Ferrier, 1897), 9.

25. Gillian T. W. Ahlgren, *Teresa of Avila and the Politics of Sanctity* (Ithaca, N.Y.: Cornell University Press, 1996), 163.

26. Angeles Arrien, foreword to *Embracing God: Praying with Teresa of Avila*, by Dwight H. Judy (Nashville: Abingdon Press, 1996), 10.

27. "Classics of Christian Devotion" class, The Southern Baptist Theological Seminary, Louisville, Kentucky, March 31, 1994.

28. Ibid.

29. Summary of Student Comments from Course Evaluations, "Classics of Christian Devotion," May 10, 1994.

30. Class handout, Student presentation on Teresa of Avila, "The Church and Western Civilization" course, Lutheran Bible Institute of Seattle, November 10, 1994.

31. After class discussion, "The Church and Western Civilization" course, Lutheran Bible Institute of Seattle, November 10, 1994.

32. Oral course evaluation, "The Church and Western Civilization," Lutheran Bible Institute of Seattle, December 1, 1994.

33. The basic modern critical biography for Teresa is Efrén de la Madre de Dios and Otger Steggink, *Tiempo y vida de Santa Teresa*, 2d ed. (Madrid: La Editorial Católica, 1977). Steven Clissold's *St. Teresa of Avila* (London: Sheldon Press, 1979; reprint, New York: Seabury Press, 1982) is still the most reliable English biographical summary, though now somewhat dated. The older biographies of E. Allison Peers, *Mother of Carmel: A Portrait of St. Teresa of Jesus* (New York: Morehouse-Gorham Co., 1946), and Marcelle Auclair (*St. Teresa of Avila*, trans. Kathleen Pond [New York: Pantheon, 1953], make for lively and insightful reading, but are now seriously dated, particularly Auclair's ignoring Teresa's *converso* background. Victoria Lincoln's detailed *Teresa, a Woman: A Biography of Teresa of Avila*, ed. Elias Rivers and Antonio T. de Nicolás (Albany, N.Y.: State University of New York Press, 1984) unfortunately often makes speculative assertions which outrun the evidence. Cathleen Medwick's recent *Teresa of Avila: The Progress of a Soul* (New York: Alfred A. Knopf, 1999) is delightful reading, despite occasional lapses into speculation. (For my review of Medwick's book, see *Church History* 69 no. 4 [December 2000]: 890-92.)

34. For examples of tensions concerning the religious role of women between Teresa and the censors of the Inquisition, see the following passages from *The Way of Perfection*, in Kavanaugh and Rodriguez, *Collected Works*, vol. 2: 3.7 (pp. 50-51), 21.3 (p. 118), 21.8 (p. 120), 22.8 (pp. 124-125), 42.4 (p. 203), and 42.5 (p. 204).

35. For example, see Teresa's lament at the beginning of *The Way of Perfection*: "At that time news reached me of the harm being done in *France* and of the havoc the Lutherans had caused and how much this miserable sect was growing" (1.2, Kavanaugh and Rodriguez, *Collected Works*, vol. 2, p. 41, my emphasis).

36. Teresa, *The Foundations* 32:46, Kavanaugh and Rodriguez, *Collected Works*, vol. 3, p. 306.

37. Joseph F. Chorpenning, *The Divine Romance: Teresa of Avila's Narrative Theology* (Chicago: Loyola University Press, 1992). Following Northrop Frye's grammar of narrative (found especially in *The Secular Scripture: A Study of the Structure of Romance* [1976; reprint, Cambridge, Mass.: Harvard University Press, 1982]), Chorpenning argues for the narrative unity of Teresa's works as romances which use literary images (archetypes) to present her theology in story form. For Chorpenning's earlier work on the transference of literary images in the development of Teresa's writings, see "The Monastery, Paradise, and the Castle: Literary Images and Spiritual Development in St. Teresa of Avila," *Bulletin of Hispanic Studies*, 62 (1985): 245-57.

38. Rowan Williams's perceptive introduction, *Teresa of Avila* (Harrisburg, Pa.: Morehouse Publishing, 1991) helpfully summarizes the results of much of this recent technical study.

39. Ibid., 16.

40. A tax exemption case involving Teresa's father in the Court of Appeal in Valladolid provides the limited information we possess on this matter (Ibid., 11-12).

41. The discovery of this hidden aspect of Teresa's story may account for much of the shift in historical assessment of Teresa. When writers of previous generations described Teresa, they falsely assumed that she embodied the "pure-blooded" Spanish ideal *(limpieza de sangre)*. For example, Alexander Whyte wrongly rhapsodizes that "no one who ever conversed with [Teresa] could for a moment fail to observe that the oldest and best blood of Spain mantled in her cheek and shone in her eye" *(Santa Teresa, 4)*.

42. For a helpful introduction to theological, historical and practical issues regarding women ministers serving in North American evangelical churches, see Stanley J. Grenz with Denise Muir Kjesbo, *Women in the Church: A Biblical Theology of Women in Ministry* (Downers Grove, Ill.: InterVarsity Press, 1995).

43. Since the Middle Ages, the Roman Catholic Church has honored a select few theologians with this title in recognition of their outstanding contributions and sanctity.

44. Perhaps the most famous of these was Isabel de la Cruz, who was arrested in 1524 (Williams, *Teresa*, 28ff.).

45. As Carole Slade argues, Teresa "transformed judicial confession, a genre that presumed the guilt of the narrator, into a vehicle for self-defense" *(St. Teresa of Avila, Author of a Heroic Life* [Berkeley: University of California Press, 1995], p. xii).

46. Ahlgren, *Teresa and Politics*, 27.

47. Ibid., 64. "If Teresa's works are viewed in their historical context, the challenges she encountered follow naturally from the climate of suspicion surrounding women's spiritual experiences" (ibid.).

48. The Spanish title of this work, *Las Moradas*, means "the dwellings" or "mansions."

49. Teresa, *The Interior Castle,* 6.4, Kavanaugh and Rodriguez, *Collected Works,* vol. 2, p. 128.

50. Teresa, *Interior Castle,* 3.1, quotation from translation of E. Allison Peers (New York: Doubleday [Image], 1961, rpt. 1989), 56.

51. Alison Weber, *Teresa of Avila and the Rhetoric of Femininity* (Princeton, N.J.: Princeton University Press, 1990), 15.

52. E. Allison Peers, *Studies of the Spanish Mystics,* vol. 1, 2nd rev. ed. (New York: Macmillan, 1951), 171. Chapter 4 (pp. 107-81) is devoted entirely to Teresa.

53. Weber, *Teresa and Rhetoric,* 145-46.

54. Ahlgren, *Teresa and Politics,* 152.

55. Ibid., 69.

56. Weber, *Teresa and Rhetoric,* 34-35.

57. For a discussion of Teresa's rhetorical use of *mujercilla* and *mujercita,* see Weber, *Teresa and Rhetoric,* 35-41.

58. Teresa, *The Book of Her Life,* 11.14, in Kavanaugh and Rodriguez, *Collected Works,* vol. 1, p. 84.

59. Teresa, *The Book of Her Life,* 28:18, in Kavanaugh and Rodriguez, *Collected Works,* vol. 1, p. 188.

60. Ahlgren, *Teresa and Politics,* 89-90.

61. See Teresa, *Meditations on the Song of Songs,* 1.9-12, 2:16–3:15, in Kavanaugh and Rodriguez, *Collected Works,* vol. 2, pp. 220-222, 229-242.

62. Teresa, *Song of Songs,* 3:15, in Kavanaugh and Rodriguez, *Collected Works,* vol. 2, p. 242. The second biblical allusion refers to Song of Songs 1:2*b.*

63. In 1577, Teresa's "little Seneca," John of the Cross, was jailed in Toledo.

64. Teresa, *Interior Castle,* 7.3.13, in Kavanaugh and Rodriguez, *Collected Works,* vol. 2, p. 442.

65. Ibid., pp. 442-43. The biblical allusions are to Psalm 42:1[2], Rev. 21:3, and Gen. 8:8-12.

66. A balanced critical historical perspective which does not simply collapse the distance between the victims of the Spanish Inquisition and the victims of contemporary fundamentalism should be maintained. The distance between Teresa's and our present-day contexts enables the process of connecting stories to build "reliable bridges" of warranted inferences, rather than indulging in the "leaps" of uncontrolled parallels.

67. Teresa, *Interior Castle,* 7; postscript, Peers trans. p. 234.

68. Williams, *Teresa,* 22.

69. Weber maintains that, "Teresa's originality lies not in doctrinal content per se but rather in her transformation of doctrine into a vital solution to her personal anguish" (Weber, *Teresa,* 75).

70. Teresa, *Foundations,* 6.15; Kavanaugh and Rodriguez, *Collected Works,* vol. 3, p. 130.

71. Teresa, *Interior Castle,* 220.

72. Cf. the discussion of Stephen Crites's analysis of "the narrative quality of experience" at the beginning of this chapter.

73. Robert Coles, *The Call of Stories: Teaching and the Moral Imagination* (Boston: Houghton Mifflin, 1989).

74. Robert Coles, *The Call of Service: A Witness to Idealism* (Boston: Houghton Mifflin, 1993), 291n. 4.

75. For a discussion of how story creates a world and an introduction to narrative theory, see Seymour Chatman, *Story and Discourse: Narrative Structure in Fiction and Film* (Ithaca, N.Y.: Cornell University Press, 1978).

76. Herbert Anderson and Edward Foley, *Mighty Stories, Dangerous Rituals: Weaving Together the Human and the Divine* (San Francisco: Jossey-Bass Publishers, 1998), 40-41.

77. I assume here that in the Christian tradition one of the marks of legitimate second-order theological language is its capacity for self-criticism. For further introductory discussion of this assumption, see my *From Scripture to Theology*, 15-17.

78. For an example of Hauerwas's narrative ethics, see *Christian Existence Today: Essays on Church, World, and Living In Between* (Durham, N.C.: Labyrinth Press, 1988), especially "I. The Practice of the Church's Story," 23-97. In an unpublished study, entitled "On Keeping Theological Ethics Theological . . . and Intelligible: An Examination of Two Ethical Strategies," Scott Becker has offered a perceptive analysis of the debate of Gustafson and Hauerwas on these issues, which has informed my understanding of both sides of this dispute.

79. See Stanley Hauerwas and William H. Willimon, *Resident Aliens: Life in the Christian Colony* (Nashville: Abingdon Press, 1989) for an example of an approach which critics accuse of sectarianism.

80. In Puritan New England in the seventeenth and eighteenth centuries, the Half-Way Covenant described the way in which persons without personal faith who belonged to the community still retained a definite status with God and the church, which enabled the baptism of their children. For a detailed study, see Robert G. Pope, *The Half-Way Covenant: Church Membership in Puritan New England* (Princeton, N.J.: Princeton University Press, 1969).

81. Anderson and Foley, *Mighty Stories, Dangerous Rituals*, 44.

82. Hannah Arendt, "Ideology and Terror: A Novel Form of Government," in Hannah Arendt, *The Origins of Totalitarianism* (New York: Harcourt, Brace & Co., 1979), 476.

83. In public situations of ministry, especially in worship, Jackie and Dale need to be careful to respect pastoral confidentiality and use wise discretion in relating to the stories of the people of Valleywood.

84. For an attractive introduction to this understanding of Christian marriage, utilizing both biblical and sociological analysis, see Diana S. Richmond Garland and David E. Garland, *Beyond Companionship: Christians in Marriage* (Philadelphia: Westminster Press, 1986).

5. Performance Models

1. Catherine Bell provides a helpful review of performance theory in recent anthropology and philosophy (*Ritual Theory, Ritual Practice* [New York: Oxford University Press, 1992], especially 37-46). Bell also insightfully observes that "the popularity of performance metaphors and theories represents something of a consensus about 'meaning' as a specifically hermeneutical conception" (p. 44).

2. For example, see Dorothy C. Bass, ed., *Practicing Our Faith: A Way of Life for a Searching People* (San Francisco: Jossey Bass, 1997); Timothy F. Sedgwick, *The Christian Moral Life: Practices of Piety* (Grand Rapids, Mich.: Eerdmans, 1999); Craig Dykstra, *Growing in the Life of Faith: Education and Christian Practices* (Louisville, Ky.: Geneva Press, 1999); and Miroslav Volf and Dorothy C. Bass, eds., *Practicing Theology: Beliefs and Practices in Christian Life* (Grand Rapids, Mich.: Eerdmans, 2002).

3. For example, Albert Blackwell argues that "the phenomenon of music, in all of its great variety, is potentially sacramental, and not only in explicitly religious contexts" (*The Sacred in Music* [Louisville, Ky.: Westminster John Knox Press, 1999], 28).

4. Jeremy S. Begbie, *Voicing Creation's Praise: Towards a Theology of the Arts* (Edinburgh: T. & T. Clark, 1991), 248-49.

5. Besides the classical performing arts, the field of theology and culture has recently shown considerable interest in film. For example, see Robert K. Johnston, *Reel Spirituality: Theology and Film in Dialogue* (Grand Rapids, Mich.: Baker Book House, 2000).

6. More specifically, *perichoresis* describes how the persons (*hypostases*) of the Trinity mutually penetrate and indwell one another, coinhering without confusion. For Fiddes's description and defense of his use of the metaphor of dance in relation to the Trinity, see *Participating in God: A Pastoral Doctrine of the Trinity* (Louisville, Ky.: Westminster John Knox Press, 2001), 72-81.

7. Fiddes, *Participating in God*, see especially 146 (prayer); 162-63,185-86 (suffering); 246 (bereavement); and 272-73 (interpretation).

8. For instance, the churches' attitudes toward music clearly reveal this pattern. For an introductory overview of the history of music in Christian worship, written from an evangelical perspective, see Don P. Hustad, *Jubilate II: Church Music in Worship and Renewal* (Carol Stream, Ill.: Hope Publishing Co., 1993), 127-276. Also, the emphasis on simplicity in worship, particularly in the Reformed tradition and the traditions of the Radical Reformation, resulted in suspicion of and opposition to the use of the arts in worship.

9. For an example of the aesthetic application of process theology to ministry, see Gordon E. Jackson, *Creating Something of Beauty: A Theology for Ministry* (St. Louis, Mo.: Chalice Press, 1998).

10. I have coined this phrase (*lex cantandi, lex credendi* in Latin) to contrast with the liturgical axiom that "the law of praying is the law of believ-

ing" (*lex orandi, lex credendi*). Further explanation will be offered later in this chapter.

11. Nicholas Lash in *Theology on the Way to Emmaus* (London: SCM Press, 1986), 37-46.

12. Ibid., 41.

13. Ibid., 45.

14. Ibid., 42.

15. Stanley P. Saunders and Charles L. Campbell, *The Word on the Street: Performing the Scriptures in the Urban Context* (Grand Rapids, Mich.: Eerdmans, 2000).

16. Ibid., 8.

17. Frances Young, *Virtuoso Theology: The Bible and Interpretation* (Cleveland, Ohio: Pilgrim Press, 1993). The book was originally published as *The Art of Performance: Towards a Theology of Holy Scripture* (London: Darton, Longman and Todd, 1990).

18. For detailed examination of the theological implications of music's temporality, see Jeremy S. Begbie, *Theology, Music, and Time* (New York: Cambridge University Press, 2000).

19. Young, *Virtuoso Theology*, 22. As Young observes, "Even a silent 'reading' of a score presupposes the possibility of physical sound" (p. 22).

20. Ibid., 25.

21. Ibid., 105.

22. Ibid., 23-24.

23. Ibid., 115.

24. Ibid., 110.

25. Ibid., 132.

26. Ibid., 46.

27. Ibid., 121-22.

28. A countrapuntal duet in classical music involves the combining of two related independent melodies into a single polyphonic musical texture. Each line retains its specific melodic character, while joining with the other in a unified harmony.

29. "Some wanted a solo with accompaniment, but two instruments, each with their own properties, were eventually allowed to play together in such a way that their contrapuntal melodies were united in one whole piece" (Young, *Virtuoso Theology*, 123).

30. Ibid., 129.

31. A cadenza typically occurs near the end of a concerto. It is a technically difficult and often brilliant solo, which is frequently improvised.

32. Young, *Virtuoso Theology*, 161. If the performance of a cadenza functions only as a means of the soloist's self-expression, then the performance will be unable to serve as bridge between the classic and the audience. Young sees a dialectic here: "On the one hand, the soloist is able to produce a show of skill,

and without the performer's total involvement—indeed projection of her per-sonality—the cadenza would be dull and uncommunicative. On the other hand, the soloist is the servant of the music—bringing out what is potentially there in the themes and harmonies of the original score" (ibid., 161).

33. Ibid., 162.

34. Carolyn J. Bohler, "God Is Like a Jazz Band Leader: Location of Divine and Human Power and Responsibility—A Call to Pastoral Theologians," *Journal of Pastoral Theology* 7 (1997): 32. Bohler's interpretation clearly reflects the influence of process theology. See also the discussion of jazz and the theology of American culture in James William McClendon, Jr., *Witness: Systematic Theology*, vol. 3(Nashville: Abingdon Press, 2000), 165-79.

35. My choice to focus upon the ecumenical Lutheran work of Gordon Lathrop reflects my own Protestant heritage, as well as the desire for a contemporary example that explicitly links liturgical performance and pastoral theology. Obviously, both the Roman Catholic and Orthodox traditions place a high value upon the performance of liturgy. Their distinctive historical and theological emphases would shape a pastoral liturgical theology directed more specifically to the life and traditions of their communities. For a useful introduction to the task of theological interpretation in liturgy from a Catholic perspective, see Joyce Ann Zimmerman, *Liturgy and Hermeneutics* (Collegeville, Minn.: Liturgical Press, 1999).

36. Gordon W. Lathrop, *Holy Things: A Liturgical Theology* (Minneapolis, Minn.: Fortress Press, 1993), 159-225.

37. Ibid., 175.

38. Ibid., 176.

39. Ibid., 33.

40. Ibid., 36-43.

41. For discussion of the significance for pastoral care of the community context of church rituals, see Elaine Ramshaw, *Ritual and Pastoral Care*, ed. Don S. Browning(Philadelphia: Fortress Press, 1987).

42. Lathrop, *Holy Things*, 193-96.

43. Lathrop characterizes the broken ritual of the liturgy as follows: "The old is maintained; yet, by means of juxtaposition and metaphor, the old is made to speak the new" (*Holy Things*, 27). The notion of broken ritual derives from Paul Tillich's concept of "broken myth," which finds the truth of myth in its capacity to refer to a new thing beyond itself. Tillich described this concept and applied it to Christianity in his popular work *Dynamics of Faith* (New York: Harper & Row, 1957), especially 52-54.

44. Lathrop, *Holy Things*, 209.

45. Ibid., 216. For instance, he maintains the church can best assist environmental reform not through "some occasional votive mass for the earth, . . . not some protest liturgy, but the *ordo* itself done clearly and well" (pp. 216-17).

46. Ibid., 216.

47. Of course, one could maintain that all Christian worship—no matter how informal or free—has some sort of practical liturgy. By "nonliturgical," I simply mean those traditions that do not order worship by a formal, written liturgy.

48. An earlier version of this research appeared as "*Lex Cantandi, Lex Credendi:* Theology and Hymnody," in *Learning from Beauty: Baptist Reflections on Christianity and the Arts: A Tribute to William L. Hendricks* (Lewiston, N.Y.: Edwin Mellen Press, 1997), 129-40. The article has been significantly revised and expanded for this chapter.

49. For a technical example of the link between formal liturgy and scriptural interpretation, see William T. Flynn, *Medieval Music As Medieval Exegesis,* Studies in Liturgical Musicology, No. 8 (Lanham, Md.: Scarecrow Press, 1999). Flynn argues that "the liturgy itself [is] the *schola* that shaped the interpretive practices of the eleventh-century church" (pp. 4-5).

50. For one detailed historical example, see Teresa Berger, *Theology in Hymns? A Study of the Relationship of Doxology and Theology According to "A Collection of Hymns for the Use of the People Called Methodists (1780),"* trans. Timothy E. Kimbrough (Nashville: Kingswood Books, 1995).

51. For an account and critique of the development of the tradition of African American hymnody, see Jon Michael Spencer, *Black Hymnody: A Hymnological History of the African-American Church* (Knoxville: University of Tennessee Press, 1992).

52. Heather Curtis has presented an insightful study on the place of hymns in the religious formation of children in American Christianity (" 'Children of the Heavenly King': Hymns in the Religious and Social Experience of Children," [paper presented to The American Society of Church History, San Francisco, Calif., January 5, 2002]).

53. For further discussion of this dual construal, see Geoffrey Wainwright, *Doxology: The Praise of God in Worship, Doctrine, and Life: A Systematic Theology* (New York: Oxford University Press, 1980), 218.

54. Wainwright traces the history of the theme and discusses its systematic implications in chapters 7 and 8 of *Doxology* (pp. 218-83).

55. See ibid., 224-26, for further detail. My exposition of Prosper's argument follows Wainwright's historical reconstruction.

56. For the Latin texts of the "pseudo-Celestine chapters," see J. P. Migne, ed., *Patrologia Latina,* 1441 vols. (Paris, 1844–64), 51, 205-12. Notice that in Prosper's text the axiom is not reversible, but the law of prayer is clearly the grammatical subject of the law for belief. The English translation I am using is given in Wainwright, *Doxology,* 225.

57. Wainwright, *Doxology,* 227-35.

58. This discussion seeks only to highlight briefly a few themes related to the practice of singing in the complex topic of music in the early church. For an extensive collection of primary texts, see James McKinnon, ed., *Music in Early Christian Literature* (New York: Cambridge University Press, 1987). For a

feminist attempt to reconstruct the history of worship from the perspective of gender, see Teresa Berger, *Women's Ways of Worship: Gender Analysis and Liturgical History* (Collegeville, Minn.: Liturgical Press, 1999). Berger specifically compares worship in the early centuries of the church with the twentieth-century liturgical movement and the more recent women's liturgical movement.

59. Ralph P. Martin, *Worship in the Early Church* (Grand Rapids, Mich.: Eerdmans, 1964), 39. Edward Foley's *Foundations of Christian Music: The Music of Pre-Constantinian Christianity*, American Essays in Liturgy (Collegeville, Minn.: Liturgical Press, 1996) offers a brief, valuable historical introduction to the context and development of liturgical music in early Christian communities.

60. Martin, *Worship in the Early Church*, 39-52.

61. For a more recent study of "Christology from below" found in popular hymns of devotion in the early church, see Daniel Liderbach, *Christ in the Early Christian Hymns* (New York: Paulist Press, 1998).

62. Théodore Gérold, *Les Péres de l'église et la musique* (Strasbourg: Imprimerie Alsacienne, 1931; reprint, Geneva: Minkoff, 1973). Gérold quotes Plato's *Protagoras* and Aristotle's *Politics* as examples.

63. Gérold, *Les Peres*, 84.

64. Johannes Quasten, *Music and Worship in Pagan and Christian Antiquity*, trans. Boniface Ramsey. (Washington, D.C.: National Association of Pastoral Musicians, 1983), 92. Quasten's citations include Clement of Alexandria (*Protrepticos*, 1.5.3) and Chrysostom (J. P. Migne, ed., *Patrologia Graeca*, 162 vols. (Paris, 1857–66), 55:104, 156, and 497 and 62:576).

65. Quasten, *Music and Worship*, 129, citing Ambrose (*De Elia et ieiunio*, [Migne, *Patrologia Latina*, 14:716]).

66. Gérold, *Les Peres*, 93. Quasten points out that Christians were sometimes forbidden even to pronounce the names of pagan gods (*Music and Worship*, p. 122, citing *Apostolic Constitutions* 5.10.2 as support).

67. Quasten, *Music and Worship*, 122.

68. Ignatius of Antioch, *Ephesians* 4.1-2, in MacKinnon, *Music*, 19.

69. Quasten, *Music and Worship*, 68-69. The reference is to Cyril of Jerusalem's *Mystagogical Catecheses* 5.6 (Migne, *Patrologia Graeca*, 33:1113).

70. For a collection of Clement's texts containing significant musical imagery, see Robert A. Skeris, "*Chrôma, Theou*": *On the Origins and Theological Interpretation of the Musical Imagery Used by the Ecclesiastical Writers of the First Three Centuries, with Special Reference to the Image of Orpheus* (Altöting: Verlag Alfred Coppenrath, 1976), 54-83. See also Skeris's interpretation of Clement on pp. 130-40.

71. Clement of Alexandria, *Protrepticus* 1.5.3-7; Migne, *Patrologia Graeca*, 8:60-61, in MacKinnon, *Music*, 30.

72. Cf. *Protrepticus* 1.4.1-5 and Skeris, *Chrôma*, pp. 57-58.

73. Cf. *Protrepticus* 1.8.3 and Skeris, *Chrôma*, pp. 61-62.

74. Cf. *Protrepticus*, 1.5.1-3 and Skeris, *Chrôma*, pp. 58-59.

75. See Origen's commentary on Psalm 32:3, Migne, *Patrologia Graeca*, 12:1304D, trans. Skeris, *Chroma*, p. 108.

76. Eusebius, *Demonstratio evangelica* 6.5.4. I am indebted to Skeris (*Chroma*, p. 108) for this reference.

77. *Apothegmeta Patrum*, as quoted in Quasten, *Music and Worship*, 95.

78. For discussion of the contested use of women's choirs to perform liturgical hymns in Syriac Christianity in late antiquity, see Susan Ashbrook Harvey, "Spoken Words, Voiced Silence: Biblical Women in Syriac Tradition," 2000 NAPS Presidential Address, *Journal of Early Christian Studies* 9 (Spring 2001): 105-31, especially 124-31. Harvey argues that "the rhetorical voices Syriac writers granted to biblical women were significantly enhanced by the performative voices of women's choirs" (p. 129).

79. *De Musica*, written in the period between 387 and 391, focuses on the question of rhythm and its implications for the philosophical issues of time and number. For discussion of *De Musica*, with special interest in the philosophy of art, see the essays in Richard R. La Croix, ed. *Augustine on Music: An Interdisciplinary Collection of Essays* (Lewiston, N.Y.: Edwin Mellen Press, 1988). Catherine Pickstock has argued for the reaffirmation of the metaphysical category of "music," as found particularly in Book VI of *De Musica*, in the context of a wider rehabilitation of the Platonic-Christian tradition (Catherine Pickstock, "Music: Soul, City, and Cosmos after Augustine," in *Radical Orthodoxy: A New Theology*, ed. John Milbank, Catherine Pickstock, and Graham Ward [New York: Routledge, 1999], 243-77).

80. Saint Augustine, *The City of God Against the Pagans*, The Loeb Classical Library, trans. David S. Wiesen (Cambridge, Mass.: Harvard University Press, 1968), 3:494-95. The Latin text reads: "*atque ita ordinem saeculorum tamquam pulcherrimum carmen.*" Wiesen translates: "the succession of the ages as if it were an exquisite poem." I, however, favor the more literal translation of "most beautiful song." I am indebted for this reference to H. I. Marrou, *Time and Timeliness*, trans. Violet Nevile (New York: Sheed and Ward, 1969), 71.

81. Augustine, *City of God*, 11.18, my paraphrase.

82. Marrou, *Time and Timeliness*, 71-72.

83. I am indebted to my colleague the Rev. Jane Plantinga Pauw for suggesting this example.

84. Augustine, *City of God*, 11.18: "*pulcherrimum carmen etiam ex quibusdam quasi antithetis honestaret.*"

85. For an examination of this theme in relation to the doctrine of the Trinity, see the concluding chapter of my *Hermeneutics as Theological Prolegomena: A Canonical Approach* (Macon, Ga.: Mercer University Press, 1994), especially 127-29.

86. For some contemporary discussion of alternative approaches to this paradox, see Stephen T. Davis, ed., *Encountering Evil: Live Options in Theodicy* (Louisville, Ky.: Westminster John Knox Press, 2001).

87. Of course, in Augustine, this view expresses his worldview of christianized Neoplatonism. I am seeking to utilize his understanding of antithesis in poetry and song without advocating the adoption of his worldview. For instance, the juxtaposition of opposites in modern surrealist art provides a contemporary visual example that is not tied to ancient philosophy.

88. I am indebted to Marrou's *Time and Timeliness* (p. 71) for these references. Augustine also discusses the usefulness of the practice of singing in worship in *Epistle* 55:18-19, responding to the reproach of the Donatists that Catholic chanting of the Scriptures is too grave.

89. Augustine, *Epistle* 138:1.5. I have used the Latin edition of Al. Goldbacher (Vindobonae: F. Tempsky, 1904), part 3, p. 130, found in *Corpus Scriptorum Ecclesiasticorum Latinorum* (Vienna, 1866ff), 44:130. The English translation is that of Sister Wilfrid Parsons, *St. Augustine: Letters* (New York: Fathers of the Church, 1953), 3:39, emphasis added.

90. Augustine, *Epistle* 166: [5], 13. *C.S.E.L.*, 44, pp. 565-66. Parsons, *Letters*, 4:19.

91. Margaret R. Miles, *Desire and Delight: A New Reading of Augustine's Confessions* (New York: Crossroad, 1992), 12-13.

92. Gillian Clark, *Augustine: The Confessions* (Cambridge: Cambridge University Press, 1993), 37.

93. Augustine, *Confessions*, 8.12.29, trans. Edward B. Pusey (London: Collier Books, 1961), 130-31, my emphasis.

94. See ibid., 9.7.15, for documentation.

95. Donald P. Hustad, *Jubilate II: Church Music in Worship and Renewal* (Carol Stream, Ill.: Hope Publishing Co., 1993), 164.

96. John M. Neale's Victorian translation of the three stanzas of Ambrose's hymn quoted in the text was widely used in English and American church services.

97. Hustad also points to the antiheretical hymns of Ephraem Syrus (c. 306-373), as an Eastern example (*Jubilate II*, 164).

98. In *Confessions* 11.27.35, Augustine specifically cites Ambrose's hymn *Deus creator omnium*, which he had mentioned as early as *De musica* 6.2.2.

99. For a detailed contemporary exposition and analysis of Augustine's understanding of time as "distention of the soul" (*distentio animi*) and its relationship to narrative, see Paul Ricoeur, *Time and Narrative*, 3 vols., trans. Kathleen McLaughlin and David Pellauer (Chicago: University of Chicago Press, 1984), 1:5-30.

100. Clark, *Confessions*, 66. Clark cites *Confessions* 11.28.38-29.39 as the primary text for her exposition. Following Clark, I disagree with the interpretation of Begbie and others who believe that in *Confessions*, as in the earlier *De Musica*, "Augustine is thinking *only* of the music of spoken words, not the music of singing or instruments" (*Theology, Music, and Time*, 84, my emphasis). Such a distinction seems to downplay the complexity of Augustine's experiences of

chanting and singing and his pastoral concerns regarding their use in worship. I think Augustine's view of music in *Confessions* is not *merely* the logical exten-sion of his concerns for rhythm and meter in *De Musica*, 6. Cf. also Augustine, *Confessions* 10.33.49-50.

101. Clark, *Confessions*, 66.

102. Augustine, *Confessions*, 10.33.49-50, Pusey trans., 176.

103. Ibid. As James J. O'Donnell observes, "The things of this world are not at fault for being beautiful, but even things of this world explicitly in the ser-vice of God, like the melodies of church music, are no less an opportunity for error than the more obvious temptations" (James J. O'Donnell, *Augustine* [Boston: Twayne Publishers, 1985], 110).

104. Richard J. Mouw, *Consulting the Faithful: What Christian Intellectuals Can Learn from Popular Religion* (Grand Rapids, Mich.: Eerdmans, 1994).

105. Mouw, *Consulting the Faithful*, 25-26.

106. Roberta Clifton Tassie, "Unified in Prayer," The *St. Matthews Baptist* 39, no. 3 (30 January 1994): 3. The article appropriately closes by quoting the words to a nineteenth century hymn by James Montgomery.

107. Cheryl A. Kirk-Duggan, *Exorcizing Evil: A Womanist Perspective on the Spirituals* (Maryknoll, N.Y.: Orbis Books, 1997), 26. Kirk-Duggan describes the theological perspective of her study: "Clarifying the activity of God and human-ity in the texts of these Spirituals leads to an interpretation of a theory and praxis of theodicy that has affected Christian transformation" (p. xiv). For an example of the study of the language of hymns incorporating ecofeminist and liberation perspectives, see Robin Knowles Wallace, *Moving Toward Emancipatory Language: A Study of Recent Hymns*, Drew University Studies in Liturgy, no. 8 (Lanham. Md.: Scarecrow Press, 1999).

108. For a clearly written introduction to the theological use and philosoph-ical difficulties of analogical language (including the debate over its relationship to metaphor), see Dan R. Stiver, *The Philosophy of Religious Language: Sign, Symbol, and Story* (Cambridge, Mass.: Blackwell Publishers, 1996), especially 23-29, 124-27. For more detailed discussions—and significantly different per-spectives—on the issues involved, compare David Burrell, *Analogy and Philosophical Language* (New Haven, Conn.: Yale University Press, 1973) and Janet Martin Soskice, *Metaphor and Religious Language* (Oxford: Clarendon Press, 1985). For constructive theological reflection on these issues, see espe-cially David Tracy, *The Analogical Imagination: Christian Theology and the Culture of Pluralism* (New York: Crossroad, 1981).

109. Of course, the Latin word *pastor* was originally used to designate "a herdsman, especially a shepherd" (C. T. Lewis and C. Short, *A New Latin Dictionary* [New York: Harper & Brothers, 1879], 1312).

110. Young, *Virtuoso Theology*, 21.

111. This difficulty encourages the development of pastoral theologies that seek to blend performance and contextual models. For a powerful recent

example, see Kathleen D. Billman and Daniel L. Migliore, *Rachel's Cry: Prayer of Lament and Rebirth of Hope* (Cleveland, Ohio: United Church Press, 1999).

112. For example, Diana Garland has cataloged sixteen different kinds of family structure in the Bible (*Family Ministry: A Comprehensive Guide* [Downers Grove, Ill.: InterVarsity Press, 1999], 345).

113. Another common worship practice that may assist Jill is extending the peace of Christ to fellow worshipers.

114. In Presbyterian polity, the session consists of the ministers and elders of a local congregation.

6. Regulative Models

1. For example, see the developing "postliberal" views of ministry described in Martin B. Copenhaver, Anthony B. Robinson, and William H. Willimon, *Good News in Exile: Three Pastors Offer a Hopeful Vision for the Church* (Grand Rapids, Mich.: Eerdmans, 1999). Charles Gerkin also utilizes Lindbeck's typology and interprets the cultural linguistic model in a narrative hermeneutical direction for pastoral care (*An Introduction to Pastoral Care* [Nashville: Abingdon Press, 1997], especially 105-13).

2. The following two sections of this chapter, as well as some material in the critical evaluation section, have been adapted from my article "Agreeing on Where We Disagree: Lindbeck's Postliberalism and Pastoral Theology," *Journal of Pastoral Theology* 8 (1998): 43-51. The intent of the description in this section is to offer readers who are not familiar with Lindbeck's approach a brief, nontechnical introduction.

3. George A. Lindbeck, *The Nature of Doctrine: Religion and Theology in a Postliberal Age* (Philadelphia: Westminster Press, 1984).

4. Of course, many Christian theologians, including a significant number of pastoral theologians, would locate themselves on a spectrum between these types. Lindbeck explicitly points to Karl Rahner and Bernard Lonergan as Catholic theologians who blend the first and second types (*Nature of Doctrine*, 16). For an application of their transcendental method to ministerial theology, see Peter Drilling, *Trinity and Ministry* (Minneapolis: Fortress Press, 1991).

5. Friedrich Schleiermacher, *On Religion: Speeches to Its Cultured Despisers*, trans. John Oman (Louisville, Ky.: Westminster John Knox Press, 1994) offers the classic exposition of this ideal type. For an examination of Schleiermacher's influence upon the discipline of pastoral theology, see Frank Milstead Woggon, "Deliberate Activity As an Art for (Almost) Everyone: Friedrich Schleiermacher on Practical Theology," *The Journal of Pastoral Care* 48 (1994): 3-13.

6. Perry LeFevre, review of *The Nature of Doctrine*, by George A. Lindbeck, *Chicago Theological Seminary Register* 74 (1984): 38.

7. Although Lindbeck uses the term "postliberal" to characterize his theology,

significant dialogue has also occurred with Protestant evangelicals. See especially Timothy R. Phillips and Dennis L. Okholm, eds., *The Nature of Confession: Evangelicals and Postliberals in Conversation* (Downers Grove, Ill.: InterVarsity Press, 1996).

8. Lindbeck, *Nature of Doctrine*, 118.

9. George A. Lindbeck, "Atonement and the Hermeneutics of Intratextual Social Embodiment," in Phillips and Okholm, *Nature of Confession*, 221-40, especially p. 227.

10. Lindbeck develops this comparison as follows: "A classical hermeneutics of social embodiment absorbs changing cultural and historical worlds into the world of the Bible: it makes the varying social, cultural, and intellectual milieus of believing communities biblically intelligible. The apologetic approach, in contrast, does the reverse. It seeks to render scriptural language intelligible by transposing it into contemporary thought forms. At its most extreme, the world absorbs the Bible: it supplies the framework within which Holy Writ is understood rather than the other way around" (Lindbeck, "Atonement," 239).

11. Stanley Hauerwas and L. Gregory Jones, "Seeking a Clear Alternative to Liberalism," *Books and Religion* 13 (1985): 7.

12. See, for example, Lindbeck, "Atonement," 239-40.

13. Hauerwas and Jones, "Seeking a Clear Alternative," 7. The cultural-linguistic approach offers an alternative to traditional cognitive-propositional approaches in its view that narratives, rather than propositions, form the basis of Christian identity. Thus it displays significant similarities to the narrative models we examined in chapter 4.

14. Lindbeck, "Atonement," 225.

15. Such a metaphysical view characterizes the cognitive-propositional model of doctrine, which in Western Christianity was decisively shaped first by Neoplatonism and then by Aristotelian scholasticism.

16. Of course, the reference here is again particularly to Friedrich Schleiermacher, whose Protestant liberalism is systematically developed in *The Christian Faith*, 2 vols., ed. H. R. Mackintosh and J. S. Stewart (New York: Harper & Row, 1963).

17. See, for example, Joseph DiNoia's discussion of the difficulties of "pluralist and inclusivist" views of Christian theology of religions which "fail to account for this inextricable connection between the particular aims of life commended by religious communities and the specific sets of descriptions they foster to promote the attainment and enjoyment of those aims" ("Varieties of Religious Aims: Beyond Exclusivism, Inclusivism, and Pluralism," in *Theology and Dialogue: Essays in Conversation with George Lindbeck*, ed. Bruce D. Marshall [Notre Dame, Ind.: University of Notre Dame Press, 1990], 257).

18. Cf. Lindbeck, *Nature of Doctrine*, 107.

19. Since 1994 I have co-chaired (first with Miriam Glover Wetherington and then with Roslyn Karaban) a study group for the Society for Pastoral

Theology that has examined both historical and contemporary case studies on the role of the church in Christian formation. The historical case study "Teresa of Avila: A Catholic Doctor for Protestant Women?" examined in chapter 4 offers a specific example of this kind of investigation.

20. For a philosophical analysis of the metaphor of the web see W. V. Quine and J. S. Ullian, *The Web of Belief* (New York: Random House, 1970). For an introductory survey of "the turn to language" in twentieth-century philosophy and religion, see Dan R. Stiver, *The Philosophy of Religious Language: Sign, Symbol, and Story* (Cambridge, Mass.: Blackwell, 1996).

21. See, for example, Clifford Geertz's advocacy of "thick description" in his classic essay "Thick Description: Toward an Interpretive Theory of Culture," in *The Interpretation of Cultures* (New York: Basic Books, 1973), 3-30; and James Hopewell's congregational studies approach in *Congregations: Stories and Structures*, ed. Barbara G. Wheeler (Philadelphia: Fortress Press, 1987). Also, the sociological analysis of American public life and the loss of community described by Robert Bellah and his colleagues, Richard Madsen, William M. Sullivan, Ann Swidler, and Steven M. Tipton, in *Habits of the Heart: Individualism and Commitment in American Life* (Berkeley: University of California Press, 1996) offers a popular North American application of this sort of analysis.

22. Lindbeck, *Nature of Doctrine*, 7, 15-19.

23. Michael Root, "Identity and Difference: The Ecumenical Problem," in *Theology and Dialogue*, 165-90. Cf. also Patrick Keifert's observation that Lindbeck's approach "provides a readily applicable means for adjudicating differences within a religious group, even providing for normative rules for articulating the faith" (Review, *Word and World* 5 [1985]: 342).

24. Root, "Identity and Difference," 180.

25. Ibid., 181.

26. Ibid., 180-81.

27. The material for this case study has been adapted from my article, "Revelation and Pastoral Theology: Historical and Methodological Reflections," *Journal of Pastoral Theology* 9 (1999): 89-103.

28. Darrel's name and other minor identifying features have been altered to protect pastoral confidentiality.

29. Bruce Marshall has persuasively argued that Lindbeck's functional view of doctrine should *not* be understood as endorsing or leading to any sort of religious relativism, despite the fears of Lindbeck's critics (Bruce D. Marshall, "Aquinas as Postliberal Theologian," *The Thomist* 53 [1989]: 353-402, especially at 364). Further discussion of this issue is offered in the following "critical evaluation" section of this chapter.

30. The traditional categories of "general revelation" and "special revelation" have historically assumed the existence of such external, universal standards. It is questionable whether many of the things claimed to be general revelation

(e.g., God in the window of nature, God in the human conscience) are revelation at all. The existence of diverse and contradictory accounts of God's revelation in nature and conscience makes suspect the claim that unaided human reason can discern such general revelation. Furthermore, the categories of general and special revelation are problematic, since for Christians and other monotheists, any authentic revelation of God would, by the nature of who God is, be *special* revelation.

31. My agreement with Lindbeck here should not be taken to mean that I endorse his postliberal theology in its entirety. For example, see my criticism of his approach in *Hermeneutics as Theological Prolegomena: A Canonical Approach* (Macon, Ga.: Mercer University Press, 1994), 111-12, as well as the critical evaluation section of this chapter.

32. Cf. Heiko Oberman's functional distinctions of Tradition 1, Tradition 2, and Tradition 3 in "*Quo vadis?* Tradition from Irenaeus to *Humani Generis*," The Dudleian Lecture, Harvard University (*Scottish Journal of Theology* 16 [1963]: 225-55).

33. One perhaps might argue that the presence or absence of explicit religious mediation leads to two different subtypes here. Yet the approach of conceiving religious mediation as a spectrum within the type of individual subjective appropriation seems to allow for a more nuanced account of the variety of ways in which both implicit and explicit religious tradition shape individual experience.

34. Within the ongoing life of a religious community all three types of revelation can occur. Whether the exclusive reliance upon one type of revelation fosters behaviors destructive to community life (e.g., delusional psychopathology, authoritarianism) is a significant topic for further exploration.

35. For further discussion of the categories of first-order and second-order religious language, see my *From Scripture to Theology: A Canonical Journey into Hermeneutics* (Downers Grove, Ill.: InterVarsity Press, 1996), 14-17. For a clearly written introduction to the complex issues of linguistic philosophy and religious language, see Stiver, *Philosophy of Religious Language*.

36. For a social psychological approach to the cognitive and moral development of college students, based upon study of students at Harvard College, see William G. Perry, Jr., *Forms of Intellectual and Ethical Development in the College Years: A Scheme* (San Francisco: Jossey-Bass Publishers, 1999).

37. "Die christologischen und trinitarischen Aussagen wurden keineswegs nur als 'grammatikalische' Regeln, sondern auch als ontologische Aussagen verstanden." Armin Kreiner, "Versöhnung ohne Kapitulation: Überlegungen zu George A. Lindbecks "The Nature of Doctrine," *Catholica*, 46 (1992): 317, my English translation.

38. Alan Padgett, review of *The Nature of Doctrine*, by George A. Lindbeck, *Theological Students Fellowship Bulletin* 8 (1985): 31. After serving on the faculty of Azusa Pacific University, Padgett became a professor at Luther Seminary. For a more erudite restatement of the same fear, see Alister E. McGrath, "An

Evangelical Evaluation of Postliberalism," in *The Nature of Confession* 23-44, especially 33-39. In a similar statement of concern, Patrick Keifert asks, "To what degree is Lindbeck's proposal funded by a rather thoroughgoing skepticism regarding ontological truth claims and, as a result, the viability of Christian evangelical outreach?" (*Word and World* 5 [1985]: 342).

39. Cf. Kreiner's assertion on the page immediately following the previous quotation: "Stated simply, the question is whether the adaptation of this approach is not very nearly a renunciation of the traditional concept of truth, and thereby tends toward either a noncognitive or a *relativistic* epistemology to which theology inevitably would have to devote itself in order to be able to take advantage of this approach" (Kreiner, *"Versöhnung,"* 318, my English translation and emphasis).

40. Marshall, "Aquinas," especially 357-70.

41. In responding to Lindbeck some Christian psychologists of religion display a rather remarkable philosophical naiveté concerning the truth of scientific method. For example, Paul Rigby, John van den Hengel, and Paul O'Grady of St. Paul University in Ottawa flatly declare, "In academic psychology, the methodological norms and the criteria for what constitutes a fact are uncontroversial" ("The Nature of Doctrine and Scientific Progress," *Theological Studies* 52 [1991]: 682). Such positivism reminds one of Freud's declaration at the end of *The Future of an Illusion,* "No, our science is no illusion. But an illusion it would be to suppose that what science cannot give us we can get elsewhere" (rev. ed., trans. W. D. Robson-Scott, ed. James Strachey London: Hogarth Press, 1962, p. 92).

42. Marshall, "Aquinas," 364. For Lindbeck's concurrence with Marshall's view, see his "Response to Bruce Marshall," *The Thomist* 53 (1989): 403. For further discussion of this question, see Miroslav Volf, "Theology, Meaning, and Power: A Conversation with George Lindbeck on Theology and the Nature of Christian Difference," in Phillips and Okholm, *Nature of Confession,* 45-66, especially 58-59.

43. See, for example, George A. Lindbeck, "Scripture, Consensus, and Community," in *Biblical Interpretation in Crisis,* ed. Richard John Neuhaus (Grand Rapids, Mich.: Eerdmans, 1988), 74-101.

44. For examination of some biblical warrants for family ministry, see Diana R. Garland, *Family Ministry: A Comprehensive Guide* (Downers Grove, Ill.: InterVarsity Press, 1999), 299-364. For critical analysis of Garland's informal correlational method, see the section "Family Ministries and Correlation" in chapter 2.

45. Lindbeck, *Nature of Doctrine,* 126.

Bibliography

Ackermann, Denise M., and Riet Bons-Storm, eds. *Liberating Faith Practices: Feminist Practical Theologies in Context*. Leuven: Peeters, 1998.

Adams, Jay E. *Competent to Counsel: Introduction to Nouthetic Counseling*. Grand Rapids, Mich.: Ministry Resources Library, 1986.

Ahlgren, Gillian T. W. *Teresa of Avila and the Politics of Sanctity*. Ithaca, N.Y.: Cornell University Press, 1996.

Arendt, Hannah. *The Origins of Totalitarianism*. New York: Harcourt, Brace & Co., 1979.

Auclair, Marcelle. *St. Teresa of Avila*. Trans. Kathleen Pond. New York: Pantheon, 1953. Reprint, Petersham, Mass.: St. Bede's Publications, 1988.

Augustine. *The City of God Against the Pagans*. Trans. David S. Wiesen. The Loeb Classical Library. Cambridge, Mass.: Harvard University Press, 1968.

———. Epistulae. Vol. 44, *Corpus Scriptorum Ecclesiasticorum Latinorum* (C.S.E.L.). Ed. Al. Goldbacher. Vindobonae: F. Tempsky, 1904.

———. *Letters*. Vols. 3 and 4. Trans. Sister Wilfrid Parsons. New York: Fathers of the Church, 1953 and 1955.

Avis, Paul. *Authority, Leadership and Conflict in the Church*. Philadelphia: Trinity Press International, 1992.

Barbour, Ian G. *Myths, Models and Paradigms: A Comparative Study in Science and Religion*. New York: Harper & Row, 1974.

Bass, Dorothy C. *Receiving the Day: Christian Practices for Opening the Gift of Time*. San Francisco: Jossey-Bass, 2001.

———. ed. *Practicing Our Faith: A Way of Life for Searching People*. San Francisco: Jossey-Bass. 1997.

Becker, Scott; "On Keeping Theological Ethics Theological . . . and Intelligible: An Examination of Two Ethical Strategies." Unpublished paper, Fuller Theological Seminary Northwest Directed Study, Seattle, Wash., spring 2000.

Begbie, Jeremy S. *Theology, Music and Time.* Cambridge: Cambridge University Press, 2000.

―――. *Voicing Creation's Praise: Towards a Theology of the Arts.* Edinburgh: T. & T. Clark, 1991.

Bell, Catherine. *Ritual Theory, Ritual Practice.* New York: Oxford University Press, 1992.

Bellah, Robert, Richard Madsen, William M. Sullivan, Ann Swidler, and Steven M. Tipton. *Habits of the Heart: Individualism and Commitment in American Life.* New York: Harper & Row, 1986.

Berger, Teresa. *Theology in Hymns?: A Study of the Relationship of Doxology and Theology According to "A Collection of Hymns for the Use of the People Called Methodists" (1780).* Trans. Timothy E. Kimbrough. Nashville: Kingswood, 1995.

―――. *Women's Ways of Worship: Gender Analysis and Liturgical History.* Collegeville, Minn.: Liturgical Press, 1999.

Bernier, Paul. *Ministry in the Church: A Historical and Pastoral Approach.* Mystic, Conn.: Twenty-third Publications, 1992.

Berryman, Philip. *Liberation Theology: Essential Facts about the Revolutionary Movement in Latin America—and Beyond.* Oak Park, Ill.: Meyer Stone, 1987.

Bevans, Stephen B. *Models of Contextual Theology.* Maryknoll, N.Y.: Orbis Books, 1992.

Bilinkoff, Jodi. *The Avila of St. Teresa: Religious Reform in a Sixteenth-century City.* Ithaca, N.Y.: Cornell University Press, 1989.

Billman, Kathleen D. "Pastoral Care as an Art of Community." In *The Arts of Ministry: Feminist-Womanist Approaches,* ed. Christie Cozad Neuger, 10-38. Louisville, Ky.: Westminster John Knox, 1996.

Billman, Kathleen D., and Daniel L. Migliore. *Rachel's Cry: Prayer of Lament and Rebirth of Hope.* Cleveland, Ohio: United Church Press, 1999.

Black, Max. *Models and Metaphors: Studies in Language and Philosophy.* Ithaca, N.Y.: Cornell University Press, 1962.

Blackwell, Albert L. *The Sacred in Music.* Louisville, Ky.: Westminster John Knox, 1999.

Boff, Leonardo, and Clodovis Boff. *Introducing Liberation Theology.* Trans. Paul Burns. Maryknoll, N.Y.: Orbis Books, 1987.

Bohler, Carolyn J. "God Is Like a Jazz Band Leader: Location of Divine and Human Power and Responsibility—A Call to Pastoral Theologians." *Journal of Pastoral Theology* 7 (1997): 23-41.

Boisen, Anton. *The Exploration of the Inner World: A Study of Mental Disorder and Religious Experience.* New York: Willett, Clark & Co., 1936. Reprints, New York: Harper & Brothers, 1952; Philadelphia: University of Pennsylvania Press, 1971.

Broughton, Rosemary. *Praying with Teresa of Ávila*. Winona, Minn.: Saint Mary's Press, 1990.

Browning, Don S. *A Fundamental Practical Theology: Descriptive and Strategic Proposals*. Minneapolis, Minn.: Fortress Press, 1991.

———. *Religious Ethics and Pastoral Care*. Philadelphia: Fortress Press, 1983.

———, ed. *Practical Theology: The Emerging Field in Theology, Church, and World*. San Francisco: Harper & Row, 1983.

Browning, Don, Bonnie J. Miller-McLemore, Pamela D. Couture, K. Brynolf Lyon, and Robert M. Franklin. *From Culture Wars to Common Ground: Religion and the American Family Debate*. Louisville, Ky.: Westminster John Knox Press, 1997.

Burghardt, Walter J., and William G. Thompson, eds. *Why the Church?* New York: Paulist Press, 1977.

Burrell, David B. *Analogy and Philosophical Language*. New Haven, Conn.: Yale University Press, 1973.

Carter, John D. "Integration of Psychology and Theology." In *Dictionary of Pastoral Care and Counseling*, ed. Rodney J. Hunter. Nashville: Abingdon Press, 1990.

Carter, John D., and Bruce Narramore. *The Integration of Psychology and Theology: An Introduction*. Grand Rapids, Mich.: Zondervan Publishing House, 1979.

Charry, Ellen T. *By the Renewing of Your Minds: The Pastoral Function of Christian Doctrine*. New York: Oxford University Press, 1997.

Chatman, Seymour. *Story and Discourse: Narrative Structure in Fiction and Film*. Ithaca, N.Y.: Cornell University Press, 1978.

Chopp, Rebecca S. *Saving Work: Feminist Practices of Theological Education*. Louisville, Ky.: Westminster John Knox Press, 1995.

Chorpenning, Joseph F. *The Divine Romance: Teresa of Avila's Narrative Theology*. Chicago: Loyola University Press, 1992.

———. "The Monastery, Paradise, and the Castle: Literary Images and Spiritual Development in St. Teresa of Avila." *Bulletin of Hispanic Studies* 62 (1985): 245-57.

———. "The Literary and Theological Method of The Interior Castle," *Journal of Hispanic Philology* 3 (1979): 121-33.

Clark, Gillian. *Augustine: The Confessions*. Cambridge: Cambridge University Press, 1993.

Clebsch, William A., and Charles R. Jaekle. *Pastoral Care in Historical Perspective*. Englewood Cliffs, N.J.: Prentice-Hall, 1964. Reprint, New York: J. Aronson, 1983.

Clissold, Stephen. *St. Teresa of Avila*. New York: Seabury Press, 1982.

Coles, Robert. *The Call of Stories: Teaching and the Moral Imagination*. Boston: Houghton Mifflin, 1989.

Collins, Gary R. *Christian Counseling: A Comprehensive Guide*. Waco, Tex.: Word Books, 1980.

————. *Psychology and Theology: Prospects for Integration.* Ed. H. Newton Malony. Nashville: Abingdon Press, 1981.

Collins, Raymond F. *Models of Theological Reflection.* Lanham, Md.: University Press of America, 1984.

Commission on Faith and Order, World Council of Churches. *Confessing One Faith: Towards an Ecumenical Explication of the Apostolic Faith as Expressed in the Nicene-Constantinopolitan Creed (381).* Faith and Order Paper 140. Geneva: World Council of Churches, 1987.

Cone, James H. *God of the Oppressed.* Maryknoll, N.Y.: Orbis Books, 1997.

Copenhaver, Martin B., Anthony B. Robinson, and William H. Willimon. *Good News in Exile: Three Pastors Offer a Hopeful Vision for the Church.* Grand Rapids, Mich.: Eerdmans, 1999.

Crites, Stephen. "The Narrative Quality of Experience." *Journal of the American Academy of Religion* 39, no. 3 (September 1971): 291-311.

Crosswell, Arthur G. "Objects and Idols: The Significance of Internal Object Relationships for the Religious Quest." *Journal of Pastoral Care* 54, no. 1 (Spring 2000): 45-54.

Curtis, Heather. " 'Children of the Heavenly King': Hymns in the Religious and Social Experience of Children." Paper presented to the American Society of Church History, 5 January 2002.

Dalferth, Ingolf U. " 'I Determine What God Is!' Theology in the Age of Cafeteria Religion." *Theology Today* 57, no. 1 (April 2000): 5-23.

Davis, Charles. "The Parish and Theology." *Clergy Review* 49 (1964): 264-90.

Davis, Stephen T., ed. *Encountering Evil: Live Options in Theodicy,* new ed. Louisville, Ky.: Westminster John Knox Press, 2001.

Dawn, Marva J. *A Royal "Waste" of Time: The Splendor of Worshiping God and Being Church for the World.* Grand Rapids, Mich.: Eerdmans, 1999.

de Certeau, Michel. "Mystic Speech." In *Heterologies: Discourse on the Other,* 80-100. Trans. Brian Massumi. Minneapolis, Minn.: University of Minnesota, 1986.

de la Madre de Dios, Efrén, and Otger Steggink. *Tiempo y vida de Santa Teresa,* 2d ed.. Madrid: La Editorial Católica, 1977.

DiNoia, Joseph. "Varieties of Religious Aims: Beyond Exclusivism, Inclusivism, and Pluralism." In *Theology and Dialogue: Essays in Conversation with George Lindbeck,* ed. Bruce D. Marshall, 249-74. Notre Dame, Ind.: University of Notre Dame Press, 1990.

Doehring, Carrie. "A Method of Feminist Pastoral Theology." In *Feminist & Womanist Pastoral Theology,* ed. Bonnie J. Miller-McLemore and Brita L. Gill-Austern, 95-111. Nashville: Abingdon Press, 1999.

Donovan, Vincent. *Christianity Rediscovered,* 2d ed. Maryknoll, N.Y.: Orbis Books, 1982.

Drilling, Peter. *Trinity and Ministry.* Minneapolis, Minn.: Fortress Press, 1991.

Dulles, Avery. *The Craft of Theology: From Symbol to System.* New York: Crossroad, 1992.

————. *Models of the Church*. Garden City, N.Y.: Doubleday, 1974. Expanded edition 1987.

————. *Models of Revelation*. Maryknoll, N.Y.: Orbis Books, 1992.

Dulles, Avery, and Patrick Granfield. *The Theology of the Church: A Bibliography*. New York: Paulist Press, 1999.

Dykstra, Craig R. *Growing in the Life of Faith: Education and Christian Practices*. Louisville, Ky.: Geneva Press, 1999.

Eliason, Leland Virgil. "A Critique of Approaches to Integrating Psychology and Theology Within Selected Evangelical Seminaries." Unpublished Th.D. Dissertation. Boston University School of Theology. University Microfilms, 1983.

Farnsworth, Kirk E. "Models for the Integration of Psychology and Theology." *Journal of the American Scientific Affiliation* 20 (March 1978): 6-9.

Fiddes, Paul S. *Participating in God: A Pastoral Doctrine of the Trinity*. Lousville, Ky.: Westminster John Knox Press, 2001.

Flynn, William T. *Medieval Music as Medieval Exegesis*. Studies in Liturgical Musicology, vol. 8. Lanham, Md.: Scarecrow Press, 1999.

Foley, Edward. *Foundations of Christian Music: The Music of Pre-Constantinian Christianity*. Collegeville, Minn.: Liturgical Press, 1996.

Foley, Gerald. *Family-Centered Church: A New Parish Model*. Kansas City, Mo.: Sheed & Ward, 1995.

Forrester, Duncan B. *Truthful Action: Explorations in Practical Theology*. Edinburgh: T. & T. Clark, 2000.

Frei, Hans W. *The Eclipse of Biblical Narrative: A Study in Eighteenth and Nineteenth Century Hermeneutics*. New Haven, Conn.: Yale University Press, 1974.

Freud, Sigmund. *The Future of an Illusion*, rev. ed. Trans. and ed. James Strachey. New York: Norton, 1975.

Fuller, Robert. "Rediscovering the Laws of Spiritual Life: The Last Twenty Years of Supervision and Training in Ministry." *Journal of Supervision and Training in Ministry* 20 (2000): 13-40.

Gadamer, Hans-Georg. *Truth and Method*, 2d rev. ed. Trans. Joel Weinsheimer and Donald G. Marshall. New York: Crossroad, 1989.

Gaede, Beth Ann, ed. *Congregations Talking about Homosexuality: Dialogue on a Difficult Issue*. Bethesda, Md.: Alban Institute, 1998.

Garland, Diana S. Richmond. *Family Ministry: A Comprehensive Guide*. Downers Grove, Ill.: InterVarsity Press, 1999.

Garland, Diana S. Richmond, and David E. Garland. *Beyond Companionship: Christians in Marriage*. Philadelphia: Westminster Press, 1986.

Geertz, Clifford. "Thick Description: Toward an Interpretive Theory of Culture." In *The Interpretation of Cultures*, ed. Clifford Geertz, 3-30. New York: Basic Books, 1973.

Gerkin, Charles V. *An Introduction to Pastoral Care*. Nashville: Abingdon Press, 1997.

————. *The Living Human Document: Re-Visioning Pastoral Counseling in a Hermeneutical Mode*. Nashville: Abingdon Press, 1984.

————. *Widening the Horizons: Pastoral Responses to a Fragmented Society*. Philadelphia: Westminster Press, 1986.

Gérold, Theodore. *Les Péres de l'eglise et la musique*. Geneva: Minkoff, 1973.

Goldberg, Michael. *Theology and Narrative: A Critical Introduction*. Nashville: Abingdon Press, 1982.

González, Justo L. *Mañana. Christian Theology from a Hispanic Perspective*. Nashville: Abingdon Press, 1990.

————. *The Story of Christianity*. 2 vols. San Francisco: Harper & Row, 1984.

Graham, Elaine L. *Making the Difference: Gender, Personhood, and Theology*. Minneapolis, Minn.: Fortress Press, 1996.

————. *Transforming Practice: Pastoral Theology in an Age of Uncertainty*. London: Mowbray (Cassell), 1996.

Graham, Larry Kent. *Care of Persons, Care of Worlds: A Psychosystems Approach to Pastoral Care and Counseling*. Nashville: Abingdon Press, 1992.

Grenz, Stanley J. *Welcoming but Not Affirming: An Evangelical Response to Homosexuality*. Louisville, Ky.: Westminster John Knox Press, 1998.

Grenz, Stanley J., and Roger E. Olson. *Twentieth-Century Theology: God and the World in a Transitional Age*. Downers Grove, Ill.: InterVarsity Press, 1992.

Grenz, Stanley J., and Denise Muir Kjesbo. *Women in the Church: A Biblical Theology of Women in Ministry*. Downers Grove, Ill.: InterVarsity Press, 1995.

Gutiérrez, Gustavo. *A Theology of Liberation: History, Politics, and Salvation*. Trans. and ed. Caridad Inda and John Eagleson. Maryknoll, N.Y.: Orbis Books, 1973.

Hahn, Celia Allison. *Growing in Authority, Relinquishing Control: A New Approach to Faithful Leadership*. Bethesda, Md.: Alban Institute, 1994.

Hall, Charles E. *Head and Heart: The Story of the Clinical Pastoral Education Movement*. Decatur, Ga.: Journal of Pastoral Care Publications, 1992.

Hall, Stuart George. *Doctrine and Practice in the Early Church*. Grand Rapids, Mich.: Eerdmans, 1992.

Hamilton, Elizabeth. *The Life of Saint Teresa of Avila*. Westminster, Md.: Christian Classics, 1985.

Harvey, Susan Ashbrook. "Spoken Words, Voiced Silence: Biblical Women in Syriac Tradition." 2000 NAPS Presidential Address. *Journal of Early Christian Studies* 9 (Spring 2001): 105-31.

Hauerwas, Stanley. *Against the Nations: War and Survival in a Liberal Society*. Minneapolis, Minn.: Winston Press, 1985.

————. *Christian Existence Today: Essays on Church, World, and Living in Between*. Durham, N.C.: Labyrinth Press, 1988.

Hauerwas, Stanley, and L. Gregory Jones. "Seeking a Clear Alternative to Liberalism." *Books and Religion* 13 (1985): 7

Hauerwas, Stanley, and William H. Willimon. *Resident Aliens: Life in the Christian Colony*. Nashville: Abingdon Press, 1989.

Heitink, Gerben. *Practical Theology: History, Theory, Action Domains: Manual for Practical Theology.* Trans. Reinder Bruinsma. Grand Rapids, Mich.: Eerdmans, 1999.

Hesselgrave, David J., and Edward Rommen. *Contextualization: Meanings, Methods, and Models.* Grand Rapids, Mich.: Baker Book House, 1989.

Hill, E. Wayne, and Carol Anderson Darling. "Using the Family Ecosystem Model to Enhance Pastoral Care and Counseling," *The Journal of Pastoral Care* 55, no. 3 (2001): 247-57.

Hiltner, Seward. *Preface to Pastoral Theology.* New York: Abingdon Press, 1958.

Holifield, E. Brooks. *A History of Pastoral Care in America: From Salvation to Self-realization.* Nashville: Abingdon Press, 1983.

Homans, Peter, ed. *The Dialogue Between Theology and Psychology.* Chicago: University of Chicago Press, 1968.

Hopewell, James. *Congregation: Stories and Structures.* Philadelphia: Fortress Press, 1987.

Hoy, David Couzens. *The Critical Circle: Literature, History, and Philosophical Hermeneutics.* Berkeley, Calif.: University of California Press, 1978.

Hustad, Donald P. *Jubilate II: Church Music in Worship and Renewal.* Carol Stream, Ill.: Hope Publishing, 1993.

Jackson, Gordon E. *A Theology for Ministry: Creating Something of Beauty.* St. Louis, Mo.: Chalice Press, 1998.

Jeanrond, Werner. "Correlational Theology and the Chicago School." In *Introduction to Christian Theology: Contemporary North American Perspectives,* ed. Roger A. Badham, 137-53. Louisville, Ky.: Westminster John Knox Press, 1998.

Jenner, Brian. "Music in the Sinner's Ear?" *Epworth Review* 16 (1989): 35-38.

Johnson, Luke Timothy. *Decision Making in the Church: A Biblical Model.* Philadelphia: Fortress Press, 1983.

————. *Scripture and Discernment: Decision Making in the Church.* Nashville: Abingdon Press, 1996.

Johnston, Robert K. *Reel Spirituality: Theology and Film in Dialogue.* Grand Rapids, Mich.: Baker Books, 2000.

Jonte-Pace, Diane, and William B. Parsons, eds. *Religion and Psychology: Mapping the Terrain: Contemporary Dialogues, Future Prospects.* New York: Routledge, 2001.

Judy, Dwight H. *Embracing God: Praying with Teresa of Avila.* Nashville: Abingdon Press, 1996.

Keifert, Patrick. Review of *The Nature of Doctrine,* by George A. Lindbeck. *Word and World* 5 (1985): 338-39, 342-44.

Killen, Patricia O'Connell, and John de Beer. *The Art of Theological Reflection.* New York: Crossroad, 1994.

Kinast, Robert L. *Making Faith-Sense: Theological Reflection in Everyday Life.* Collegeville, Minn.: Liturgical Press, 1999.

————. *What Are They Saying About Theological Reflection?* New York: Paulist Press, 2000.

Kirk-Duggan, Cheryl A. *Exorcizing Evil: A Womanist Perspective on the Spirituals.* Maryknoll, N.Y.: Orbis Books, 1997.

Koyama, Kósuke. *Waterbuffalo Theology.* Maryknoll, N.Y.: Orbis Books, 1974.

————. *Mount Fuji and Mount Sinai: A Critique of Idols.* Maryknoll, N.Y.: Orbis Books, 1985.

Kraft, Charles H. *Christianity in Culture: A Study in Dynamic Biblical Theologizing in Cross-cultural Perspective.* Maryknoll, N.Y.: Orbis Books, 1979.

Kreiner, Armin. "Versöhnung ohne Kapitulation: Überlegungen zu George A. Lindbecks 'The Nature of Doctrine,'" *Catholica* 46 (1992): 307-21.

Kuhn, Thomas S. *The Structure of Scientific Revolutions.* Chicago: University of Chicago Press, 1962.

La Croix, Richard R., ed. *Augustine on Music: An Interdisciplinary Collection of Essays.* Lewiston, N.Y.: Edwin Mellen, 1998.

Lash, Nicholas. *Theology on the Way to Emmaus.* London: SCM Press, 1986.

LeFevre, Percy. Review of *The Nature of Doctrine,* by George A. Lindbeck. *Chicago Theological Seminary Register* 74 (1984): 37-38.

Lessing, Gotthold Ephraim. "On the Proof of the Spirit and of Power" (1777). In *Lessing's Theological Writings,* ed. Henry Chadwick, 51-56. Stanford, Calif.: Stanford University Press, 1956.

Liderbach, Daniel. *Christ in the Early Christian Hymns.* New York: Paulist Press, 1998.

Lindbeck, George A. "Atonement and the Hermeneutics of Intratextual Social Embodiment." In *The Nature of Confession: Evangelicals and Postliberals in Conversation,* ed. Timothy R. Phillips and Dennis L. Okholm, 221-40. Downers Grove, Ill.: InterVarsity Press, 1996.

————. *The Nature of Doctrine: Religion and Theology in a Postliberal Age.* Philadelphia: Westminster Press, 1984.

————. "Response to Bruce Marshall." *The Thomist* 53 (1989): 403-6.

————. "Scripture, Consensus, and Community." In *Biblical Interpretation in Crisis: The Ratzinger Conference on Bible and Church,* ed. Richard John Neuhaus, 74-101. Grand Rapids, Mich.: Eerdmans, 1989.

Loftus, John Allan. "The Integration of Psychology and Religion: An Uneasy Alliance." Whitinsville, Mass.: Affirmation Books, 1981.

Loomer, Bernard. "On Committing Yourself to a Relationship." *Process Studies* 16, no. 4 (1987): 255-63.

MacIntyre, Alasdair. *After Virtue: A Study in Moral Theory,* 2d ed. Notre Dame, Ind.: University of Notre Dame Press, 1984.

Maier, Gerhard. *The End of the Historical-Critical Method.* Trans. Edwin W. Leverenz and Rudolf F. Norden. St. Louis, Mo.: Concordia Publishing House, 1977.

Mann, Alice. *The In-Between Church: Navigating Size Transitions in Congregations.* Bethesda, Md.: Alban Institute, 1998.

Marrou, H. I. *Time and Timeliness.* Trans. Violet Nevile. New York: Sheed and Ward, 1969.

Marsden, George M. *Fundamentalism and American Culture: The Shaping of Twentieth-century Evangelicalism, 1870–1925.* New York: Oxford University Press, 1980.

Marshall, Bruce D. "Aquinas as Postliberal Theologian." *The Thomist* 53 (1989): 353-402.

————, ed. *Theology and Dialogue: Essays in Conversation with George Lindbeck.* Notre Dame, Ind.: University of Notre Dame Press, 1990.

————. *Trinity and Truth.* New York: Cambridge University Press, 2000.

Martin, David A. *The Breaking of the Image: A Sociology of Christian Theory and Practice.* New York: St. Martin's Press, 1980.

Martin, Ralph P. *Worship in the Early Church.* Grand Rapids, Mich.: Eerdmans, 1975.

McClendon, James W., Jr. *Systematic Theology: Doctrine.* Nashville: Abingdon Press, 1994.

————. *Systematic Theology: Ethics,* 2d ed. Nashville: Abingdon Press, 2002.

————. *Systematic Theology: Witness.* Nashville: Abingdon Press, 2000.

McGrath, Alister E. "An Evangelical Evaluation of Postliberalism." In *The Nature of Confession: Evangelicals and Postliberals in Conversation,* ed. Timothy R. Phillips and Dennis L. Okholm, 23-44. Downers Grove, Ill.: InterVarsity Press, 1996.

McKinnon, James, ed. *Music in Early Christian Literature.* New York: Cambridge University Press, 1987.

McLaughlin, Eleanor Como. "Equality of Souls, Inequality of Sexes: Women in Medieval Theology." In *Religion and Sexism: Images of Women in the Jewish and Christian Traditions.* Ed. Rosemary Radford Ruether, 213-66. New York: Simon and Schuster, 1974.

Medwick, Cathleen. *Teresa of Avila: The Progress of a Soul.* New York: Alfred A. Knopf, 1999.

Meland, Bernard Eugene. *Essays in Constructive Theology: A Process Perspective.* Chicago: Exploration Press, 1988.

Metz, Johann Baptist. *The Emergent Church: The Future of Christianity in a Postbourgeois World.* Trans. Peter Mann. New York: Crossroad, 1981.

Milbank, John, Catherine Pickstock, and Graham Ward, eds. *Radical Orthodoxy: A New Theology.* New York: Routledge, 1999.

Miles, Margaret R. *Desire and Delight: A New Reading of Augustine's Confessions.* New York: Crossroad, 1992.

Miller-McLemore, Bonnie. "The Human Web: Reflections on the State of Pastoral Theology." *Christian Century* 110, no. 11 (7 April 1993): 366-69. Revised and expanded version published as "The Living Human Web: Pastoral Theology at the Turn of the Century." In *Through the Eyes of Women: Insights for Pastoral Care,* ed. Jeanne Stevenson Moessner, 9-26. Minneapolis, Minn.: Fortress Press, 1996.

Miller-McLemore, Bonnie J., and Brita L. Gill-Austern, eds. *Feminist & Womanist Pastoral Theology*. Nashville: Abingdon Press, 1999.

Moessner, Jeanne Stevenson, ed. *Through the Eyes of Women: Insights for Pastoral Care*. Minneapolis, Minn.: Fortress Press, 1996.

Mouw, Richard J. *Consulting the Faithful: What Christian Intellectuals Can Learn from Popular Religion*. Grand Rapids, Mich.: Eerdmans, 1994.

Mudge, Lewis S. and James N. Poling, eds. *Formation and Reflection: The Promise of Practical Theology*. Philadelphia: Fortress Press, 1987.

Myers, Ched. "Embodying the Great Story: An Interview with James W. McClendon." *The Witness* (December 2000): 13-15.

Neuger, Christie C., ed. *The Arts of Ministry: Feminist-Womanist Approaches*. Louisville, Ky.: Westminster John Knox Press, 1996.

Neuhaus, Richard John, ed. *Biblical Interpretation in Crisis: The Ratzinger Conference on Bible and Church*. Grand Rapids, Mich.: Eerdmans, 1989.

————, ed. *Theological Education and Moral Formation*. Grand Rapids, Mich.: Eerdmans, 1992.

Niebuhr, H. Richard. *The Meaning of Revelation*. New York: Macmillan, 1962.

————. *The Purpose of the Church and Its Ministry: Reflections on the Aims of Theological Education*. New York: Harper, 1956.

O'Donnell, James J. *Augustine*. Boston: Twayne Publishers, 1985.

Olmedo, Félix G. "Santa Teresa de Jesús y los predicadores del siglo de oro." *Boletín de la Real Academia de la Historia* 84 (1924): 165-75 and 280-95.

O'Meara, Thomas F. *Theology of Ministry*, rev. ed. New York: Paulist Press, 1999.

Padgett, Alan. Review of *The Nature of Doctrine*, by George A. Lindbeck. *Theological Students Fellowship Bulletin* 8 (1985): 31.

Pattison, Stephen. *Pastoral Care and Liberation Theology*. New York: Cambridge University Press, 1994.

Patton, John. *Pastoral Care in Context: An Introduction to Pastoral Care*. Louisville, Ky.: Westminster John Knox Press, 1993.

Peers, Edgar Allison. *Mother of Carmel, A Portrait of St. Teresa of Jesus*. New York: Morehouse-Gorham, 1946.

————. *Saint Teresa of Jesus and Other Essays and Addresses*. London: Faber and Faber, 1953.

————. *Studies of the Spanish Mystics*, 2nd rev. ed. Vol. 1. New York: Macmillan, 1951.

Perry, William G., Jr. *Forms of Intellectual and Ethical Development in the College Years: A Scheme*. New York: Holt, Rinehart & Winston, 1970.

Phan, Peter C. "Contemporary Theology and Inculturation in the United States." In *The Multicultural Church: A New Landscape in U.S. Theologies*. Ed. William Cenkner, 109-30. New York: Paulist Press, 1996.

Philipchalk, Ronald P. *Psychology and Christianity: An Introduction to Controversial Issues*. Lanham, Md.: University Press of America, 1987.

Phillips, Timothy R., and Dennis L. Okholm, eds. *The Nature of Confession:*

Evangelicals and Postliberals in Conversation. Downers Grove, Ill.: InterVarsity Press, 1996.

Placher, William C. *The Domestication of Transcendence: How Modern Thinking About God Went Wrong.* Louisville, Ky.: Westminster John Knox Press, 1996.

Poling, James N. *The Abuse of Power: A Theological Problem.* Nashville: Abingdon Press, 1991.

Poling, James N., and Donald E. Miller. *Foundations for a Practical Theology of Ministry.* Nashville: Abingdon Press, 1985.

Pope, Robert G. *The Half-Way Covenant: Church Membership in Puritan New England.* Princeton, N.J.: Princeton University Press, 1969.

Powell, Robert C. *Fifty Years of Learning Through Supervised Encounter with Living Human Documents.* New York: The Association for Clinical Pastoral Education, 1975.

Primavesi, Anne. *From Apocalypse to Genesis: Ecology, Feminism, and Christianity.* Minneapolis, Minn.: Fortress Press, 1991.

Purves, Andrew. *Pastoral Theology in the Classical Tradition.* Louisville, Ky.: Westminster John Knox Press, 2001.

———. *The Search for Compassion: Spirituality and Ministry.* Louisville, Ky.: Westminster John Knox Press, 1989.

Quasten, Johannes. *Music and Worship in Pagan and Christian Antiquity.* Trans. Boniface Ramsey. Washington, D.C.: National Association of Pastoral Musicians, 1983.

Quine, W. V. O., and J. S. Ullian. *The Web of Belief,* 2d ed.. New York: Random House, 1978.

Rahner, Karl. *Theology of Pastoral Action.* Trans. W. J. O'Hara. New York: Herder and Herder, 1968.

Ramsey, Ian T. *Models and Mystery.* London: Oxford University Press, 1964.

Ramshaw, Elaine. *Ritual and Pastoral Care.* Philadelphia: Fortress Press, 1987.

Ricoeur, Paul. *Freud and Philosophy: An Essay on Interpretation.* Trans. Denis Savage. New Haven, Conn.: Yale University Press, 1970.

———. "The Hermeneutics of Testimony." Trans. David E. Stewart and Charles E. Reagan. In Paul Ricoeur, *Essays on Biblical Interpretation,* ed. Lewis S. Mudge, 119-54. Philadelphia: Fortress Press, 1980.

———. "Psychoanalysis and the Movement of Contemporary Culture." Trans. Willis Domingo. In Paul Ricoeur, *The Conflict of Interpretations: Essays in Hermeneutics.* Ed. Don Ihde, 121-59. Evanston, Ill.: Northwestern University Press, 1974.

———. *The Rule of Metaphor: Multi-disciplinary Studies of the Creation of Meaning in Language.* Trans. Robert Czerny. Toronto: University of Toronto, 1977.

———. *Time and Narrative.* Vol. I. Trans. Kathleen McLaughlin and David Pellauer. Chicago: University of Chicago Press, 1984.

Rigby, Paul, John van den Hengel, and Paul O'Grady. "The Nature of Doctrine and Scientific Progress." *Theological Studies* 52 (1991): 669-88.

Rogers, Jack. *Claiming the Center: Churches and Conflicting Worldviews.* Louisville, Ky.: Westminster John Knox Press, 1995.

Root, Michael. "Identity and Difference: The Ecumenical Problem." In *Theology and Dialogue: Essays in Conversation with George Lindbeck,* ed. Bruce D. Marshall, 165-90. Notre Dame, Ind.: University of Notre Dame Press, 1990.

Rosenblatt, Roger. "A World of Lost Connections." *Time* (3 September 2001): 98.

Ruether, Rosemary Radford. "Feminism and Religious Faith: Renewal or New Creation?" *Religion and Intellectual Life* 3, no. 2 (Winter 1986): 7-20.

Sanderson, William Ashman. "Christian Empiricism as an Integrating Perspective in Psychology and Theology." *Christian Scholars Review* 8 (1978): 32-41.

Saunders, Stanley P., and Charles L. Campbell. *The Word on the Street: Performing the Scripture in the Urban Context.* Grand Rapids, Mich.: Eerdmans, 2000.

Scalise, Charles J. "Agreeing on Where We Disagree: Lindbeck's Postliberalism and Pastoral Theology." *Journal of Pastoral Theology* 8 (1998): 43-49.

――――. "Developing a Theological Rationale for Ministry: Some Reflections on the Process of Teaching Pastoral Theology to M.Div. Students." *Journal of Pastoral Theology* 1 (1991): 53-68.

――――. *From Scripture to Theology: A Canonical Journey into Hermeneutics.* Downers Grove, Ill.: InterVarsity Press, 1996.

――――. *Hermeneutics as Theological Prolegomena: A Canonical Approach.* Macon, Ga.: Mercer University Press, 1994.

――――. "Historical 'Snapshots' of Ministry: The Changing Language of Case Studies." *Review and Expositor* 96, no. 3 (Summer 1999): 423-40.

――――. "Integration." In *The New Dictionary of Pastoral Studies,* ed. Wesley Carr, 179-80. Grand Rapids, Mich.: Eerdmans, 2002.

――――. "Lex Cantandi, Lex Credendi: Theology and Hymnody." In *Learning from Beauty: Baptist Reflections on Christianity and the Arts: A Tribute to William L. Hendricks.* Ed. David M. Rayburn, Daven M. Kari, and Darrell D. Gwaltney, 129-40. Lewiston, N.Y.: Edwin Mellen Press, 1997.

――――. "Revelation and Pastoral Theology: Historical and Methodological Reflections." *Journal of Pastoral Theology* 9 (1999): 88-103.

――――. Review of *Teresa of Avila: The Progress of a Soul,* by Cathleen Medwick. *Church History* 69, no. 4 (December 2000): 890-92.

――――. "Teresa of Avila: Teacher of Evangelical Women?" *Cross Currents: The Journal of the Association for Religion and Intellectual Life* 46 (1996): 244-49.

Schleiermacher, Friedrich. *On Religion: Speeches to Its Cultured Despisers.* Trans. John Oman. Louisville, Ky. Westminster John Knox Press, 1994.

――――. *The Christian Faith.* 2 vols. Ed. H. R. Mackintosh and J. S. Stewart. New York: Harper & Row, 1963.

Schön, Donald A. *The Reflective Practitioner: How Professionals Think in Action.* New York: Basic Books, 1983.

Schreiter, Robert J. *Constructing Local Theologies.* Maryknoll, N.Y.: Orbis Books, 1985.

———. *The New Catholicity: Theology Between the Global and the Local.* Maryknoll, N.Y.: Orbis Books, 1997.

Segundo, Juan Luis. *The Liberation of Theology.* Trans. John Drury. Maryknoll, N.Y.: Orbis Books, 1976.

Shorter, Aylward. *Toward a Theology of Inculturation.* Maryknoll, N.Y.: Orbis Books, 1989.

Sine, Thomas. *Cease Fire: Searching for Sanity in America's Culture Wars.* Grand Rapids, Mich.: Eerdman's, 1995.

———. *Mustard Seed vs. McWorld: Reinventing Life and Faith for the Future.* Grand Rapids, Mich.: Baker Books, 1999.

Skeris, Robert A. *'Chrōma Theou': On The Origins and Theological Interpretation of The Musical Imagery Used by the Ecclesiastical Writers of the First Three Centuries, with Special Reference to the Image of Orpheus.* Altöting: Verlag Alfred Coppenrath, 1976.

Slade, Carole. *St. Teresa of Avila: Author of a Heroic Life.* Berkeley, Calif.: University of California Press, 1995.

———. "Saint Teresa's *Meditaciones sobre los cantares*: The Hermeneutics of Humility and Enjoyment." *Religion and Literature* 18 (1986): 27-43.

Soskice, Janet Martin. *Metaphor and Religious Language.* Oxford: Clarendon Press, 1985.

Spencer, Jon Michael. *Black Hymnody: A Hymnological History of the African-American Church.* Knoxville: University of Tennessee Press, 1992.

Stevenson-Moessner, Jeanne, ed. *In Her Own Time: Women and Developmental Issues in Pastoral Care.* Minneapolis, Minn.: Fortress Press, 2000.

Stiver, Dan R. *The Philosophy of Religious Language: Sign, Symbol, and Story.* Cambridge, Mass.: Blackwell Publishers, 1996.

Stone, Bryan P. *Compassionate Ministry: Theological Foundations.* Maryknoll, N.Y.: Orbis Books, 1996.

Stroup, George. W. *The Promise of Narrative Theology: Recovering the Gospel in the Church.* Atlanta: John Knox Press, 1981.

Sullivan, Mary C. "From Narrative to Proclamation: A Rhetorical Analysis of the Autobiography of Teresa of Avila." *Thought* 58 (1983): 453-71.

Tassie, Roberta Clifton. "Unified in Prayer." *The St. Matthews Baptist* 39, no. 3 (30 January 1994): 3.

Tavard, George H. *A Theology for Ministry.* Wilmington, Del.: Michael Glazier, 1983.

Teresa de Jesús. *Obras completas.* Ed. Efrén de la Madre de Dios and Otger Steggink. Madrid: Bilbioteca de Autores Christianos, 1974.

———. *Obras completas.* Ed. Enrique Llamas Martínez et al., under the direction of Alberto Barrientos. Madrid: Editorial de Espiritualidad, 1984.

———. *Obras completas.* Ed. Maximiliano Herraíz. Salamanca: Ediciones Sigueme, 1997.

Teresa of Avila. *The Collected Works of St. Teresa of Avila.* 3 vols. Trans. Kieran

Kavanaugh and Otilio Rodríguez. Washington, D.C.: Institute of Carmelite Studies, 1976–85.

———. *Interior Castle*. Trans. and ed. E. Allison Peers. Garden City, N.Y.: Doubleday, 1961. Reprint, 1989.

———. *The Interior Castle*. Trans. Kieran Kavanaugh and Otilio Rodríguez. New York: Paulist Press, 1979.

———. *The Life of Saint Teresa of Avila by Herself*. Trans. J. H. Cohen. New York: Viking Penguin, 1957.

Thiel, John E. *Nonfoundationalism*. Guides to Theological Inquiry Series. Minneapolis, Minn.: Fortress Press, 1994.

Thiemann, Ronald F. *Revelation and Theology: The Gospel As Narrated Promise*. Notre Dame, Ind.: University of Notre Dame Press, 1985.

Tilley, Terence. *Story Theology*. Collegeville, Minn.: Liturgical Press, 1990.

Tillich, Paul. *Dynamics of Faith*. New York: Harper, 1957.

———. *Systematic Theology*. 3 vols. Chicago: University of Chicago Press, 1951–63.

———. *Theology of Culture*. Ed. Robert C. Kimball. New York: Oxford University Press, 1959.

———. *Writings in Philosophy of Culture*. Ed. Michael Palmer. New York: De Gruyter, 1990.

Townsend, Loren. "Theological Reflection, Pastoral Counseling, and Supervision." *The Journal of Pastoral Theology* 12, no. 1 (2002): 63-74.

Tracy, David. *The Analogical Imagination: Christian Theology and the Culture of Pluralism*. New York: Crossroad, 1981.

———. *Blessed Rage for Order: The New Pluralism in Theology*. Chicago: University of Chicago Press, 1996.

———. "The Foundation of Practical Theology." In *Practical Theology: The Emerging Field in Theology, Church and World*. Ed. Don S. Browning, 61-82. San Francisco: Harper & Row, 1983.

———. "Practical Theology in the Situation of Global Pluralism." In *Formation and Reflection: The Promise of Practical Theology*. Ed. Lewis S. Mudge and James N. Poling, 139-54. Philadelphia: Fortress Press, 1987.

VandeCreek, Larry, and Arthur M. Lucas, eds. *The Discipline for Pastoral Care Giving: Foundations for Outcome Oriented Chaplaincy*. New York: Haworth Pastoral Press, 2001.

Volf, Miroslav. "Theology, Meaning, and Power: A Conversation with George Lindbeck on Theology and the Nature of Christian Difference." In *The Nature of Confession: Evangelicals and Postliberals in Conversation*. Ed. Timothy R. Phillips and Dennis L. Okholm, 45-66. Downers Grove, Ill.: InterVarsity Press, 1996.

Volf, Miroslav, and Dorothy C. Bass. *Practicing Theology: Beliefs and Practices in Christian Life*. Grand Rapids, Mich.: Eerdmans, 2002.

Villacéque, Sol. "Rhetorique et pragmatique: La transformation de code dans le *Libro de la vida* de Thérèse d'Avila." *Imprevue* 2 (1985): 7-27.

Wainwright, Geoffrey. *Doxology: The Praise of God in Worship, Doctrine, and Life: A Systematic Theology.* New York: Oxford University Press, 1980.

Wallace, Robin Knowles. *Moving Toward Emancipatory Language: A Study of Recent Hymns.* Lanham, Md.: Scarecrow Press, 1999.

Weber, Alison. *Teresa of Avila and the Rhetoric of Femininity.* Princeton, N.J.: Princeton University Press, 1990.

Welch, John. *Spiritual Pilgrims: Carl Jung and Teresa of Avila.* New York: Paulist Press, 1982.

Whitehead, Evelyn E. and James D. Whitehead. *Community of Faith: Models of Strategies for Developing Christian Communities.* New York: Seabury, 1982.

Whitehead, James D., and Evelyn E. Whitehead. *Method in Ministry: Theological Reflection and Christian Ministry.* Minneapolis, Minn.: Seabury Press, 1980.

Williams, Rowan. *Teresa of Avila.* Harrisburg, Pa.: Morehouse Publishing, 1991.

Wilson, Edward O. *Consilience: The Unity of Knowledge.* New York: Random House, 1998.

Wimberly, Edward P. *Counseling African-American Marriages and Families.* Louisville, Ky.: Westminster John Knox Press, 1997.

Wittgenstein, Ludwig. *Philosophische Untersuchungen/Philosophical Investigations.* Trans. G. E. M. Anscombe. Oxford: Basil Blackwell, 1967.

Woggon, Frank Milstead. "Deliberate Activity As an Art for (Almost) Everyone: Friedrich Schleiermacher on Practical Theology." *The Journal of Pastoral Care* 48 (1994): 3-13.

Wolfe, David L. "Reflections on Christian Empiricism: Thoughts on William Sanderson's Proposal." Christian Scholars Review 8 (1978: 42-45.

Young, Frances *Virtuoso Theology: The Bible and Interpretation.* Cleveland, Ohio: Pilgrim Press, 1993.

Zimmerman, Joyce Ann. *Liturgy and Hermeneutics.* Collegeville, Minn.: Liturgical Press, 1999.

Subject Index

Index of Names